ign and Comparative Studies/South Asian Series 7

Caste in Tamil Culture: The Religious Foundations of Sudra Domination in Tamil Sri Lanka

Bryan Pfaffenberger

Maxwell
School of Citizenship
and Public Affairs
Syracuse University

For more than two decades, teaching and research within the Maxwell School of Syracuse University have reflected a strong concern with the world outside our national borders. The contemporary crises in world population, food, and energy have served to dramatize anew the interdependence of nations and regions, and the importance of external events and forces. The Foreign and Comparative Studies Program, created in 1975 by the unification of existing programs in East African, Latin American, South Asian, and Soviet and East European Studies, reflects the Maxwell School's continuing awareness of the imperative for attention to developments and circumstances outside the United States. The Program maintains the resources and activities associated with each of the earlier area programs. It also encompasses foreign area interests of a broadly comparative nature without focus on a specific geographical region, and those not formerly represented in the earlier, regional programs.

The Foreign and Comparative Studies Publications are a central part of the Program's activities. Currently included are an African Series, a South Asian Series, and a Latin American Series. These constitute a medium for publishing manuscripts of a length greater than that of a journal article, but less than usual book length. Other materials, such as symposia papers, are occasionally included. Manuscripts are published on many aspects of the historical, social, cultural, economic, and political institutions relevant to the peoples of the areas within the Program's scope. Scholars are invited to submit manuscripts for consideration in these series.

Foreign and Comparative Studies Program Susan S. Wadley, Director

South Asian Series Editorial Committee

Susan S. Wadley, Chair
David Beatty
Tej K. Bhatia
Robert N. Kearney
David E. Sopher

Foreign and Comparative Studies Program
Syracuse University
119 College Place
Syracuse, New York 13210

CASTE IN TAMIL CULTURE

The Religious Foundations of Sudra Domination in Tamil Sri Lanka

Bryan Pfaffenberger

Foreign and Comparative Studies/South Asian Series, No. 7
Maxwell School of Citizenship and Public Affairs
Syracuse University
1982

Library of Congress Cataloging in Publication Data

Pfaffenberger, Bryan, 1949-
Caste in Tamil culture.

(Foreign and comparative studies. South Asian series ; no. 7)
Bibliography: p.
Includes index.
1. Tamils--Sri Lanka. 2. Caste--Sri Lanka.
3. Shudras. 4. Hinduism--Sri Lanka. I. Title.
II. Series.
DS489.25.T3P43 1982 305.5'122'095493 82-7321
ISBN 0-915984-84-9 AACR2

For Suzanne, Julia, and Roger

FRONTISPIECE. A Sudra landholder performs prostrate worship, in fulfillment of a vow, at the subsidiary shrine of a temple near Chavakachcheri, Sri Lanka.

This world is
because even though they receive the god's ambrosia
some will not drink it savoring its sweetness alone;
they do not bear rancor;
they are not indolent even though they fear
  what others fear;
for fame they will give even their lives,
but if it brings blame, they will not take it,
even though they might have the world;
they are not indifferent;
and, even though they are so great,
they do not spend their exertions for themselves
but strive for others.
This world is because these men are.

--*Puṟanāṉūṟu* 182

(trans. Hart 1979:28)

NOTE ON TRANSLITERATION

Tamil terms are transliterated according to the system used by the University of Madras' Tamil Lexicon; other Indic terms are transliterated according to established conventions in the literature. To avoid confusion, the plural of an Indic term (e.g. Tamil: sg. teyvam, pl. teyvaṅkaḷ) is not transliterated, but is formed by the addition of a dash and an s (e.g., teyvam-s). Improperly transliterated Indic terms in quotations are not corrected. Names of castes, ethnic groups, places, and deities are capitalized but not italicized. Many Tamil terms cannot be readily translated by a single English gloss; cummā, for example, can mean, in differing contexts, "freely" or "ordinarily." In the text, a single gloss is often provided to epitomize the sense of the term as it is used in its particular context; it might be used in a different sense elsewhere. The glossary (Appendix I) sums up the various meanings of frequently used Indic terms, and should be consulted during the reading of the text.

CONTENTS

Note on Transliteration vi

Illustrations viii

Acknowledgments ix

1. Introduction 1
   - *The Problem of Sudra Domination* 1
   - *The Rise of the Dravidian Social Formation* 19
   - *Jaffna and South India* 26
2. The Form of Sudra Domination in Tamil Jaffna 35
   - *The Rise of Tamil Culture in Jaffna* 35
   - *The Symmetry of the Anomalous Ranks* 52
3. Temples, Patrons, and the Frailty of Sudra Authority 61
   - *Temples and Patrons* 61
   - *The Frailty of the Veḷḷāḷar Achievement* 82
4. The Ritual Organization of Disorder 95
   - *The Religious Meaning of the Imposed Features* 95
   - *The Confrontation with Wilderness* 124
   - *The Pre-Aryan Substratum* 135
5. The Ritual Design of Sudra Domination 147
   - *The Achievement of Order* 147
   - *The Ritual Regulation of Feminine Power* 150
   - *The Ritual Confrontation of Demons* 179
   - *The Threats Posed to Order* 193
   - *Rituals of the Calendrical Cycle* 209
6. The Nature of Sudra Domination 223

Appendix I. Glossary of Indic Terms 231

Appendix II. The Ritual Roles of the Castes of Jaffna 237

Bibliography 243

Index 253

Note on the Author 258

TABLES

I. The Castes of Jaffna in Rank Order.......................... 39

II. The Castes of Jaffna: Population (estimated)............. 47

III. The Bad Sights.. 103

IV. The Cosmic Forces of the Four Directions................. 129

V. Pollution Times of the Castes of Jaffna.................. 197

VI. The Days of the Week.. 211

VII. The Months of the Year..................................... 215

VIII. The Seasons in Jaffna...................................... 217

FIGURES

I. The Symmetry of Rank in the South Indian Social Formation. 16

II. The Configuration of Rank in the Jaffna Peninsula......... 57

MAPS

I. The Tamil-Speaking Lands of India and Sri Lanka........... 3

II. Jaffna District and Its Environs.......................... 37

PLATES

I. A Sudra landholder performs prostrate worship in fulfillment of a vow at the subsidiary shrine of a temple near Chavakachcheri, Sri Lanka........................ *frontispiece*

II. A Paḷḷar (Untouchable) woman, accompanied by her daughter and son, weeds a Veḷḷāḷar-owned rice paddy near Chavakachcheri, Sri Lanka.................................... 48

III. A Paṟaiyar drummer of the Jaffna Peninsula................ 53

IV. Brahman priests of a Jaffna *ākama* temple performing a fire sacrifice (*hōma*).. 75

V. *Kāvaṭi* vow-fulfillment (*nērttikaṭan*) at an Ammaṉ shrine in Jaffna.. 177

Preface and Acknowledgments

The pages to follow recount an attempt to comprehend the tradi- ional caste system of the Tamil lands of South Asia in terms of the eligious beliefs and world view of Tamil culture, which is without loubt one of the most distinctive of Hindu civilization's variant egional traditions. This study focuses, in particular, on the high ank of dominant cultivating castes of the Sudra (Servant) status in raditional Hindu ranking terms, and seeks to explain why it is that, among Tamil folk and Dravidians generally, such castes rank far igher than they would if caste statuses were judged solely in terms of the traditional, textual criteria of rank. Rooted in a study of itual among the Sudra agriculturalists of Sri Lanka's Jaffna Penin- ula, this monograph seeks to reveal a quintessentially Tamil recast- ng of the classical Hindu tradition of ranking and, what is more, to ncover the distinctively Dravidian view of the universe in which the uzzling caste statuses of the traditional Tamil caste system were onstituted with meaning and legitimacy. Whatever negative value we ay assign to the caste relations that they legitimate, it is none- heless true, as I hope to show, that the religious foundations of udra domination constitute one of the most creative and architec- onic achievements of the world's traditional cultures. This study s intended to contribute to our emerging awareness of the distinctive enius of Tamil civilization.

That we have thus far failed to recognize the distinctive egional character of Tamil culture has much to do, I believe, with he ahistoricism of much modern anthropology. Tamil culture arose in complex historical process by which the civilization of the Gangetic lains diffused to the South. We are little encouraged to apprehend ts nature by refusing to consider how modern Tamil culture is in cer- ain respects a product of that process. Of course, much nonsense has een written about the history of the Tamils, not a little of it being olored by the anti-Brahman and Tamil separatist movements of this cen- ury. Much of what has been written about Tamil history is well escribed in the terms Radcliffe-Brown would have used for it: pseudo- istorical speculation. But Radcliffe-Brown admonished us to abandon istory, not because there was anything wrong with history as such indeed, he believed that it was only through historical analysis that ne could explain the appearance of particular social forms in particu- ar places), but rather because the type of societies normally studied y anthropologists lacks the records which would make history possible. he history of Tamil culture is indeed possible, as Stein (1980) has hown, for there are abundant historical sources--such as the many housands of temple inscriptions--that offer a foundation for historical nterpretation.

My interpretation of caste in Tamil culture is founded squarely on he premise that our understanding of the meaning of caste statuses in he Tamil tradition--an understanding that has thus far eluded scholar- hip--emerged only when Tamil culture is understood both anthropolo- ically and historically. On grounds both of training and temperament, feel much more comfortable with the anthropological approach than I do ith the historical, and on that account I have simply appropriated the fine historical interpretations which have recently been offered by Stein (1980) and Ludden (1978). Even so, these historical understandings have been subjected to an essentially anthropological methodology, one recently employed by Geertz (1980) and well outlined by Dumont:

> What is known of the past, on the plane of general and, more or less, preliminary information, is useful to the anthropologist . . . [but] the present has an advantage over the past.. . . The intensive study of the present by the anthropologist, because it is complete by definition . . . is incomparable for bringing to light relations, configurations, or structures in the social datum, in contrast to historical data, always fragmentary. Once such a configuration is isolated in the present . . . one may hope to find something of it in the past, and to use it to put in an intelligible order what often appears in the hands of classical indology . . . as a purely accidental collection (1980:xxv).

The first two chapters below attempt to isolate the configuration with which I am concerned, namely the high status and privileges of Sudras in Tamil culture, both in light of the ethnology of South India (chapter one and my own studies in Sri Lanka's Jaffna Peninsula (chapter two). There follows an interpretation of the historical process by which Tamil cultu arose, one that I believe sheds light on certain quintessentially South Indian institutions--such as the distinction between right- and left-han castes--that have not been satisfactorily explained in historical terms alone. In so doing I have modified very slightly the interpretations of the South Indian social formation offered by Stein and Ludden, but only very slightly, and, it is to be hoped, with profit.

The research on which this monograph is based was conducted in Sri Lanka during 1973 and 1974-75 with the kind assistance of the Institute for International Studies, University of California, Berkeley; that university's Department of Anthropology; and a Foreign Area Fellowship of the Social Science Research Council and the American Council of Learned Societies. A fellowship from the National Endowment for the Humanities permitted me to situate my Sri Lanka evidence in the wider co text of the literature on Tamil India, and provided a year of release ti from my teaching duties. Knox College generously supported the typing o the manuscript. I am indeed grateful for the support which has been giv to this study. The opinions and interpretations expressed in the pages follow are, however, mine alone, and do not necessarily reflect the posi tion of any agency named here.

To Gerald Berreman, George L. Hart, III, and Burton Benedict, all o the University of California, Berkeley, go my warm thanks for their guidance and support during the latter phase of my graduate studies at Berkeley. Thanks are due as well to William Simmons, John Gumperz, Euge Irshick, George DeVos, and Alan Dundes for moral support and intellectua guidance at Berkeley. I am deeply indebted to the many Sri Lankans who took it to be their personal responsibility to see that my time in that verdant isle was happy and productive; in particular, I wish to thank warmly the people of Kaccay South and Sanghitanai (the two Jaffna villag that cheerfully welcomed my attempt to describe their religious and soci life), as well as Aelian Fernando, N. Ramachandra Iyer, K.J. Chelvarajar K. Nadarajah, and C.M.S. Nathan. My colleagues at Knox--particularly Jon Wagner--cheered me on during the redrafts (more numerous than I care to mention) of this monograph, and Susan Wadley made many sage and helpful suggestions during its final incarnation. Mary Beth Ritter combed out many of the more glaring inconsistencies and kurram-s ("faults, sins") present in the text, and cheerfully typed--the manuscript. I think it obvious that this project has received kind assistance from very many people indeed; if I have failed to profit from it, the onus is mine alone to bear.

Galesburg, Illinois
Spring, 1982

Chapter 1

INTRODUCTION

> "As for the regional sphere, . . .the South, more religious about impurity, does not fit into the varna theory, as it lacks the two intermediate varnas. This raises the problem, let us say, of a Tamil pattern. . . .To be able to articulate all of this, I think the first step was to posit a general Indian formula [of caste ideology]. It was a necessary stage, but it was only a stage; more limited and specific studies that have thus been made, if not possible, at least surer and directly fruitful, will enrich, modify, and perhaps transform the global view."
>
> --Louis Dumont (1981:xxxvii)

I. The Problem of Sudra Domination

Few who have traveled widely in South Asia have failed to be captivated by the unique character of Dravidian culture, the tradition of the many millions of South Indians and Sri Lankans who speak the Dravidian tongues (Tamil, Malayalam, Kannada, and Telegu). Epitomized by the cultural life of the Tamil people, Dravidian culture strikes one, in the first instance, as at once fully (and vigorously) Hindu in the most orthodox sense, for South Indian Hindus adhere very scrupulously to the ancient rules concerning purity and pollution as they are mandated by the classical socio-legal code books (Dharmaśāstra-s). Those code books, which were composed in Sanskrit verse during the early centuries of the Christian era (Basham 1954:112f), contain the very essence of the Hindu social philosophy, as it had been laid down in the development of high civilization in North India's Gangetic Plains. And yet Dravidian culture also strikes one--especially when South Indian social life is compared more closely to the Sastric social ideal--as quite clearly divergent, Dravidian, and unique.

Nowhere in India, of course, does social reality approach the form mandated in the Dharmaśāstra-s (Mandelbaum 1970:I, 22ff). Nonetheless, as Stein has noted (1980:52), the contemporary society of rural North India approaches that ideal far more accurately than does the society of the Dravidian lands. That this is so is puzzling indeed, for South Indian Hindus perceive themselves (and are deemed by others) to be more traditional than their northern counterparts (Dumont 1981:58). Compounding the enigma is the evidence that much of what South Indian villagers would identify as the very heart of their tradition --ritual and worship--makes little sense in terms of the religious philosophy of the Gangetic civilization (Elmore 1915:4f). Any attempt to address South Indian culture, to explain it or merely to describe it, must begin by acknowledging this paradox: it is at once fully within the compass of what is essential to the Hindu life, and yet retains its own distinctive and variant ethos.

The pages to follow recount an attempt to comprehend one of the most enigmatic aspects of the South Indian tradition, its caste system. The caste system of South India, epitomized (as are most things South Indian) by the social formation of the Tamil-speaking lands (Map I), is if anything even more rigid and redolent of the hierarchical ethos than that of North India. And yet--here, of course, is the uniquitous paradox with which South Indian presents us--the Tamil caste system comprises features which are not only unknown in North India but are also without any clear foundation in the Sastric lore. So divergent is the southern system that one is tempted to say, with Raghavan (n.d.:117) that the Śāstra-s have "little application" to the Tamil caste system, which should be analyzed in purely Dravidian terms. But to do so is to forget the fundamental challenge with which Dravidian culture presents us, namely, to see it

MAP I.

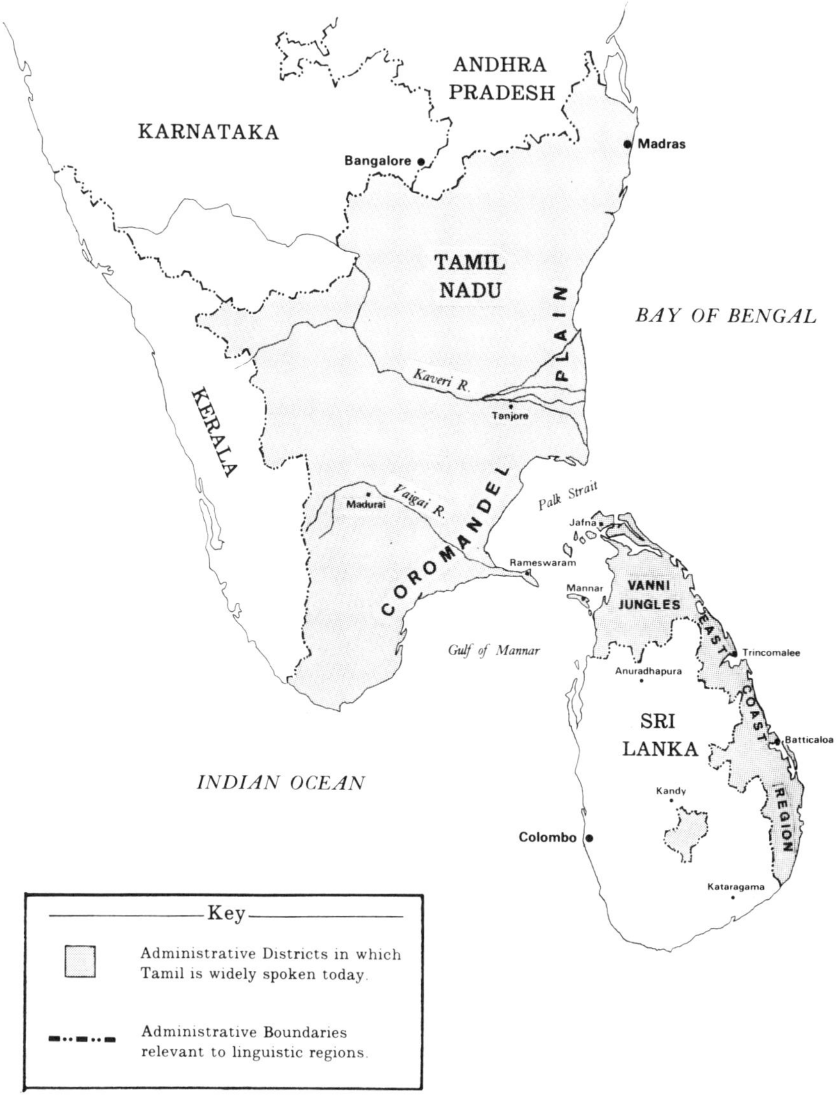

The Tamil-Speaking Lands of India and Sri Lanka.

as a regional variant of the Gangetic tradition of Hinduism.

We are obliged to observe, for instance, that the highest and lowest ranks of the Tamil caste hierarchy--that of the Brahman and of the scavenging Paṟaiyar Untouchables--are perfectly explicable in Sastric terms. The traditional South Indian Brahman--learned, of high Gangetic ancestry, and orthodox in his observance of the manifold rules of personal and caste purity--well illustrates the combination of life-style attributes that Hindus, throughout time, have rewarded by conferring on Brahmans the highest standing among men. The South Indian Brahman indeed exemplifies purity, which is a state of sanctity brought about by distancing the self (and the caste) from the tainting, debilitating processes of life and death. And the lowly Paṟaiyar--unlettered, of no dignified lineage, and saturated with the pollution that comes of handling the carcasses of cattle--equally well exemplifies the opprobrious features that, in the ancient texts as well as among Hindus today, condemn a caste to a despised status. To argue that the Sastric ranking ideology has "little application" to the Tamil caste system is to ignore the challenge that South India presents to ethnology.

Yet it is also true that, in the middle ranges of the Tamil caste hierarchy, the ranking categories and overall form of the Gangetic caste tradition are very poorly reproduced. The most striking aspect of this anomaly--the one with which this monograph is chiefly concerned--is the enigmatic status of certain non-Brahman cultivating castes, which are traditionally of the Sudra (or Servant) rank in Sastric terms and which are epitomized by the cultivating Veḷḷāḷars* of the Tamil hinterland. Throughout South India, in those areas in which Brahmans are not the chief landowners, Sudra cultivating castes often possess what Srinivas

---

*There appears to be more than one spelling of this caste name. Most Jaffna Veḷḷāḷars spell their caste name as it is given here, but one often encounters the spelling Vēḷāḷar.

has termed "decisive dominance" (1959). Numerically predominant in an area and endowed with the lion's share of the land, the dominant caste believes itself to be entitled to rule the villages in which it resides, and does not shrink from the use of force to maintain what it sees as its legitimate privileges (Mandelbaum 1970:II, 358ff).

Judged in purely Sastric terms, the non-Brahman dominant caste of South India--a caste which possesses only the lowly Sudra rank in the Sastric tradition of caste categories (*varṇa*-s)--should not merit a very high caste rank. Yet, proclaiming themselves to be very pure and respectable indeed, Veḷḷāḷars, for instance, are judged to stand in public esteem just below the Brahmans. That Veḷḷāḷars are so acknowledged is actually quite mysterious, for Veḷḷāḷar castes, at the same time that they proclaim their great purity, in fact tend to lead a fairly impure lifestyle. Veḷḷāḷars, for instance, do not eat beef, but they very often eat other kinds of meat; drink alcohol; carry on close relations with impure, Untouchable laborers; supervise blood sacrifices; drink the blood of sacrificial victims; remarry widows; and, in general, throw themselves lustily into the tainting affairs of day-to-day life. These practices are very much out of keeping with the other-worldly, ascetic-like customs of the pure castes, and according to the classical doctrine, the Veḷḷāḷars' rank should be low indeed. Yet Veḷḷāḷars, throughout the Tamil lands, are ranked very high. Furthermore, they are ranked higher in public esteem than certain non-Brahman castes that emulate the Brahmanical ideal of purity, a situation that, for Dumont (1981:88), indicates that the classical ranking ideal is "in abeyance." The contradiction between Veḷḷāḷar claims to purity and the realities of their worldly lifestyle emerges clearly, according to Beck, in the symbolism of plowing. Brahmans, since the most ancient times, have disdained the plow, believing that "plowing land is a polluting activity since overturning the soil threatens the life within it." Brahmans hire non-Brahman laborers to do their plowing for them. Yet Vel̤l̤āl̤ars esteem the act and advertise their association with it, as if to flaunt Brahmanical ideals and drive home tauntingly the idea that they possess a high rank that they do not deserve (Beck 1970:782-83, n. 12).

When measured against the ranking paradigm of the Dharmaśāstra-s, the status of Vel̤l̤āl̤ars appears to be both irreligious and artificially inflated. The Dharmaśāstra-s outline the Hindu notions of an interdependent, caste-based social order, in which the greatest merit (both social and religious) attaches to those who adhere to their ascribed status. These notions, collectively known as the varṇāśrama dharma ("duties of the four caste categories and four stages of life [aśrama]"), reflect the most essential theme of Indian social thought: as in Plato's Republic, there is outlined, for each man, "a place in society and a function to fulfill, with its own rights and duties" (Basham 1954: 138). Dumont terms the spirit of the varṇāśrama dharma "holistic": "the stress," he asserts, "is placed on society as a whole, as collective Man; the ideal derives from the organization of society with respect to its [religious] ends (and not with respect to individual happiness); it is above all a matter of order, of hierarchy; each particular man in his place must contribute to the global order, and justice consists in ensuring that the proportions between social functions are adapted to the whole" (1981:9). That Vel̤l̤āl̤ars claim a rank higher than the one they deserve seems to flaunt the very essence of the Sastric social ideal, as it was expressed in the Laws of Manu: "it is better to do one's own duty [svadharma, the ascribed occupation and duty of a caste] badly than another's well" (cited in Basham 1954:138).

The duty of Sudras, according to the Dharmaśāstra-s, is to serve the higher caste-categories (varṇa-s) with humility. The three higher varna-s, Brahman (priests and scholars), Ksatriyas (warriors and rulers), and Vaisyas (commoners), were collectively known as the twice-born (dvija), due to their ritual rebirth in the orthodox Vedic initiation rites. As the purest and, from a religious standpoint, the most powerful of men, Brahmans were deemed to have dominion over all others. In practice, however, the religious duties of Brahmans--studying and teaching the Vedas--were considered sufficiently challenging to warrant for them not wordly dominion, but rather a life of "plain living and high thinking" (Kane 1974:110). The practice of worldly dominion (war and government) was therefore left--at least in classical theory--to Ksatriyas, with the understanding that even the most powerful Ksatriya king was still subordinate in status to Brahmans. To Vaisyas was left the day-to-day business of life. Below them all, and despised for their impurity (āśauca),were the lowly Sudras.

In the Śāstra-s (Lingat 1973; Kane 1974) Sudras were likened to burial grounds, which are among the most impure of places. They were forbidden to study the Veda, to consecrate sacred fires, to carry on certain life-cycle ceremonies (saṁskāra, including the crucial initiation rite), to give gifts to Brahmans save under great restrictions, to claim a short pollution period after a kinsman's death, to give food to Brahmans, to come close to Brahmans, to perform ascetic acts, or to claim prestige. They were enjoined to esteem their poverty, for the wealth of Sudras was held to be a vexation to Brahmans. So far from seeking riches, they were admonished to serve the higher varṇa-s with humility. The status of Sudras in the Śāstra-s, in sum, was depicted as a very lowly one, although, to be sure, there was an even lower status, that of the cāṇḍāla-s or Untouchables. Nonetheless, it is quite clear that the classical tradition mandates a life of poverty and service for Sudras, and it is equally clear that the scriptural mandate is regularly contravened in practice by the Sudra dominant castes of the South.

So distant is the varṇa scheme from actual social reality that many scholars discount its relevance or utility for the analysis of caste anywhere in the South Asian culture area. Yet to do so is to ignore the fact that Hindus themselves view the Śāstra-s as the fons et origo of their social design. Whether or not the Sastric scheme applies exactly to the actual form of caste ranking, Hindus all over South Asia--including the Dravidian South--use the language and the ideology of those scriptures to conceptualize their social relations. Furthermore, it is quite clear that the North Indian caste system, at least, conforms in principle to the overarching design of the texts. Positions of respectability, of domination, of wealth, and of landholding are held almost universally in North India by persons who claim, and are thought by others, to possess the twice-born status (see, for instance, Gould 1964:35). It is believed in North Indian villages that the twice-born, who are scrupulous in their maintenance of domestic purity and orthodox customs, possess the right to dominate others because of their religious merit (acquired in a former life) and because of their purity (Wadley 1976).

The Sudra dominant caste of the South clearly does not possess the Sastric entitlement to dominate other castes. Nonetheless, Veḷḷāḷars, for instance, believe themselves to possess the right to claim the honor, respect, and services of a wide variety of non-Brahman subordinate castes. Among them are professional castes--potters, watchmen, carpenters, and many more--whose statuses, if lower than that of Veḷḷāḷars, are nonetheless fairly respectable. (Certain professional castes whose duties involve the routine handling of impurities, such as tonsure or the washing of menstrual cloths, rank much lower, at or below the line which separates the touchable from the untouchable castes.) As much as thirty percent of the population belongs, not to these respectable professional castes, but rather to very low ranking and impoverished castes called Untouchables (or, with polite circumlocution, "Original Dravidians" [ātiṭirāviṭa]; alternatively, "children of God" [harijans]). So low and despised are these castes, which are epitomized by the Paḷḷar and the Paṟaiyar of the Tamil lands, that people of respectable caste rank believe their touch to be defiling. For centuries, lowly Untouchables (the retainers of Veḷḷāḷar masters) have performed the backbreaking labor--weeding, transplanting, harvesting--that has helped to bring luxuriant harvests to the rice paddies and gardens owned by the high caste folk (Beck 1972, 1976; Banks 1957, 1960). On the whole, castes of the Ksatriya and the Vaisya varṇa-s --the ones who would be legitimately entitled, in the Sastric sense, to claim the privilege of domination--have been absent or nearly so in the South (Mandelbaum 1970:I, 23; Dumont 1981:73).

The Tamil social formation has often been characterized in Sastric terms as comprising only Brahmans, Sudras, and Untouchables (Béteille 1969:3), but even this formulation obscures far more than it clarifies. It takes no account, for instance, of the persistent and enigmatic distinction of castes into "right" and "left" categories, a distinction that in fact represents one of the most important and pervasive social features of the South Indian system (Beck 1970). It is quite evident that, in contradistinction to North India, the actual caste system of South Indian villages can be interpreted even by the most sympathetic analyst to conform only vaguely to the Sastric ranking paradigm.

The high rank of Sudra dominant castes perhaps best characterizes the gap between the Sastric ideal and southern practice. Claiming as they do a rank and a set of privileges that lacks scriptural foundation, Veḷḷāḷars and other South Indian Sudra cultivating castes would appear to be engaged in what can only be described as a wily subversion of tradition, relying on their wealth, the coercive force that they possess, and their stranglehold on the land to guarantee their seemingly inflated status claims. Precisely this case has been made, for instance, by Mandelbaum with regard to the Sudra dominant caste of a village in Andhra Pradesh:

> The dominant landowners there are Raj Gonds, a jati [caste] of tribal origin. When Dube studied the village in the early 1950's, the Raj Gonds were still performing cow sacrifice and eating beef, traits that would have consigned them to the lowest depths of defilement among other Hindus. But in this village Hindus of all but two jatis took water from them [a gesture conceding the water-giving caste's superiority] and the lower jatis also took food from them.. . . The example of the Raj Gonds indicates that under especially strong conditions of power, even the most heinous of polluting acts can be overlooked by otherwise orthodox Hindus (Mandelbaum 1970:I, 208).

On the surface, this interpretation of the evidence has much to recommend it, not in the least because it resonates so well with the common-sense notion Western scholars have of power and its role in human affairs. The Sudra, as we have depicted him, has seized for himself and his castefellows a privileged rank in village social life; his aim, we assume, is mastery and domination over those his endeavors expose to be weak. His claim to purity, no less than his claim to his laborers' impurity, is (as some would say of all such claims by the powerful) an artifice: "more or less cunning," as Geertz has put it, "more or less illusional, and designed to facilitate the prosier ends of rule" (1980:122). To depict the strategy of Sudra domination in these terms is to suggest that it is founded not on shared belief and consensus, but rather on delusion and coercion.

It is therefore not surprising that Mandelbaum has interpreted the political role of the dominant caste as one of "regulation," emphasizing not the ideology of rule so much as its coercive foundations. A truly dominant caste, he notes correctly, is willing and able "to field a band of determined men who will discourage dissidents by force. . .

[and] dispossess other villagers of their livelihood" (1970:I, 358-59). From this interpretation emerges a view of how Sudra domination has been reproduced over the centuries, despite its lack of legitimacy in traditional ranking terms. Sudra domination has persisted, it would appear, because the power of the dominant caste in its village has been so pervasive and so adept that the dominated have been forced to accept it, even though it cannot be justified by reference to the religious notions of rightful domination that can be found in the Dharmaśāstra-s.

Against this interpretation it can be argued, as would Dumont (1981:153), that even though the Sudra dominant castes of southern India do not claim the Ksatriya rank they nonetheless seek to emulate the legitimate function of Ksatriyas, for whom a certain dispensation is made with regard to the niceties of purity restrictions. After all, a ruler can hardly be expected to do his job if, like the Brahman, he must live the Śāstra-mandated life of plain living and high thinking. He must be a man of action, and indeed the texts depict the king expressly as immune to impurity (āśauca) because he was pervaded with the power of the gods (Gonda 1969:15). That power was conferred upon him in the royal installation ritual (Inden 1978:28ff).

There is no small evidence that the Ksatriya dominant castes of North India indeed deem themselves to possess a right to ignore purity restrictions. The North Indian Rajput, for instance, "regards it as a kind of warrior's dispensation that he is permitted to hunt, eat meat, drink liquor, and eat opium" (Hitchcock 1958:220, cited in Mandelbaum 1970:I, 207). In Central India, Rajputs, notwithstanding their impurity, claim to rank higher than members of other non-Brahman castes that emulate the purity ideal, and the consensus of public opinion is in agreement (Mayer 1966:35). It would appear, then, that there exists a traditional basis by which the dominant "warrior" or "royal" castes of Indian villages may ignore purity rules and yet claim high rank: they aim to "reproduce the royal function," and therefore are exempt from purity restrictions (Dumont 1981:291).

Nonetheless, there is clear and compelling evidence that this interpretation, applied to the Sudra dominant castes of the south, flies in the face of the social facts. Traditional Sudra powerholders, epitomized by the dominant Veḷḷāḷar castes of Tamilnadu, do not conceive themselves to be eligible for the crown (Thurston 1909:VII, 363) and have seldom claimed membership in the Ksatriya varna (Béteille 1969:97). Nor do they fancy themselves to be "warriors." It is true, to be sure, that warlike castes such as the Kallars and Maravars of South India maintain a martial tradition and deem themselves to be Ksatriyas, but the Ksatriya model of domination has never found currency in the heartland of the South, the rice-growing lowlands (Stein 1980: 70-71). As will be seen, Kallars are peripheral to the agrarian social formation with which we are concerned. The dominant non-Brahman castes of the southern heartland, epitomized by the Veḷḷāḷars, have for two millenia regarded themselves (and have been regarded) as people of peace. In one of the early Tamil texts, Tolkāppiyan's grammar, Veḷḷāḷars were expressly differentiated from warriors, and of them it was said that they had no other occupation save the tilling of the soil (cited in Thurston 1909:VII, 369). One and one-half millennia later, the Madras Census Report described Veḷḷāḷars in terms that well apply to the Veḷḷāḷars of Jaffna today: "a peace-loving, frugal, and industrious people" (cited in Thurston 1909:VII, 370).

We would seem to be left, then, with Mandelbaum's suggestion that temporal power elevates the rank of the impure, and that the dominant caste's claim to be "pure" is little more than artifice invented to clothe its naked power in the fabric of traditional authority. This authority-seeking strategy does not, however, wholly overthrow the classical ranking scheme, for the dominant caste still recognizes and honors the Brahman's absolute superiority. For Dumont, the ranking situation in villages controlled by the dominant caste shows that, while the classical tradition provides the ultimate ground of ranking ideology, naked force makes itself felt in the middle range of the caste hierarchy and "distorts" the classical scheme (1981:153). For this reason, Dumont argues, we must acknowledge the presence on the Indian scene of a "shamefaced," but nonetheless present, version of the self-interested, arbitrary calculation and action associated with the bourgeois individualism of the modern West (1981:353).

The role of South India's dominant castes in distorting the traditional Sastric ranking framewok is witnessed, Dumont suggests, not only in the artificially high rank of the dominant caste itself, but also in the artificially low rank of certain dominated Untouchables. To be sure, Paraiyars, the lowest of castes among Tamils, possess a rank that would seem genuinely to reflect the absolute odium of impurity. Yet throughout southern India, there are certain Untouchable castes, nominally impure, whose status is not explicable in the Gangetic religious framework. Sudras call these castes, epitomized by the Pallars, "impure" (tuppuravu illai), pointing out, for instance, the castes' allegedly unclean occupation, their shoelessness, their partial nudity, their non-vegetarian diet, and their close identification with rituals involving blood sacrifice. On close inspection, however, it is very difficult to tell just why it is that these traits are impure--particularly when many of them are also carried on by respectable Sudra landholders.

Consider, for example, the traditional status of the palmyra-climbing Nadars of Tamilnadu. Of them it was said in the Ramnad Manual that they were, in the nineteenth century, "inferior to Sudras and superior to Parayas" (Hardgrave 1969:21, n. 17). The Bishop Caldwell noted their rather anomalous status:

> In some respects the position of the Shanars [Nadars] in the scale of castes is peculiar. Their abstinence from spiritous liquors and from beef, and the circumstance that their widows are not allowed to marry again, connect them with the Sudra group of classes. On the other hand, they are not allowed as all Sudras are, to enter the temples; and where old native usages still prevail, . . . their women, like those of the castes still lower, are obliged to go uncovered from the waist upwards (cited in Hardgrave 1969:22).

Notwithstanding their estimable customs, it could be claimed that the Shanars' impurity stems from their occupation: tapping palmyra trees for toddy, an alcohol-bearing drink. Liquor is specifically condemned in the Dharmaśāstra-s as an impure, foul substance. And yet the toddy they tapped was no doubt destined for Sudra consumption, a point that Caldwell failed to appreciate. If it is polluting to tap toddy, then surely it is even more so to drink the fermented beverage. Yet Sudras, particularly powerful, landholding Sudras like the Veḷḷāḷars of Tamilnadu, rank very high--notwithstanding the fact that, in reality, their domestic customs in cuisine and ritual are hardly distinguishable from "Untouchables" like the Nadars.

It would appear, then, that the higher-ranking Untouchables are "impure" only because powerful Sudras wish to call them impure, and so degrade them to the Sudras' servitude. Toward this end, it has been argued, landholding Sudras force these "Untouchables" to demarcate themselves in public as equivalent to Paṟaiyars: like Paṟaiyars, for instance, Nadars were traditionally forbidden to wear shoes and, in consequence, it is said of the Nadars that they are impure. But, as Louis Dumont has noted, wearing shoes--even leather ones, leather being very odious to a strict Hindu--can hardly be said to degrade an Untouchable vis-à-vis Sudras:

> In the . . . district of Tinnevelly, I saw the marks of blows on the back of an Untouchable, blows which he had received for having crossed

> the village of a martial caste (the Maravar) wearing sandals. The inhabitants themselves wear leather sandals, blows have never removed impurity, and it is clear that the village was not polluted, but that villagers had simply wanted to uphold a symbol of subjection (Dumont 1981:82).

According to Dumont's interpretation, the features of dress that powerful Sudras impose on castes like the Nadars are only apparently sensible in terms of the Gangetic notions of pure and impure. At first sight, these imposed features would seem to be "particularly clear examples of hierarchy." Yet, Dumont asserts, "closer inspection shows that these features derive more from power than from the hierarchical principle" (*Ibid.*). They do not issue from custom, although they are phrased in terms of it, but rather from the desire of the dominant caste to regulate and to subordinate persons who, by being linked with Untouchables, can be exploited for their labor.

What is so striking about the South Indian system, then, is that its anomalous ranks display a very intriguing reverse symmetry. The Sudra landholding caste presents itself as "pure" and wins a rank second only to that of the Brahmans; the toddy-tapping Untouchables are presented as "impure" and win a rank penultimate to the lowly Paraiyars (Figure 1). While the status of the Brahman and Paraiyar would appear to be explicable in terms of the Gangetic ranking ideology, the two anomalous ranks quite clearly contradict it.* The consensus of scholarship on this curious pattern is that

---

*It could be argued that the Sastric ranking paradigm still applies in that Vellālars and Pallars exhibit, respectively, less purity than the Brahman and less impurity than the Paraiyar, and that the two castes therefore deserve the medial positions that they occupy in the hierarchy. But to do so ignores the truly anomalous feature of the Tamil ranking paradigm, for Vellālars rank higher than genuinely pure non-Brahmans, just as Pallars rank lower than genuinely impure non-Paraiyars.

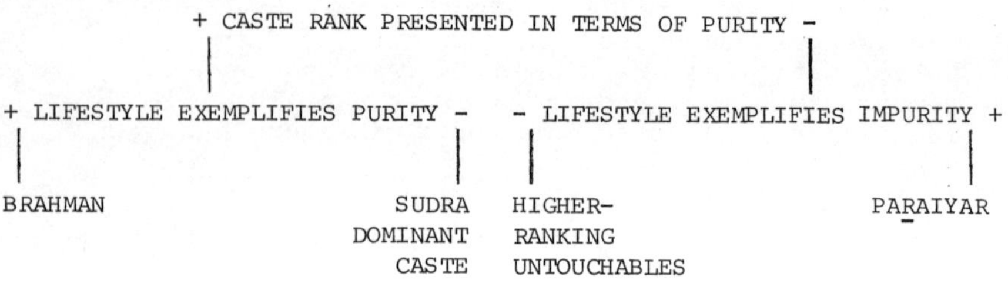

FIGURE 1. The Symmetry of Rank in the South Indian Social Formation

the power held by the landholding Sudra caste of an area permits them to grant themselves a very high rank, one that they do not deserve, while at the same time degrading the rank--one equally undeserved--of the toddy-tapping Untouchables. This warping of the hierarchical principle does not, however, wholly overthrow the Gangetic framework. At the extremes of the hierarchy, the Gangetic principles hold; in the middle, they are controverted by a substratum of power.

Whatever magnetic attraction this view of the evidence may hold for us, it is well to remember that in embracing it we shirk the challenge of understanding South Indian culture as a genuine variant of the Gangetic mold. We have denied, a priori, any uniquely Southern cultural understanding of the two anomalous ranks. There is, to be sure, much apparent credit to the argument that no such cultural understanding exists, for it is not represented in Dravidian languages of caste relations. In Jaffna, for instance, Hindus use the ranking paradigm of the *Dharmaśāstra*-s--especially the concepts of purity (*cuttam*) and impurity (*tīṭṭu* or *tuppuravu illai*)--to describe the statuses of Veḷḷāḷars and of Paḷḷars, notwithstanding the concepts' inaccuracy. Yet, if we are to accept the argument that a cultural understanding can be demonstrated to exist only when we have discovered linguistic terms that label it, we must assume, in the face of all the evidence for a regional cultural tradition, that South Indian thought has made no contribution to the cultural understanding of caste in the Dravidian lands.

There is--thanks to major, recent advances in social anthropology--another kind of language to which we can listen: the language of ritual. Leach, for instance, has defined ritual as that aspect of customary behavior which communicates something, and argues that ritual plays an essential role in social relationships by reaffirming (often by exaggerating) status differences (1968:524). Throughout southern India, people of many different castes have roles to play in village ritual events, both in the context of household and of temple rites. If these rituals communicate the meaning of traditional status arrangements, then through an analysis of them we may learn something about the Dravidian understanding of caste statuses.

That these rituals do indeed state a Dravidian ideology of caste relations is the contention of this monograph. Through an analysis of the rituals carried on by the Sudra cultivators of Sri Lanka's Jaffna Peninsula, the center of Tamil culture in that island country, I wish to show that there is a Dravidian cultural understanding of Sudra domination and of the two anomalous statuses, one that invests them with the deepest religious meaning and with the most profound legitimacy. At once true to its Hindu sources and its Dravidian roots, this essentially southern caste ranking tradition does not stand in conflict with the Sastric tradition, but on the contrary extends and develops the classical tradition within the framework of a distinctively Dravidian world view. An analysis of this tradition helps us to understand, furthermore, not only the curious forms of the southern caste system, but also other aspects of southern social life (such as the distinction between "left" and "right" castes) that have thus far resisted analysis. To grasp the religious foundations of Sudra domination is to grasp, as well, the place of the Dravidian cultural design within the overarching confines of the Hindu cultural universe.*

The idea that there is a "Dravidian substratum" underlying the customs of southern India, notwithstanding their northern veneer, has prompted a great deal of fruitless speculation--so much so that, in fact, modern scholarship tends to shy away from it. For many years, Indology seemed to assume that anything and everything that could be defined as "civilized" was of Aryan origin, while all "primitive" customs--such as, for example, shamanism, blood sacrifice, or even (in some accounts), the *pūja* ritual--were Dravidian. An account of the ethnocentric, if not blatantly racist, assumptions underlying these definitions would constitute a valuable contribution to the sociology of knowledge. Gonda (1965), in a masterly essay, has shown very convincingly that the customs of modern Hinduism such as *pūja*, which are thought to stem from Dravidian influence on the formerly pure Vedic religion of the Aryans, can in fact be shown to be entirely consistent with the orthodox, Gangetic tradition.

Yet not every aspect of the southern caste system is consistent with the classical social thought of Gangetic India. If we are to assume that the *varṇāśrama dharma*, with

---

*Because I intend to unmask an essentially Dravidian ideology of caste ranking--an ideology that represents a fundamental recasting in Dravidian terms of the Sastric tradition--I have not attempted to assess the utility for this project of the "ethnosociology" school of caste studies associated with the recent work of McKim Marriott (1976). That school assumes the Hindu ideology of caste relations to be codified in the *Dharmaśāstra*-s, an assumption that for crucial methodological reasons I am here unwilling to make. Nonetheless, it will become clear in the pages to follow, at least to those familiar with Marriott's theory, that this study bears implications for the ethnosociology project (once it is made more sensitive to regional variation), but it is not my aim here to assess them.

its social code calling for hierarchy and interdependence on the basis of birth-ascribed groups, is the only possible ideology of caste in Indian civilization, then we are left with only one recourse when confronted with the South Indian evidence. We must explain the discrepancies between Gangetic code and the southern practice by reference to the Sudras' willful manipulation of their tradition to suit their political and economic goals. For many, this interpretation may seem quite satisfactory. And yet it resonates, perhaps too well, with the Western (and particularly the British and American) notion of Economic Man, who is forever and everywhere poised in tension with his cultural traditions as he attempts, as it is said, to "maximize" his wealth and power. Remarkably enough, Dumont himself--an author who has more clearly than any other called into serious question the relevance of the Economic Man model to South Asian ethnology--has, when faced with the scarcely traditional rank of the non-Brahman landholding caste, admitted the existence of a sort of "maximizing," one carried on within cultural limits, on the Indian scene.

Whatever position one wishes to take on the universality of Economic Man, it is my conviction that, as a fundamental principle of anthropological methodology, we should not use a theoretical construct that we suspect to be ethnocentric until we have at least explored the alternatives. At the present time the option open to us, as Dumont himself has recently and very clearly foreseen, is to study regional patterns and configurations of caste in terms of regional ideological traditions (1981:xxxvi). And that is precisely the aim of this study.

II. The Rise of the Dravidian Social Formation

The origins of traditional Dravidian society are shrouded in mystery, but it is fairly clear that in the centuries preceeding the birth of Christ, there were two separate areas of civilizational development in India: the Gangetic Plain of the North and the Coromandel Plain of southeastern India, presently Tamilnadu (Stein 1980:32). In antiquity, the culture of the Gangetic Plain was surely the more advanced of the two. At the time that Chandragupta Maurya (c. 322-298 B.C.) dwelt in his graceful capital at Pāṭaliputra, the indigenous folk of the Coromandel Plain lived the life of the tribal Iron Age (Maloney 1975:6). The realm of the Hindus was then expressly stated to include only North India; below the Vindhya mountains separating North and South India, was the land of the mleccha-s, barbarians, and vratya-s, good Aryan folk who had degenerated into barbarianism.

Between 200 B.C. and 300 A.D., incipient civilization (by which is meant the beginnings of writing, cities, widespread trade, monumental construction, and political centralization) had apparently emerged in the South (Ibid., p. 33). Stimulated by civilizational development in nearby Sri Lanka, and by sea trade with northeastern India, this early Tamil civilization was founded on irrigated rice agriculture. Its centers of political and cultural development were the centers of early achievements in irrigation. There were three such centers or core areas of technical and political development: the Kaveri river and delta, the Tambaraparanai and Vaigai drainages to the south, and the lushly watered littoral of Kerala. Corresponding to these three centers were the three ancient "kingdoms" of South India, the Chola, Pandya, and Chera (Ibid., p. 12).

The degree of political centralization achieved by these "kingdoms" was, as Stein has argued for most of South Indian history, slight, and in most areas people lived under conditions that doubtless approximated what anthropologists would call statelessness (Stein 1977). Villagers continued to live in the ways of the Iron Age, carrying on a folk tradition that many scholars believe to have represented a uniquely South Indian branch of the prehistoric technological tradition of South Asia (Maloney 1975:8,13). The palace, the city, and the village were to come under the increasing influence of Gangetic civilization during the first centuries of the Christian era; still, it is reasonable to assume that, since this process was entirely peaceful and very gradual, the indigenous traditions of the South Indian hinterland village were not wholly erased by acculturation. Adding weight to this interpretation is the decidedly autochthonous nature of the earliest stratum of Tamil literature, the Caṅkam poetry (dated by some as early as the first to third centuries A.D.). Despite the presence of Sanskritic concepts in the poems, they appear to reveal a world view little influenced by North Indian thought (Hart 1975).

The rise of the Tamil social formation as we know it oday may be traced, according to Stein (1980), to the period ubsequent to the Caṅkam era, when Brahmans became important igures in rural affairs. By the eighth or ninth century .D., there had crystallized throughout the Coromandel Plain n agrarian social order which was to endure without radical lteration for one thousand years. This social formation, tein has argued, was the achievement of Brahmans, the cariers of the Gangetic tradition, working together in the ural hinterland with their allies, indigenous Dravidian ultivating groups (typified by the Veḷḷāḷar).

The Brahman-peasant alliance was of mutual benefit to oth parties. Brahmans benefited from the rich gifts and ndowments peasants gave them for temples and for their mainenance. Peasant cultivators benefited as well, for reasons hat are best understood when we consider the growth of the grarian order. Spreading out from the core centers of irriated agriculture, the agrarian social formation of early uth India encountered areas still inhabited by fierce ibal folk of the dry plains and hills. Not only was it cessary to subdue these folk, but the conquered tribes had be assimilated into the agrarian order--ever voracious for labor--at the lowest status levels, without threatening the status of the original peasant cultivators (Stein 1980:73ff; Ludden 1978:5-8). Brahmans provided these peasant cultivators with a ranking ideology that defined the peasants as "next only to Brahmans in moral standing. They were accorded the status of sātvik, or men of a respectable way of life, and thus distinguished from the lower orders of the population" (Stein 1980:84).

By the ninth century A.D. the social structure of this agrarian order in the irrigated rice-growing regions had tak a clear and persistent form. Its most important caste status as Ludden has remarked, were the same then as they were in 1900: Brahmans, Veḷḷāḷars, Paḷḷars, and Paṟiayars (1978:5). Rice and other lands were controlled, in the main, by group of Veḷḷāḷars, who held hereditary rights (kāṇi) to control agrarian production on a particular plot of land (thus, kāṇ yatcikkāraṉ, "land-controllers"). Since holdings were not allocated to individuals, but on the contrary only to group membership in these Veḷḷāḷar land-controlling groups was ta tamount to access to land. Brahmans provided Veḷḷāḷars wit the ideology they needed to defend their privileges and pos tion by defining Veḷḷāḷars as a morally excellent and distinct caste. In public ritual events at the temples, Veḷḷāḷar donors were rewarded with honors indicating their high status and legitimate rights. In return for this service, Brahmans were accorded, by means of ritualized endowments, legitimate claims to a portion of the Veḷḷāḷar-controlled harvest (Ludden 1978:5-6). Paḷḷar and Paṟaiyar laborers, who were being continuously recruited from the periphery of the expanding order, were--if we may extrapola from contemporary evidence--similarly compensated by ritua allocations at the threshing-floor distribution. They were thereby provided, to offset their low status, with a secure niche in the local economy (Ibid., p. 8).

Accompanying the emergence of a definite Tamil social :ormation in the irrigated rice lands was an enigmatic dis- :inction between "right" (valaṅkai) and "left" (iṭankai) :astes (Appadurai 1974; Beck 1970; Stein 1980). Contem- orary survivals of the division suggest that it represented thoroughgoing bifurcation of the social order into two ival segments, save that Brahmans were deemed to stand bove the split. On the one hand were the "right" castes rouped around the dominant Veḷḷāḷar cultivators, who deemed hemselves committed to reproduce the social ideal of the lassical Gangetic tradition. Among these castes the predom- nant themes were agrarian ideals, a lusty involvement in ife, lack of concern with purity restrictions, and caste nterdependence. On the other hand were the "left" castes, ed by the artisans, who shirked the world of agrarian inde- endence in favor of a town life emphasizing the Brahmanical leal of purity and saintliness. However neat this pattern ay appear, it was contradicted in the lower status levels the "right" division (Beck 1972). Paḷḷars, closely tied Veḷḷāḷars and representing the agrarian laborer par cellence, were--and this is puzzling indeed--of the "left" bdivision (Stein 1980:477, Table VIII-6).

Another persistent social cleavage was founded, as Lud- n (1978) has argued, on the ecological dichotomy of rice- owing lowland versus dry uplands. The characteristic cial formation of the irrigated lowlands, the hierarchical der of Brahmans, Veḷḷāḷars, Paḷḷars, and Paṟaiyars, was t reproduced on the upland plains and hills. Agriculture ere was predominantly of the rainfall-dependent, slash-and- rn variety, which requires little coordination of labor. e upland areas were controlled by warlike castes such as e Kallar and Maravar, whose links with the irrigated low- nds were few and antagonistic until the kings of the late dieval period strove to subdue them.

It was only in the irrigated lowlands that anything roaching a well-integrated social order emerged. In light of Wittfogel's analysis of Oriental despotism (1957), it is very tempting to link the emergence of this "hydraulic society" to the achievement of highly centralized state power. The kings of the period indeed claimed for themselves exalted titles and enormous realms. Yet the evidence strongly suggests a different picture. Throughout most of this period the political organization of the Coromandel Plains resembled not so much a centralized state as a chiefdom, with the territorial segments of the agrarian order (the many <u>nāṭu</u>-s) possessing almost complete autonomy. Far from the royal center conditions doubtless bordered on statelessness (Stein 1977).

The agrarian order of the lowlands was integrated, Ludden (1978) has argued, not by the political power of the state, but rather by means of a comprehensive system of ritual entitlement. The constituent elements in this ritually organized order were caste groups, whose status in the nexus of social relations was defined and legitimated by moral and religious valuations. Brahmans, through temple rituals, invested Veḷḷāḷars with the right to control agrarian reproduction; by denying Paḷḷars and Paṟiayars this ritual entitlement, Brahmans condemned the laborers to landlesness, servitude, and low status. So elaborate was this system of ritual entitlement that "every inch of land, every act of public life, and every necessary interaction in economic processes became infused with ritual meanings and moral valuations" (Ludden 1978:6). And so effective was the ritual legitimation of rights and statuses that no massive component of state power was necessary to buttress the system of inequality or to organize public works. On the whole, the system grew "in a cellular, segmented manner: similar, allied, but staunchly independent units were merely added on as population and irrigated acreage increase" (<u>Ibid</u>., p. 8).

That the agrarian order of medieval Tamilnadu was integrated chiefly on the strength of ritual entitlements and local authority mandates all the more a consideration of how the ranks of Veḷḷāḷars and Paḷḷars were legitimated. As will be seen below, it is quite clear that describing Veḷḷāḷars as "pure" in the Sastric sense is as false as describing Paḷḷars as "Untouchables." It seems highly unlikely, given the decentralized political conditions of medieval Tamilnadu, that this agrarian order could have persisted and grown if half of its component statuses (indeed, three-quarters, for neither Brahmans nor Paṟaiyars were numerous) were founded on a mockery of the Sastric ranking tradition.

The key to this puzzle is to realize--and this is precisely my thesis--that the ritual entitlements on which the whole edifice of Veḷḷāḷar domination is founded are not solely of Gangetic derivation. It has already been suggested that the indigenous village folk culture of the South could well have survived the diffusion of Gangetic culture from the North, a process that appears to have been entirely peaceful and mutually acceptable to all parties concerned. In recognition of this point, Stein has argued that South Indian civilization is an achievement, not of urban intellectuals, but rather of rural Brahmans and peasant cultivators. "An inevitable outcome of millennia of social and cultural propinquity and interaction of Sanskritic and non-Sanskritic cultures," Stein has argued, "was a single cultural system" (1980:6), blending the two traditions into an architectonic whole. In the following chapters, I shall argue that the ritual life of the Tamil people today indeed reveals to us a design for legitimate Veḷḷāḷar domination and Paḷḷar servitude, one rooted in a quintessentially Tamil --and fully Hindu--grasp of the universe.

III. Jaffna and South India

My evidence for this argument is drawn from a study of the ritual organization of traditional authority in Sri Lanka's Jaffna Peninsula. But the use of the Jaffna evidence to stand for the whole of South India requires justification, not in the least because almost all of the scholars who have written on the subject consider Jaffna to be a "marginal" or "interstitial" area, poised between the great centers of mainland Tamil and of Sinhala civilization (see, e.g., Banks 1960:61).

Jaffna, easily the most Indian (and, more to the point, the most Tamil) region of Sri Lanka, has been very wrongly depicted as marginal to the South Indian pattern due to a persistent misunderstanding in the literature. The first studies of South Indian society suggested very strongly, but erroneously, that its most telling and ubiquitous feature was the high rank (both in economic and in religious terms) of Brahmans (see, e.g., Suntheralingam 1974:7f). This impression grew not a little from ethnographic studies in regions like central Tanjore (e.g., Gough 1955, 1960) where Brahmans, through medieval royal entitlements, became dominant landholders in many villages. Thus Nyrop _et al_., for instance, argue that in mainland South India the characteristic social trait is that Brahmans, "as ritually the purest and temporally the most influential group, dominate society" (1971:107). Stein has argued that this trait is distinctively Dravidian (1980:52ff). However, Brahmans are few in Jaffna, numbering only about one percent of the population (Banks 1957:fig. 1), so Nyrop _et al_.(1971) and Dumont (1981:216) distinguish Jaffna from the mainland as a marginal and distinct region.

There are several objections that can be raised to the idea that the high secular rank of Brahmans identifies regions as distinctively Dravidian. First, Brahmans are often the most powerful of castes in certain North Indian villages (see, e.g., Wiser 1958). Second, even in those

South Indian regions where Brahmans now predominate, there is a legend (which possesses, no doubt, at least some historical validity) that the area was formerly dominated by Veḷḷāḷars (Mencher 1970:202). Third, to emphasize the high secular status of Brahmans in defining quintessentially Dravidian areas is to divert attention from what is certainly the most distinctive feature of Dravidian society, namely, the Brahman-Sudra alliance. What is most distinctive about the South Indian social formation is that, even where secular power is in the hands of Sudras, Brahmans--though they might be poor and powerless--are nonetheless accorded the highest rank, and are supported by Sudras. The rise of Brahman secular power in the South is a phenomenon of medieval politics, for the kings of precolonial times sought to enhance the legitimacy of their rule through the granting of entire villages to Brahmans.

The close alliance of Brahmans and high-ranking Sudra dominant castes is not clearly evident in those areas in which royal entitlements wholly obscured the older and more characteristically South Indian pattern. In fact, if we wish to study the ancient patterns of the Brahman-Sudra alliance, we are far more usefully situated when we study not in one of the core areas of royal entitlement, such as Tanjore, but rather in a peripheral and recently settled area like Koṅku Nāṭu (Coimbatore District) or the Jaffna Peninsula. These areas best preserve the social and ritual features of Sudra domination. As Beck has noted, "it is into just such areas that well-organized outside groups [aspiring to the status of the Sudra dominant caste] migrated during times of political and economic prosperity.. . . Once established, such castes continue to dominate local institutions and to structure them to their advantage" (1976:257). In Koṅku Nāṭu, for instance, the dominant Koṅku Veḷḷāḷars (or Kavuṇṭars) believe themselves to have migrated to the region circa the tenth to twelfth centuries A.D.

under the sponsorship of the Chola kings (Beck 1976:281). Jaffna Veḷḷālars maintain precisely the same legend regarding the origins of civilization in the Jaffna Peninsula. In Koṅku Nāṭu, Brahmans--with whom the Koṅku Veḷḷālars are closely allied--comprise only one percent of the Coimbatore District's population (Beck 1972:58, table 1.3). By Nyrop's and Dumont's criterion, we should have to say that Koṅku Nāṭu and Beck's rich evidence can teach us nothing about mainland South India.

That this position is ludicrous should open the way for the admission of the Jaffna evidence to the debate on South Indian civilization. Indeed, Jaffna, so far from representing a marginal area of little comparative interest, is--as I wish to show--an extremely conservative and very South Indian region which to this day preserves, as does Koṅku Nāṭu, the very heart of the South Indian cultural design. To make this suggestion is not to argue that Jaffna is some sort of cultural fossil of the medieval era; nor is it to argue that the culture of Jaffna contains no regionally idiosyncratic elements. It is simply to insist that, since every Tamil region necessarily contains the generative heart of South Indian civilization, the Brahman-Sudra alliance, Jaffna is at least as capable as any other South Indian region to illuminate the general pattern of civilization tha Brahmans and indigenous Sudras achieved in their millenium of alliance.

Yet it may still be objected that Jaffna's ritual life which I propose to describe to reveal the character of Sudra domination, represents little more than a curious and rather odd "folk" tradition from which few general consider ations may be drawn about mainland culture. Underlying thi view is the depiction of folk society first offered by Redfield (1962) and now entrenched in much anthropological thought. In Redfield's view, cultures are integrated by cities (Redfield and Singer 1954); the folk village, in contrast, is relatively isolated from the city's homogenizi influence and, in consequence, maintains its own provincial customs, which are quaint and distinctive. According to this interpretation of South Indian peasant society, the rites of Jaffna are, ipso facto, a divergent tradition save in those instances where "urban influences"--e.g., "Sanskritized" rituals founded on literate models--can be shown. But to interpret the rituals of Dravidian villages in these terms is to place Dravidian society forever beyond the grasp of our understanding. Dravidian civilization, as Stein (1980) has argued, was not an urban but a rural achievement, rooted in the long juxtaposition of indigenous Sudra cultivating castes and their Brahman allies. The result of this juxtaposition was the crystallization, all over the Tamil-speaking areas and beyond, of a comprehensive civilizational design, one aspect of which, I wish to show, was a thoroughgoing marriage of what some would call "Sanskritic" and "non-Sanskritic" rituals. Jaffna rites certainly reveal provincial themes and elements, but their basic design reflects what must be understood to be a widely distributed civilizational achievement. It has recently been noted that, furthermore, there is "an impressive similarity [of 'folk' ritual] practice and concepts over a wide area of South India" (Shulman 1980:5), long evidenced in such texts as Thurston (1912), Oppert (1978), Elmore (1915), and Whitehead (1916).

The wide distribution of a definite Dravidian ritual tradition argues strongly, especially in the context of Stein's analysis of the Brahman-Sudra alliance, that "folk" rituals were part of the pattern which crystallized into traditional Tamil civilization. But the point is best demonstrated by the contemporary evidence. The rituals of Jaffna--rituals whose basic patterns are found all over the Dravidian culture area--reveal to us that the process by which dominant cultivating castes came to be invested with the right to manage agrarian affairs included not only

Brahmanical rites (chiefly, those of the temple), but also a wide array of non-Brahman rites that have long been presumed to reflect little more than an illiterate religion of superstition and fear (Whitehead 1916), or a desire to secure "pragmatic" gains (Mandelbaum 1966). This unfortunate and ethnocentric misconstruction, which has identified any rite not immediately located in the Sanskritic scriptures as a manifestation of a primitive and utilitarian consciousness, has for many long years made it impossible for us to perceive the unity of the Dravidian ritual design, which unites that which is Brahmanical and non-Brahmanical into an architectonic whole of astonishing coherence and of a distinctively Dravidian sensibility. It is part of the aim of this study to unveil this design, as Jaffna has revealed it to us, and to point out that it represents one of the most remarkable achievements of traditional civilization anywhere in the globe.

The marriage of Brahmanical and non-Brahmanical rites in the Dravidian ritual tradition very probably occurred precisely because the Brahmanical tradition alone, as we have seen, could not establish the high rank and privileges of Sudra landholders. The syncretism of the two produced a system of ritual status definitions that, for its Dravidian context, was far more powerful. Rooted in a quintessentially Dravidian grasp of the universe, which everyone in the system shared, the Brahmanical-cum-Dravidian ritual tradition invested all parties to the system of agrarian caste relations with statuses that could not be questioned. Indeed, so rooted is the Tamil "caste system" in a system of ritual depictions of status that it is probably not accurate to call it a "caste system" at all. Many groups in Tamil society, to be sure, are appropriately called "castes," in the sense of occupationally distinct groups of persons thought to be related to one another and possessing an ascribed, inflexible status. But to interpret Tamil society in these terms is to lose sight entirely of the comprehensive ritual design through which these statuses consistently emerged and acquired meaning in Tamil social relations. Rather than speaking of the agrarian social formation of the irrigated lowlands in terms of four castes (Brahman, Veḷḷāḷar, Paḷḷar, and Paṟiayar), it is far more accurate to say, as Ludden has recently perceived (1978), that these statuses emerged and were sustained in a process of ritual relations which established their rights and responsibilities in the total agrarian order.

To the extent that these four "caste" statuses are widely distributed throughout the Tamil lands, and to the extent that they were sustained by an equally widespread ritual design, it should hardly surprise us to find that any Tamil region is essentially exemplary of the whole culture area. The rituals of Jaffna inform us about the religious meaning of statuses in the traditional South Indian social formation because the society of Jaffna displays precisely the same social pattern (chapter two). Jaffna stands, in fact, uniquely poised to instruct us well on the ancient coherence of the Brahman-Sudra achievement and the process by which agrarian caste statuses were created and sustained. Unlike South India, the Jaffna Peninsula has experienced no anti-Brahman movement at all. On the mainland, where entrenched Brahman political and economic power was strengthened even further by British colonial practices, a virulent anti-Brahman political movement emerged in the late nineteenth century (Suntheralingam 1974) and, by the mid-twentieth century, at the height of the movement, Gough described the Brahmans of Tanjore as a people scorned for their conservatism and their seigneurial aspirations (1955: 38). Village rituals, which formerly dramatized the unity among the village's many castes, were dying out all over the Tanjore District, and in some areas had been abandoned altogether (1955:47-48). Jaffna, far from the currents of Indian politics and language conflict which exacerbated the anti-Brahman movement in the mainland, has known no anti-Brahman sentiment (Banks 1960:69), and in its hinterland villages the ancient coherence of the Brahman-Sudra alliance is even now plain to see.*

A study purporting to isolate a Tamil caste ranking ideology inevitably runs the risk of getting confused with the program of Tamil nationalism, which wishes to celebrate that which is purely Tamil and to label as "cultural imperialism" the Brahmanical or Sanskritic element in Tamil culture. Whatever satisfaction or political expediency this program provides, it is nonetheless false to the tradition which has, in fact, prevailed for a millennium in the Tamil lands. It is certainly true that much of modern Tamil culture issues from a northern source, but the northern element has been inextricably woven together with indigenous Tamil cultural traits to produce a remarkable synthesis, true to the essence of both traditions. To deny this synthesis and to differentiate the two traditions, as if they were only artificially joined, is to rip apart the coherence of the Tamil view of the world and to place it forever beyond the grasp of scholarship. It is my conviction that we have failed to comprehend the nature of Tamil culture because we have been too eager to differentiate between the Brahmanical and the non-Brahmanical, the civilized and the primitive, the "great tradition" and the "little tradition," the "transcendental" and the "pragmatic" (Srinivas 1968; Redfield and Singer 1954; Mandelbaum 1966). Were this study to follow the program of Tamil nationalism, the mistake would only be repeated. The coherence and unity of Tamil culture are achievements of Brahmans and Sudras working together for a thousand years. Although the two have recently parted ways politically, the unity of Tamil culture yet stands, and doubtless moderates the schism.

---

*Jaffna's extreme cultural conservatism has played no small role in the increasingly violent Tamil separatist movement in Sri Lanka (see Pfaffenberger 1981).

It must also be stressed here that, since the nineteenth century, the dominant castes of the Tamil lands have not deemed themselves to be Sudras, save in Jaffna, that most conservative of Tamil regions. The objection may be raised that many non-Brahmans in South India will find the term Sudra offensive, to the extent that it applies to them. The evidence, however, strongly suggests that, prior to the nineteenth century, Sudra rank was not an embarrassment to such castes as the Vel̤l̤āl̤ars. They proclaimed that status, for instance, on temple inscriptions. It was only after the coming of the British censuses in the nineteenth century that Vel̤l̤āl̤ars began to claim for themselves a higher rank in the Sastric terms, and they did so under circumstances that are indeed telling. The British colonial officials, as would later ethnologists, tried to interpret South Indian caste statuses in terms of the status categories of the Dharmaśāstra-s, that is, the four-fold status configuration of varṇa-s (Brahmans, Ksatriyas, Vaisyas, and Sudras). The British asked Vel̤l̤āl̤ars if they were not, as the texts asserted, indeed to be classed as servants of the three higher varṇa-s; the reaction, predictably enough, was one of vehement indignation. In 1871, for instance, Vel̤l̤āl̤ars claimed that "they had been seriously injured in reputation, and handled with great injustice, in being classified as Sudras by the Municipal Commissioners of Madras. . .the very idea of service is, as it needs must be, revolting to the Vellala, whose profession teaches him perfect independence. . . .Hence a Vellala cannot be of the Sudra or servile class (Thurston 1909:VII, 366-67). What was considered an injustice by nineteenth century Vel̤l̤āl̤ars was to be defined as Sudras in Sastric terms, as if the textual codification of that status could never have been reinterpreted in the subsequent cultural evolution of Indian society. My aim here is to expose the Tamil notion of the Sudra status, which prior to the British incursion was enthusiastically claimed by Vel̤l̤āl̤ars, without being blinded either by excessive emphasis on the Sastric meaning of statuses or by the webs of defensive ideology that twentieth century Tamils have erected in the face of misinformed colonial policy.

It should be noted that, in dealing with South India as a cultural region, I follow Stein (1980) in placing emphasis not on the drawing of precise boundaries, but rather on the core or nuclear area in which the regional civilization of southern India was created and from which South Indian culture radiates. That center, he argues, is the irrigated, lowland basin of the Tamil plain, where for more than a millennium Brahmans and Sudras worked together to create the South Indian cultural design. It was from this core area that Veḷḷāḷar folk emigrated, during the heyday of the great South Indian kings, to create between the tenth and the fourteenth centuries such classic zones of Sudra domination as Koṅku Nāṭu and the Jaffna Peninsula. The field of South Indian studies is well justified in assigning methodological primacy to the study of Tamil culture, for it was from the Tamil wellspring that South Indian civilization arose. This study no doubt bears implications for the analysis of society in such regions as Kerala, Andhra Pradesh, and even contemporary North India, but I leave aside here any attempt here to assess them. The aim here is to unveil the Tamil cultural underpinnings of the Tamil caste system.

Chapter 2

THE FORM OF SUDRA DOMINATION IN TAMIL JAFFNA

"Agriculture is no agriculture,
unless it is performed by Vellalas."

--South Indian proverb (cited in Thurston 1909:VII, 388)

I. The Rise of Tamil Culture in Jaffna

Just when Tamil Hindus first came to Jaffna is not nown, but intensive settlement probably did not begin until fter the demise of the great, ancient center of Sinhala ivilization, the irrigated plains of Rājaraṭṭha (the northentral region) (Indrapala 1969). After Sinhala settlement ad drifted to the central highlands and the southwest, a indu kingdom arose in Jaffna, with its capital at Nallur, ot far from present-day Jaffna Town (Banks 1957:18-30, 419-7; Pathamanathan 1978). The kingdom's historical chronicles uggest that Veḷḷāḷars played an important role in its ffairs. The raison d'être of kingly rule seems to have centered on the fostering of settled, ordered society, and owards that end the kings appear to have organized coloniation programs in which prominent Brahmans, famed Veḷḷāḷars, nd the "eighteen kuṭis"--the conventional epithet for the eḷḷāḷars' subordinates (Hutton 1961:67)--were brought from outh India (Anonymous 1827:52). No king could rule without he support of his Veḷḷāḷar ātikars, or chieftains, who were uite prepared to conspire against him if his rule did not uit their interests. It was by interfering in the internal olitics of Jaffna that the wily Portuguese brought down the ast Hindu king of Jaffna in 1618 (Pieris 1914:127ff).

Portuguese rule in Jaffna was fairly short-lived (1618-658). The Portuguese army destroyed the peninsula's hundreds of temples, and forced the population to convert (nominally, save for the fishing castes) to the Roman Catholic Church (Navaratnam 1964:34). Under the Dutch (1658-1795), firm administrative control was established, with the aim not of transforming the indigenous social system, but rather of extracting from it as much profit as possible (Banks 1957: 421). Under Dutch rule, the status of the lowly Untouchable --the praedial Naḷavars and Paḷḷars, in particular--was defined as "slavery" in the sense of Roman law, an act that deepened Veḷḷāḷar control and dominance over the Untouchable and, as will become evident, well lined Dutch pockets. To understand the effect of Dutch rule, we must look closely at the structure of Jaffna's caste system and at the peninsula' ecology.

Philipus Baldeus, a Dutch missionary, reported that the "Bellalas" of seventeenth century Jaffna were agricultur alists, surrounded by their cattle, their verdant fields, an their servants. Proud of their ancestry and resolutely endo gamous, Veḷḷāḷars deemed themselves superior to the "Nal-louas" (Naḷavars) and "Parreas" (Paṟaiyars), whom Baldeus termed "nasty and dirty" folk. Veḷḷāḷars regarded them with a "wonderful contempt," and set them to work tilling the ground, caring for cattle, watering plants, and performing "the most disagreeable and dirty offices in life." These "despised and vile" people were expected to show an "extra-ordinary respect" for the highest castes: "on an inferior passing a superior he must show his insignificance by a deep and respectful bow to the earth" (Baldeus 1958-59:372). Veḷ-ḷāḷars, even though they were proud and everywhere "the wealthiest people," held Brahmans in the highest regard, due without doubt to the Brahmans' great purity and cleanliness, which impressed Baldeus. In his eyes the Brahmans of Jaffna were "as modest in their deportment, as could be wished; they are sober, alert, clean, civil and friendly and very moderate in eating and drinking and never touch any strong drink. They wash twice a day, and abstain from eating

MAP II.

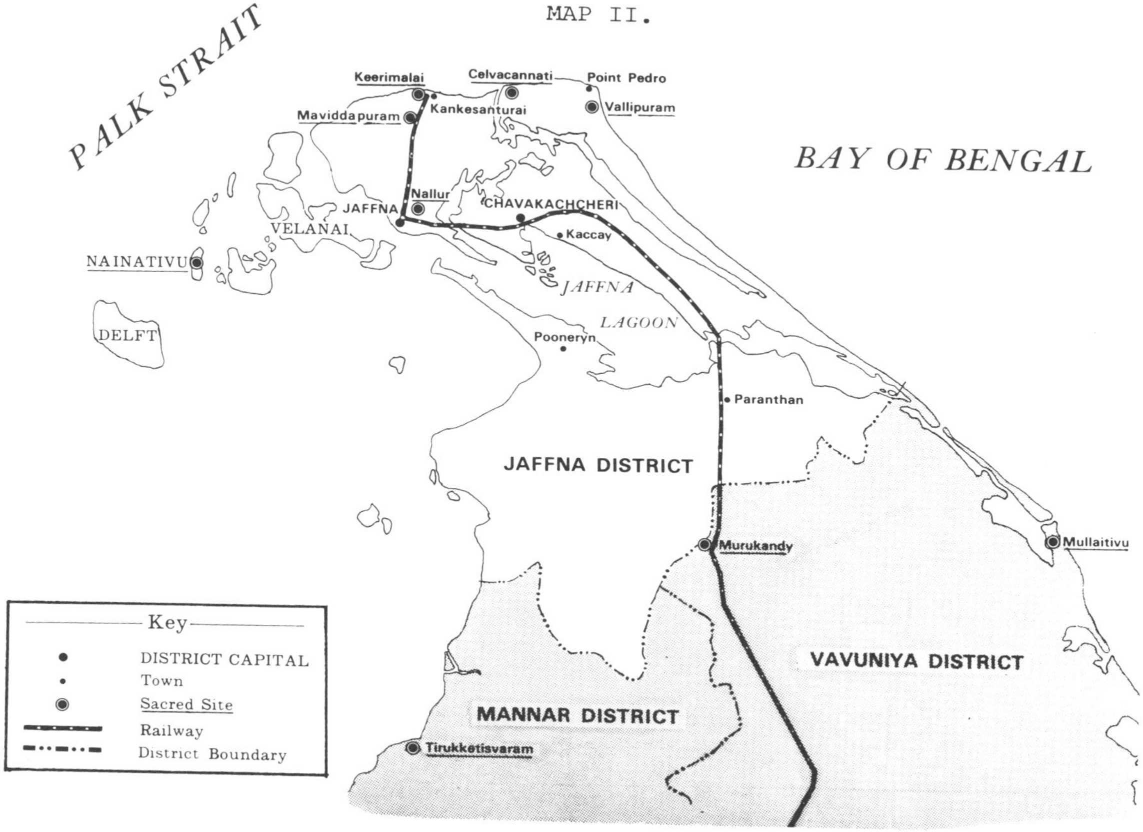

Jaffna District and Its Environs.

anything that was endowed with or can produce life" (Ibid., p. 354). Seventeenth century Jaffna reiterated, in sum, the pattern of social organization that has been said to typify Tamil culture: a rural status ladder composed of pure and esteemed Brahmans; of a non-Brahman, dominant agricultural caste; of despised, praedial laborers of Untouchable rank; and of a number of small, professional castes (artisans, washermen, barbers, and musicians).

The ethnology of Jaffna has shown that, in Vellālar eyes, this social system should be centered and focused exclusively on them (Banks 1960:71). In the old days, before British liberalization (ca. mid to late nineteenth century) altered the picture to some degree, the Vellālar is said to have lived like a chieftain, or as one Tamil put it to A.M. Hocart,

> like a feudal lord with all his vassals round about him. He had therefore slaves and vassals to serve him on all occasions, and these slaves and vassals represented different castes who served him in such capacity whenever occasion demanded. The vassals were called kudimai and the slaves adimai (1950:7).

The kutimai castes, roughly homologous to the "right-side castes" of South India,* were not slaves; they could not be bought or sold. But families of these castes were obliged to particular Vellālar lords, and had to perform their traditional secular and ritual occupations at the lords' beck and call. Among these castes in precolonial times were the five artisan castes (Goldsmiths, Blacksmiths, Carpenters, Temple Carvers, and Coppersmiths) and the other professional castes (Potters, Masons, Washermen, Barbers, and Paraiyars) (Banks

---

*The right-side versus left-side distinction is, to my knowledge, unknown in Jaffna, but it can be argued that the atimai-kutimai distinction retains the spirit of its South Indian counterpart. The link between the two distinctions will become clearer when the South Indian distinction is explored in more detail below (chapter three, II.1).

TABLE I

THE CASTES OF JAFFNA

	Tamil Name	English Name	Traditional Occupation	Aṭimai-Kuṭimai Status
Touchable Castes	Pirāman	Brahman	temple priest	--
	Śaiva Kurukkal	Śaiva priest	temple priest for non-Brahman shrines	--
	Veḷḷāḷar	--	landholder, farmer	--
	Paṇṭāram	Garland maker	temple helper	--
	Ciṟpācāri	--	temple sculptor	--
	Kōviyar	--	domestic servant	aṭimai
	Taṭṭar	Goldsmith	goldsmith	kuṭimai
	Kaṟaiyar	--	deep sea fisher	--
	Taccar	Carpenter	carpenter	kuṭimai
	Kollar	Blacksmith	blacksmith	kuṭimai
	Nattuvar	Musician	auspicious music	--
	Kaikular	Weaver	weaver	--
	Cāṇṭar	Oil monger	sesame oil maker	--
	Kucuvar	Potter	potter	kuṭimai
	Mukkuvar	--	lagoon fisher	--
	Vaṇṇar	Dhoby	washerman	kuṭimai
Untouchables	Ampaṭṭar	Barber	barber	kuṭimai
	Paḷḷar	--	praedial labor	aṭimai
	Naḷavar	--	praedial labor	aṭimai
	Paṟiayar	--	drummer	kuṭimai

SOURCE: Kenneth David, 1974:47.

1957:439). The notion underlying the *kuṭimai* category is that these castes possess certain skills, which have been intensified by repeated intermarriage. Thus it is said in Jaffna today that "the son of the blacksmith will excel even his father."

The fitness of each *kuṭimai* caste extends to its ritual role as well. Only the Barber can shave, and only he can perform certain indispensable ritual services during life-cycle ceremonies in the Veḷḷāḷar home. These services will be discussed in detail later in this study; here it should be noted that the proper Veḷḷāḷar household should have a full complement of *kuṭimai* servants, the word itself being synonymous with a Veḷḷāḷar family's respectability. The root *kuṭi-* means, according to Fabricius, "family, tribe . . .inhabitation, dwelling, house" (1910:203). Thus the *kuṭimai* castes were called the *kuṭimakkaḷ*, the "children of the house," indicating the ideal that they should be closely, and personally, associated in a warm, quasi-familial way with the Veḷḷāḷar lord and his family who depend on them.

With one exception, the slaves (*aṭimai*) were praedial rather than domestic, this distinction being found elsewhere in South India (Srinivas 1952:20f). There are said to have been four *aṭimai* castes at one time: the Naḷavars, Paḷḷars, Kōviyars, and a fourth caste called the Dutch Chiandos (Banks 1957:441). The last is said to have been none other than today's Cāṇṭars, but Dutch records seem to distinguish the two groups. The "Chiandos" were, in 1697, "few in number" (Raghavan n.d.:118-19). From an economic standpoint, the two most important *aṭimai* castes were the menial laborers, the Naḷavar and Paḷḷar, both Untouchables in caste status and similar to the "left-side" Paḷḷars of South India. The Untouchable slaves lived apart from their Veḷḷāḷar masters, often in palmyra groves where they were permitted to forage and to garden for their subsistence.

However, their master had the right to call them to work at any time, and when he did so, he was obliged to provide them only with meals and clothing (Banks 1957:443).

To use the word "slaves" with regard to the aṭimai castes is probably misleading. To be sure, the Dutch regarded them as such. And yet studies of slavery in South India suggest quite strongly that the status of slaves like the Paḷḷars is not accurately described by the conventions of Roman law: that the slave is unfree, and that the full power of the State lies behind that condition. It appears, in precolonial South India, that slaves had always open to them the sanction of deserting a cruel master, just as the whole countryside might desert a cruel chieftain (Kumar 1965:32; Srinivas 1952:22). The sanction might have been chosen only under severe circumstances; nonetheless, there have been tracts of virgin forests or dry lands throughout South India (until recently) in which a single family could set up subsistence, slash-and-burn agriculture (Ludden 1978:3). This is true of Jaffna as well; lying just to the south are vast tracts of the Vanni jungles. To be sure, they are infested with malaria and populated by wild animals, but the aṭimai slaves could take refuge in them under severe, trying circumstances, and live virtually undetected.

The availability of desertion as a sanction against cruel treatment suggests that the relation between Veḷḷāḷar master and aṭimai "slave" was not quite so harsh as one might imagine. Without envisioning a "golden age" in which slaves esteemed their status, we can nevertheless suggest that, given the option of desertion, the aṭimai castes were given certain traditional privileges to go along with their disabilities. As Bremen notes,

> The servant in traditional India was not only a laborer but also a client, and as such he was entitled to affection, generosity, and intercession on the part of his master, who, as a patron, had to guard and promote the interests of his subordinate. Conversely, the servant owed his master respect and loyalty (1974:20).

By defining the atimai Untouchables as slaves in the sense of Roman law, and in particular, as enslaved persons attached to a specific master irrespective of rights to land, the Dutch unleashed forces which were to insulate Vellālar domination from later administrative efforts (on the part of the British, ca. 1844-1948, and of the modern Sinhala-dominated independent government) to destroy it. The immediate effect of the Dutch changes was the near-monstrous growth of a slave-based export economy, a point best appreciated in light of the peninsula's ecology.

Forlorn and arid in its natural appearance, the peninsula would hardly seem to hold much promise for farming. Standing within the country's arid zone, Jaffna receives little rain, averaging between 25 and 50 inches per year. Much of the rain falls in the northeastern monsoon, which begins in November and tapers off by January. The southwestern monsoon (from May to October) which so lushly water the wet zone of the southwest, is cut off by the central highland massif and brings little rain to Jaffna (Farmer 1957:750f). There are, furthermore, no rivers in Jaffna, and on that account rice agriculture must depend on rain. Rice is grown in low-lying paddies dug out to collect rainfall. The excavations must have involved much labor, and local legends attribute the paddies to the heroic, single-handed efforts of a great, legendary Vellālar hero, an ātikar, who was given the land by the Hindu kings of Nallur When the monsoon rains fall on time, and evenly, throughout the monsoon period, the rice paddies, having collected the rains, flourish with a lovely carpet of young shoots. The bunds of the paddies are constructed very carefully to hold the rainfall, which nourishes the plants. The hot, dry weather of late January and February ripens the grains, and the harvest is gathered by February. Yet the monsoon is as likely to fall unevenly--often in one violent storm of twenty-four hours duration--as it is to fall properly.

Rice agriculture is, even in the best years, only marginally economic; however, Veḷḷāḷars were traditionally obliged to grow rice because the State demanded tribute in kind, to be paid over to the State's representative at the threshing-floor distribution (Banks 1957:426).

Far more productive are the garden lands (<u>tōṭṭam</u>). The soils of Jaffna are of decayed limestone, and while they are not naturally fertile, they are nonetheless loamy and well aerated. In the small garden plots, Jaffna farmers bury into the soil a variety of humus-bearing material, including manure, decayed palmyra thatch, green leaf manure, and household garbage. The demand for humus has shaped many details of Jaffna rural life. Fences are made of a living bush, which propagates easily from cuttings and produces a luxurious canopy of green leaves. Cattle are tethered to sheds, which are placed over the fallow soil. Walls and roofs are made, at least in the villages, of palmyra thatch, which is renewed occasionally, the decayed thatch then being dug into the soil. Nothing is wasted.

When properly fertilized, the soil must be watered from wells, which tap a seemingly inexhaustible supply of fresh ground water. Jaffna's abundant ground water supply demarcates it firmly from the central plains to the south, and has ensured its prosperity. Jaffna gardens are independent of rainfall, so the peninsula is protected to some extent from famine owing to drought. If rice is unavailable, there is an abundant, compensating resource: the palmyra. From it issues stout timber, a staple flour, an edible fruit, an alcoholic beverage (toddy), a molasses-like sugar (jaggery), and extremely useful fronds, from which are made fences, mats, caps, fans, umbrellas, and even paper (Tennent 1860:519ff).

The combination of hot sun, dependable water supply, sedulous manuring, and a population protected from drought encourages the profitable production of crops destined for curry pots: onions, gourds, chillies, turmeric, ginger, pumpkins, eggplant, and gourds. Among the other food crops grown are cabbage, melon, sweet potatoes, gram, millet, and pulses. Tobacco is extensively planted in Jaffna, and the crop consumed by a local cigar industry. The productivity of the garden or tōṭṭam lands depends, however, on the farmer's ability to make a prodigious investment in labor. Gathering humus, digging it into the soil, drawing water from wells, and watering the plants requires much effort, and on the whole, it is human effort which is required. So long as labor is available, Jaffna farmers can reap astonishing profits from even an acre of tōṭṭam land (Selvanayagam 1966:174; Thuraisingham 1953).

The Dutch encouraged cash-crop tōṭṭam agriculture by defining the Untouchables as slaves of Veḷḷāḷars, importing thousands of additional slaves from South India, and doing away with the final instances of revenue payments in rice (Banks 1957:428). It appears that a wholesale shift from rice agriculture to tōṭṭam style gardening then took place, with the result that Jaffna became a rice-importing area, which it remains to this day. The Dutch grew rich from the export trade, and Jaffna came to be regarded as one of the most prized of Asian holdings. The shift was accompanied, in addition, by the destruction of the legal framework by which Untouchables or other castes possessed rights in the Veḷḷāḷars' harvest. Land appeared on the market, and was exchanged on the market, without any reference to the traditionally recognized rights of Untouchables to be transferred with it. In this process, there may well have been a collusion of sorts between the Dutch concept of private property and the indigenous idea of garden lands, which were even in the traditional context never subject to intervening claims.

These changes altered the traditional form of Veḷḷāḷar domination, but they also served to insulate Veḷḷāḷars from the later attempts of more liberal administrators to legislate social justice and equality. The Dutch changes exacerbated the economic differentiation between Veḷḷāḷars and Untouchables by denying, in effect, the rights in land that Untouchables traditionally held. Untouchables, so far from being guaranteed a minimum income, were relegated to membership in a landless class, whose members were exposed to--and victimized by--the impersonal forces of the market. These forces were prodigious indeed. During the nineteenth and twentieth centuries, Veḷḷāḷars monopolized the economic, educational, and political resources generated by the British presence in Sri Lanka (1795-1948)(Kearney 1973: 188). They invested their resulting riches not only in land, but also in elaborate domestic ceremonies, which Untouchables were forbidden to emulate (Banks 1957:435). This prestige-oriented, agrarian "capitalism" did not produce general prosperity, but rather set off repeated cycles of land price inflation. By 1952-1954, as Banks noted, land prices were "exceptionally high." Garden land cost Rs.8,000/=per acre in Jaffna, whereas an acre of equivalent land in Kandy cost only Rs. 500/=. Jaffna land was at that time more expensive than land in East Anglia, England (1957:28); moreover, opening up waste lands is even more expensive than buying arable land.

Since neither Untouchables nor any other non-Veḷḷāḷars can easily afford to buy land, the dominance of the Veḷḷāḷars in Jaffna's affairs remains effectively unchallenged. To be sure, social change has altered at least to some extent the pattern of Veḷḷāḷar domination in Jaffna. British liberalizations permitted many of the *kuṭimai* castes to pursue their occupations in the expanding economies of towns and rural marketplaces, and so many of the artisan castes established a fierce independence from Veḷḷāḷar control. The *aṭimai*-*kuṭimai* distinction collapsed, and what was left of the Veḷḷāḷars' traditional cadre of servants was grouped together under the label *kuṭimakkaḷ* (Kōviyars, Naḷavars, Paḷḷars, Barbers, Washermen, and Paṟaiyars can still be found carrying on traditional relations with Vellāḷar lords). Veḷḷāḷars see the present days as a "sad decline from the golden age when Vellālas ruled all" (Banks 1960:71), but it is nonetheless true that, for the Untouchable <u>aṭimai</u> castes, reform has brought precious little change (Banks 1957:72). Present-day Jaffna Untouchables are called, by polite circumlocution, "Minority Tamils." They constitute about one-fifth of Jaffna's population (Table II). According to many high-caste folk in Jaffna, the Untouchables are unclean (<u>tuppuravu illai</u>) and deserve the social disabilities--servitude, landlessness, poverty, and lack of access to wells, temples and cremation grounds --that Veḷḷāḷars still try to impose on them. A Prevention of Social Disabilities Act was passed in 1957, and was strengthened considerably in 1971, but in 1974-1975 many of the Veḷḷāḷar-imposed disabilities were still endured by Untouchables. Despite these and other liberal reforms, the traditional relations of dominance and submission between Veḷḷāḷars and the <u>aṭimai</u> Untouchables "have continued without much disturbance" (Banks 1957:446).

The radical transformation of Jaffna's agrarian system raises the quite legitimate question of whether the Jaffna evidence should be interpreted as a sign of Tamil tradition or of a bastardized, postcolonial melange of East and West. To be sure, the economic forces and social relations of the peninsula's mode of production, together with the political and legal framewords in which they are situated, have experienced very great change. And yet, on the highest superstructural level, that of religion and ritual, it is quite apparent that radical change has <u>not</u> occurred. On the contrary, Veḷḷāḷars and their clients (of what is now a subordinate <u>class</u>) still try to conceptualize their relationship in the old way. Veḷḷāḷars, for instance, maintain rice paddies even though they are at best marginally economic, for it is felt that the genuine Veḷḷāḷar is one who grows rice and compensates his servants with it (Banks

TABLE II

THE CASTES OF JAFFNA: POPULATION
(estimated)

Tamil Name	English Name	Proportion of Jaffna's Tamil Population
Pirāman	Brahman	0.7
Śaiva Kurukkal	Śaiva priest	0.2*
Veḷḷāḷar	--	50.0
Paṇṭāram	Garland maker	1.0
Ciṟpācāri	--	0.5*
Kōviyar	--	7.0
Tattar	Goldsmith	0.6
Kaṟaiyar	--	10.0
Taccar	Carpenter	2.0
Kollar	Blacksmith	0.4
Nattuvar	--	0.2
Kaikular	Weaver	0.5*
Cāṇṭār	Oil monger	0.5*
Kucuvar	Potter	0.5*
Mukkuvar	--	2.0*
Vaṇṇar	Dhoby	1.5
Ampaṭṭar	Barber	0.9
Paḷḷar	--	9.0
Naḷavar	--	9.0
Paṟaiyar	--	2.7
Other Castes		0.8*

SOURCE: Banks 1957:figure 1, n.p. This figure is based on a survey of village headmen. Banks' figures are, however, incomplete. Figures marked with an asterisk reflect the author's estimate, and are not as reliable as Banks'.

PLATE II.

A Paḷḷar (Untouchable) woman, accompanied by her daughter and son, weeds a Veḷḷāḷar-owned rice paddy near Chavakachcheri, Sri Lanka.

1957:13). This example suggests the inertia of superstructures, which may remain resolutely entrenched even though the mode of production in which they first arose has undergone considerable modification.

The superstructural framework of traditional Veḷḷāḷar domination is still very apparent in Jaffna, and it is on that basis that I would suggest, with caution, that the Jaffna evidence is relevant to the debate on the curious social forms of South Indian caste. Similarly radical changes have doubtless afflicted the South Indian evidence; every datum, if it is to stand as a sign of tradition, should be considered with caution. But the best argument, perhaps, is to stress that, so far from representing a peripheral area of limited interest, Jaffna in fact preserves the perplexing forms of South Indian caste--especially the Brahman-Sudra alliance--with astonishing accuracy. Jaffna has protected these forms from the twentieth-century, anti-Brahman movements which have obscured, at least, an ancient and characteristic Tamil institution in South India. Jaffna, as noted earlier, has had no anti-Brahman movement at all.

The puzzlingly high rank of the Sudra Veḷḷāḷars is quite apparent in the evidence, and so is the enigmatic status of the supposedly impure <u>aṭimai</u> Untouchables. That they are called "unclean" is rather remarkable, for judged strictly in the terms supplied by the classical ranking criteria of the <u>Dharmaśāstra</u>-s, it can well be argued that Naḷavars and Paḷḷars are hardly more impure than the Peninsula's very worldly Veḷḷāḷars. Most Naḷavars and Paḷḷars in Jaffna avoid eating beef, especially carrion. To scavenge carrion is the role of the Paṟaiyar, and it is because the <u>aṭimai</u> Untouchables refuse this role that they are ranked higher than Paṟaiyars (Banks 1957:36). The diet of the <u>aṭimai</u> Untouchables is on the whole indistinguishable from that of the Veḷḷāḷars, who do eat meat, although they abstain from beef. And yet it is said of the Untouchables in general that "beef-eating is the caste custom of these castes," notwithstanding the seemingly contradictory assertion that Nalavars are higher than Pallars because the former do not eat beef (Banks 1957:198-201, 363-64).

Even if Pallars and Nalavars avoid the role of scavenging, they are in the Vellālar view still guilty of it:

> Some groups of Pallas have the reputation of stealing and slaughtering cows of Vellalas to eat them secretly. They are said to kill the cow and cook it that night and eat the whole animal so that there is no trace left. This is thought very wicked on ritual grounds, apart from the objection to theft; in fact the action is believed so horrible that it is usually discussed in a lowered voice. Whether it actually occurs or not is uncertain, as it is always said to be done by Pallas of neighbouring villages; 'our Pallas'--those directly employed and controlled by the Vellalas speaking--are good Pallas, and never do such things. In Chirrupiddi, the Woombadi Pallas were thought to be wicked in this way, but the Vellalas of the village Puttur, where the Woombadi Pallas lived, denied these accusations and said their Pallas were 'good', and accused yet a third group of Pallas of doing this (Ibid., p. 364).

No less contradictory and strained is the assertion that the two castes' traditional occupation, palmyra-climbing, is impure. To be sure, there is an old and fully orthodox Hindu ban on liquor, the making of which is one object of climbing palmyras. Smṛtyarthasāra, for instance, listed as sources of extreme pollution "excreta, urine, semen, blood, fat, marrow, liquor, and intoxicants" (Kane 1975:IV, 316). This view is certainly held in Jaffna with regard to cocoanut whiskey (arrack), beer, wine, and western spirits, which many Vellālars will not touch. But it is emphatically not held with regard to palmyra toddy.

Toddy, in contrast to whiskey, is felt to be "nicely cool" (nalla kuḷir), health-giving, and wholesome. Vellālars, particularly if they work hard during the day, consume it eagerly and in copious amounts. There is nothing about toddy-drinking that is held reprehensible, save among a few "teetotalers" who are influenced by Christian missionaries or who are Christians themselves. Notwithstanding that much of the toddy they tap is destined for Veḷḷāḷar refreshment, Naḷavars and Paḷḷars are nonetheless held to be impure on account of toddy-tapping. That this accusation does not make much sense has been noted by Banks:

> Teetotalers, but no one else, sometimes explain that toddy-tapping and selling toddy are very wicked and contrary to religion.. . . But this reason is obviously an ad hoc justification, as palm tree climbing for even the most legitimate reasons, for example to cut branches for fodder, is thought equally debased.. . . The degradation of palm climbing is somehow associated with the actual technique of climbing these trees. This involves clasping the tree with arms and legs, the feet being tied together with cord; this cord is used as a grip while the arms are raised, after which the legs are rapidly raised up and a new grip obtained. With this method of climbing, the genitals of the climber are sometimes exposed by mistake. . .[and] it is shameful for men to expose their genitals publicly (1957:397-98).

Yet this interpretation is only Banks' conjecture, and he notes that he was "never able to get a direct statement about why this sort of climbing was thought so degrading" (*Ibid.*) Clearly it may be shameful to expose one's genitals, but it is inconsistent with the northern, classical tradition to suggest that exposure makes a man unclean.

Consider, further, that Untouchables must remain shoeless. To be without shoes is surely not a polluting condition. According to the purity ideology, Untouchables *should* wear shoes; then they would be polluted by the leather, just as Paṟaiyars are supposed to be polluted by their drumskins (Moffatt 1979:112). In fact, shoes are thought unclean in Jaffna and should never be worn in sacred places--that is, in homes, temples, and interestingly enough, in fields: "One [old] . . .pensioner who had worn shoes for many years and whose feet were also sore, was forced by public opinion, despite his pain, obvious reluctance, and considerable influence, to stop wearing shoes when visiting his field" (Banks 1957: 359-60). Obviously, it is more pure to be barefoot, and forbidding Untouchables to wear shoes would seem to enhance their purity.

A list of the lifestyle features that Jaffna Veḷḷāḷars impose on Untouchables should help to drive home the features irrelevance to the purity and pollution concepts. In Jaffna, Untouchable women traditionally were forbidden to cover their breasts, to wear gold earrings, to be the object of Brahaman-officiated life-cycle rites, or to live in a concrete home. Untouchable men were forbidden to wear shirts, to cut their hair, to use umbrellas, or to ride bicycles. All Untouchables were forbidden to sit higher than Veḷḷāḷars, to buy land, to cremate their dead, to enter temples, to enter Veḷḷāḷar homes to enter teashops, to walk on pavements if Veḷḷāḷars were using them, to insult Veḷḷāḷars, or to marry without Veḷḷāḷar permission. All of these features add up to a lifestyle that, Veḷḷāḷars say, epitomizes pollution (*tīṭṭu*). Yet many of these imposed features make no sense at all in terms of the pollution concept.

II. The Symmetry of the Anomalous Ranks

Jaffna's remarkable social formation preserves, in sum, precisely the enigmatic status configuration that has been observed throughout southern India: within the encompassing and fully orthodox ranks of the genuinely pure Brahman and the genuinely impure Paṟaiyar, there are two statuses that simply do not make sense: that of the falsely pure Veḷḷāḷar and the falsely impure *aṭimai* Untouchable, who are hardly distinguishable on the grounds of purity of custom. And yet, puzzlingly enough, the Veḷḷāḷars rank *higher* than the artisans who emulate the purity ideal, and the *aṭimai* Untouchables in fact rank *lower* than certain castes which are involved in impurity (the Barbers and Washermen). The Veḷḷāḷar and *aṭimai* statuses in fact seem to display a reverse symmetry, as if they were mirror images of each other.

PLATE III.

A Paṟaiyar drummer of the Jaffna Peninsula.

Caste origin myths in Jaffna reveal another aspect of the reverse symmetry by which the two anomalous ranks differ from each other and so diverge from the Sastric mold. In keeping with the South Indian tradition, Jaffna Paṟaiyars regard themselves as fallen Brahmans, while the aṭimai Untouchables deem themselves to be fallen persons of dominant caste rank. Jaffna Paṟaiyars say that, long ago, "two brothers were the pusaris [priests] in a Mariammam temple. The elder brother decided to fast and to observe a vow of silence. He wanted his younger brother to watch over the temple. So he said to the people, 'Nān parrayan, tampi pārpār,' 'I will be silent, my younger brother will watch.' But the people misunderstood him and thought he said, 'Nan paraiyan, tampi pārpār,' 'I am the drum person [parai; "funeral drum"; an, "person"], younger brother is the priest [tampi, "younger brother"; pārpār, from pār "to see"; "seer, wise one, priest"] (David 1976:189-90).

There is, in fact, considerable confusion between the ranks of the Brahman and Paṟaiyar. Paṟaiyars in Jaffna, remarkably enough, claim to be higher than Brahmans. Banks comments that "in a sense . . . [the Paṟaiyar claim] is a joke to the higher castes, but a joke with an element of truth in it and an ambiguity for which there is no local explanation" (1957:394). Like Brahmans, Paṟaiyars are cultivated, reserved, clean and well-spoken, civilized and likable (Ibid., 189-90). In South India, Paṟaiyar origin myths usually "explain" the low Paṟaiyar status by providing a reason for their association with meat--a reason that shows their good intentions: "They have a very exalted account of their lineage, saying that they are descended from the Brāhman priest Sāla Sāmbavan, who was employed in a Śiva temple to worship the god with offerings of beef, but who incurred the anger of the god by one day concealing a portion of the meat, to give it to his pregnant wife, and was therefore turned into a Paṟaiyan. The god appointed his brother to do duty instead of him, and the Paṟaiyans say tha

Brāhman priests are their cousins. For this reason they wear a sacred thread at their marriages and funerals" (Thurston 1909:VI, 84).

Pallars tell this tale:

> Pallaṉ and Veḷḷāḷaṉ, both farmers were annan and tampi (older and younger brother). Pallaṉ had many children; Veḷḷāḷaṉ had only four children. There was a horrible thunderstorm and a cyclone which destroyed Pallaṉ's land, tools, and crop but left Veḷḷāḷaṉ's intact. Pallaṉ had no food and had to ask his younger brother for something to eat.
>
> Veḷḷāḷaṉ felt sorry for his elder brother, but Veḷḷāḷaṉ's wife was a bad woman. He was afraid of her. Veḷḷāḷaṉ asked his wife to give Pallaṉ and his family shelter and food. For two days she obeyed although she did not wish to do so. On the third day Veḷḷāḷaṉ's wife scolded Pallaṉ and told him to go away. Veḷḷāḷaṉ was so sad that he died of shock. . . .
>
> Veḷḷāḷaṉ's wife became the sole owner of the property, and Pallaṉ and his family had to take food from her hands. She soon told them to go away. They started crying, and she then made them work for her. She made her husband's elder brother plow, sow, harvest, draw water, and do other (menial) work; Pallaṉ's wife had to cook for her. Pallaṉ's children had to look after the cattle. Having kept an account of all the food she gave them, she bought all the land once held in Pallaṉ's name. After acquiring all the land, she said: 'You must share-crop on your own land. You must cut and plow'.. . . Veḷḷāḷaṉ's wife continued to live on the raised land . . . Pallaṉ lived on the low land (paḷḷam)which was more suitable for irrigation and cultivation. Their name derives from the term for low land (David 1976:189-90).

Pallars, in sum, deem themselves to be fallen Veḷḷāḷars, whose low status was forced upon them when they appeared landless, while the Paṟaiyars deem themselves to be fallen Brahmans, whose status was forced upon them when they appeared polluted.

III. The Ideology of Sudra Domination

Let us now consider, in retrospect, the forms of southern caste, with particular reference to the relation of the global ideology, the purity versus impurity distinction of the *Dharmaśāstra*-s, and its apparent opposite, the notions underlying the two anomalous ranks in South India. In fact this configuration is an expected feature of an ideological system in general, ideologies quite commonly asserting, according to Dumont, a "maximal," "encompassing" value (e.g., the pure as superior to the impure), and a "secondary," or "encompassed," value (e.g., the landholding caste as superior to the poverty-stricken caste). It must be noted that, according to Dumont, the global ideology is ultimately superior, while the secondary ideology is "neutralized" or "repressed" to a degree (1981:xxix). Despite its repressed, "shamefaced" status, the secondary ideology is, in fact, the "opposite" of the global ideology, and therefore contradicts it in practice--but only up to a point. In the South India caste system, for instance, the statuses of the pure Brahman and impure Paṟaiyar (the "fallen Brahman") are, evidently, genuine signs of the global ideology's encompassing, superior status. The global ideology indeed provides the terms for describing the anomalous statuses in the middle ranges. Nonetheless, these statuses are governed by the "shamefaced," secondary ideology, and thus appear contradictory: the powerful Veḷḷāḷar caste is falsely described as pure, while the powerless *aṭimai* Untouchables are falsely desribed as impure.

The crucial issue may now be stated. Does the "secondary" or "encompassed" ideology that governs the middle statuses resemble the secular ideal of *artha* (the Ksatriya's self-interested action), or is it not some other, religious ideology, whose nature and identity we have completely failed to guess? The evidence, beginning with the fact that Sudra dominant castes like Veḷḷāḷars expressly reject the Ksatriya ideal, commands the latter interpretation. What differentiates the Veḷḷāḷar from the *aṭimai* Untouchable is not simply wealth versus poverty, or power versus powerlessness. They are also differentiated in that Veḷḷāḷars invest

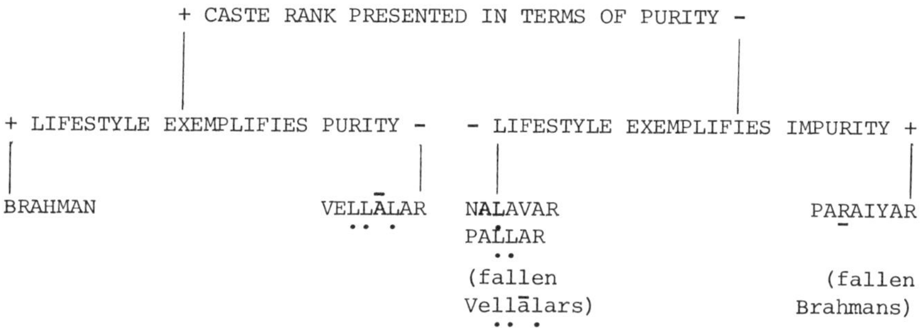

FIGURE II. The Configuration of Caste Rank in the Jaffna Peninsula

very substantially in ritual, claim title to the reproductive resources of farming life, and seem eager to validate their status claims by distributing the rice they have grown to their _kuṭimakkaḷ_ clients. The _aṭimai_ Untouchables, in contrast, constitute very precisely a mirror image of the Veḷḷāḷar caste. Just as Paṟaiyars are embarrassed by their association with impurity, so too the _aṭimai_ Untouchables would seem to be embarrassed by their alienation from titles to reproductive resources, their inability to invest in rituals, and the necessity of begging for rice.

What appears to underlie the Veḷḷāḷar/_aṭimai_ Untouchable distinction is that the former win from their investment in ritual a culturally recognized right or entitlement to control agrarian reproduction, while the latter--strangers to the rites that confer the entitlements--are legitimately deprived of that control, and thus embarrassed by their poverty. This thesis not only ties together the evidence; it helps us to understand why Veḷḷāḷars in Jaffna continue to grow rice and to maintain _kuṭimakkaḷ_ servants, despite the collapse of any real economic or political incentives for doing so. To win an entitlement in ritual, and to validate it by giving rice, is even today to possess enormous prestige and fame in Jaffna, a fact that surely reveals the persistence and vitality of an old status ideology.

To comprehend the nature of the Vellālar and *aṭimai* Untouchable statuses, we must, therefore, examine the ritual design by which these statuses emerge and are sustained. Throughout southern India, Vellālars invest prodigiously in a great variety of rituals that, in their final effect, establish and legitimate the ranking of persons in these two categories. The ritual design calls for rites that establish the proper Vellālar home; maintain its supernatural welfare despite the vagaries of the life and calendrical cycles; foster rain and fertility by controlling the masculine and feminine disorder inherent in localities; and win the protection and help of the gods. While these rites benefit the whole community indirectly, they are actually focused on Vellālar patrons, and produce in them, it is thought, a condition so auspicious that it makes their impurity irrelevant. That condition, spoken of as the benefit (*palan*) of ritual, is best defined as a supernatural force possessed by great Vellālar men, a force that brings to them, as Tamils says, "increase": abundant progeny, the flourishing increase of stock, the bounteous outcome of harvests, and an ever-growing fortune. The mystical, generative power of Vellālars, a potency stemming from ritually induced order, invests Vellālars with the right--indeed the responsibility--to possess that which reproduces, namely, the stock and the crops.

The ritual order prevailing in Vellālar lives is most tellingly apparent when compared to the ritual disorder of the *aṭimai* and other Untouchables, whose deep stigma will be explored in the chapters to follow. Just as Vellālars receive their potency as masters of reproduction from rituals so too do Untouchables receive their potency--a dark, dangerous power arising from disorder--from the same ritual process The Untouchables' condition, the antithesis of the Vellālars' is created and sustained when Untouchables are not only prevented from benefiting from the rites, but are also required, in their various ritual capacities, to imbibe or to manipulate the very substance of the autochthonous, evil powers which are thought to afflict this world. The resulting afflicted condition (*tōṣam*) negates fertility, good fortune, and health. Just as the Veḷḷāḷar is obliged to become the custodian of growing, reproducing things, the Untouchable is obliged to remain deprived of them; and the Untouchables' poverty, in the *post hoc ergo propter hoc* thinking of Tamil caste relations, amply justifies the disabilities of the Untouchable status.

Within the framework of the Gangetic ranking ideology of purity and impurity, then, there is hidden--as will be seen in the following pages--an unspoken southern ranking ideology, which underlies the Veḷḷāḷar and Untouchable statuses and invests them with a legitimacy unquestioned in the system. In its essential principles, the southern ideology, and the ritual design that issues from it, are indeed quintessentially Tamil achievements, revealing to us an ancient and characteristically Tamil world view. We shall see that this world view, now that the essential configuration has been isolated, can in fact be viewed plainly in the earliest stratum of Tamil literature. This is not to deny that in some measure this ideology can be shown to have a northern source: the postclassical Gangetic tradition of temple worship, in fact, provides precisely the notion of order that Veḷḷāḷars now epitomize, although this notion was extended and completed when united with southern traditions. But the notion of disorder, I wish to argue, is purely a Tamil one, of very ancient, southern provenance. In essence, the total synthesis, while having both northern and southern sources, is a distinctively Tamil achievement. Yet it is fruitful to begin our analysis of that achievement with a study of the temple worship tradition, for it is by looking at that tradition's realization in southern culture that we shall see the reason for the more comprehensive synthesis.

Chapter 3

TEMPLES, PATRONS, AND THE FRAILTY OF SUDRA AUTHORITY

> "Let him who wishes to enter the worlds that are reached by [Vedic] sacrificial offerings build a temple to the gods, by doing which he attains both the results of the sacrifice and the performance of religious obligations."
>
> --Bṛhat Saṃhita (cited in Kramrisch 1974:139)

I. Temples and Patrons

I.1. The Greatness of the Temple Patron

Throughout the Jaffna Peninsula, the landscape is dotted with Hindu shrines, risen anew since the British colonial regime restored freedom of religious choice in the nineteenth century. The larger of them, the Brahman-staffed ones featuring concrete construction and sculpture, are called ākama kōyilkaḷ by educated Jaffna Hindus. The term means "shrines [built according to] the temple scriptures [ākama-s]." The scriptures were first composed, evidently, in Sanskrit, but they are of medieval and South Indian provenance (Cartman 1957:26). In nearly every case, ownership of the temple is invested, not in the Brahmans who perform the complicated rites of the ākama temple's daily and annual calendar, but rather in one or several Veḷḷāḷar lineages (cantati) (Banks 1960:67ff). While the rites at the ākama shrine appear to be generally beneficial in that they regenerate the cosmos (Clothey 1969; Michell 1977:61ff), the lion's share of the benefits is thought to accrue not to the general public but rather, as will be seen, to the lineages of the patrons (yajamāna-s) who build the temple and pay for the rites.

To support temples is an act that, throughout the Tamil lands, is constitutive of a Sudra's greatness. Everywhere, Veḷḷāḷars play conspicuous roles as temple patrons, providing funds for the construction of temples, for the maintenance of priests, for festival expenses, and for routine operating costs. One important contribution that Veḷḷāḷars make to temple ceremonial is the provision of rice from their own fields. The rice is cooked by temple Brahmans in the kitchen attached to the shrine, and is then offered to the deity. Thus consecrated, food--as well as other offered substances and objects--is taken out of the temple for distribution to the assembled worshippers. In this distribution the *yajamāna* has no small prominence. According to Appadurai and Breckenridge, in South India "the largest garland (*mālai*) worn by the deity during a specified ritual period, and in some cases the silk vestments of the deity (*parivaṭṭam*) are bestowed upon the donor, who is also given a share of the left-over food of the deity (*prasātam*) and priority in drinking the water (*tīrttam*) sanctified by contact with the deity's ablutions or meals" (1976:197). The objects, food, and water given to the *yajamāna* are called *mariyātai*, or "honors." From the generous support that Veḷḷāḷars give to temples eventually issues what is, for Hindus, a convincing --and what is more, a public--display of primacy and high rank.

This point was driven home to me throughout my field research among the Veḷḷāḷars of Jaffna. When visiting the Jaffna home of a very wealthy and prominent Colombo businessman, a Veḷḷāḷar of noble ancestry, I was taken to visit the family's temple nearby at *pūcai* (*pūja*, or flower offering) time. Having bathed and dressed in clean clothes, I, as a Westerner, was defined as an ordinary Sudra of touchable caste for purposes of temple entry, and on that account was permitted to enter the temple gate and to stand outside the first hall of the temple. My host stood with me until the priest came out of the sanctum sanctorum with the consecrated offerings. I was left there to find that my host, with a haughty expression, had bolted into the first, outer hall, motioning me to remain where I was, and received the first offerings from the priest. With evident pride, he took the offerings from the priest and then, walking out of the first hall into the inner courtyard, gave them to me.

This rite is one of the most stratifying in Hindu society, for he who gives is the great one. At the conclusion of the pūcai, the Brahman priests of Jaffna hand over to the temple owner several brass bowls containing piracātam, or consecrated offerings. Generally, these consist of holy ash (vīpūti), sandalwood paste (cantanam), flowers (pū), and vermilion powder (kuṅkamum). This exchange takes place in the inner hall. The temple owner then walks toward the rest of the worshippers, who are lined up in the outer hall to receive the consecrated offerings. They cup their hands and the temple owner drops the offerings into their palms. In the Tamil social context, this is a ranking symbol of note: only a superior may drop something into the cupped hands of another person; furthermore, cupping the hands to receive is a deferential gesture. Indeed, it is so deferential that it is said to be servile in most other contexts to fully cup both hands. Elsewhere, an inferior would receive something with his right hand, indicating deference by deftly grazing his right elbow with his left hand. In the temple context, however, a worshipper is expected to cup both hands, or at least to grasp his right wrist firmly with his left hand. Thus, the temple owner has scored a point, so to speak, against his castefellows by forcing them to acquiesce to his superiority in a public context. As one Jaffna Vel̤l̤āl̤ar put it, "If they must come to worship the temple owner at the pūcai, then they will have to worship him at his house too--he will be a big man in the village."

There is, of course, a religious rationale for comprehending the greatness of the patron. Serving as a patron is far more beneficial than merely visiting the shrine. Jaffna

Hindus say that visiting a temple without serving as a patron is certainly worthwhile, but one cannot expect miracles. To go to a temple to which one does not donate is to go, as they say, "freely, without restraint, and without entailing reciprocity," all of which are the meanings of the term cummā. When a Hindu says that he has gone cummā to a temple, it is meant that he has no special relation to the deity. The visit does not entail any reciprocity between worshipper and deity, and its value in the total religious picture is rather unimportant. In practice, the people attending the pūcai-s are the very (not a few would say "overly") pious--generally old people and women--and a few curious children. The visit does little more than remind them of the deity and give them a positive and lucky experience of a subtle nature.

Were this benefit the only one that could be derived from temple worship, it is doubtful that temples would merit the lavish investment they receive. Tamil Hindus seek from their shrines not only the subtle benefit of audience with the deity, and not only the merit (puṇṇiyam) accruing to that act, but also tangible benefit (palaṉ): "produce, result, gain, advantage, reward," or, in a word, "increase." While this aim is the central one in all forms of ākama temple worship, it is particularly pronounced at the shrines of the elephant-headed Piḷḷaiyār (Gaṇeśa). While Piḷḷaiyār is hardly felt to be a paragon of timeless mysteries and deep religion among Hindus, he is nonetheless dearly loved for his great partiality to those who honor him. That partiality translates very readily, Jaffna Hindus believe, into material benefit.

The North Indian, Sanskrit mythology about the god, a son of Śiva, fits Piḷḷaiyār's role in Jaffna worship quite well. In one myth, it is said that the gods were angry with Śiva because his other son, Skanda (or, as he is known to Tamils, Murukaṉ) was giving salvation to all and sundry at his pilgrimage centers ("baths," tīrttam). In consequence, no one was bothering any more with the Vedic rites, and heaven was getting overcrowded. So the gods, wishing to keep heaven as a private club for themselves, begged for relief. Out of pity for them, Parvatī, Śiva's consort, made Gaṇeśa, "who created obstacles for men going to heaven by diverting their longing for pilgrimage to desire for the acquisition of wealth" (O'Flaherty 1976:254).

Most of the Veḷḷāḷar-owned __ākama__ shrines of Jaffna are, in fact, Piḷḷaiyār shrines, repeating an old South Indian tradition that Piḷḷaiyār temples are more numerous than those of his brother (Stein 1978:22). That this is so is hardly surprising. Serving as a patron for a Piḷḷaiyār shrine is thought to confer on a man and on others of his lineage the ability to grow copious harvests. The association of __ākama__ shrines and agriculture is conspicuous in the fact that, in Jaffna, Piḷḷaiyār's temples are often found at the edges of the green, bountiful rice paddies. It is believed that donating part of the proceeds of the harvest to the temple both increases the yield and obviates the vicissitudes of the seasons. A tale is told about a man who owns a big rice plot; half of its produce is given over to a temple every year, and because of this gift, the field is said to produce more than twice the yield of its neighbors, thus compensating the owner quite handsomely. It is always green, it is said, even if there is a weak monsoon.

The village Piḷḷaiyār temple is the object of myriad vows concerning enterprises, for which the deity's blessing is sought at the beginning. Once again, these benefits (__palan__-s) are available mainly (some would say, "only") to the temple patrons. Among the enterprises are (1) __cōtanai__, "exams." Jaffna Tamils value education very highly, but it is nonetheless true that very many of them regard educational success as first and foremost a matter of an __ākama__ temple deity's blessing rather than individual merit. Whatever endowments a person may have by nature, they say that no progress can be made in the modern world without Piḷḷaiyār's approval and blessing, which are the real, underlying reasons for spectacular success on examinations. A student will not fail to study in most cases, but the really crucial step before the examination is the vow before a Piḷḷaiyār shrine. The same is true for interviews (*nērmuka parīṭsai*). (2) *pirayāṇam*, "journey." A vow must be made to Piḷḷaiyār before setting out on a journey, particularly one involving some length or the crossing of the sea. (3) *payir ceytal*, "growing food." Before sowing paddy, a vow should be made to Piḷḷaiyār at one of his *vayalkkōyilkaḷ*, or "rice field temples," asking his aid in return for a proportion of the rice crop (as much as one twentieth of the harvest) to be given to the temple. (4) *nāḷānta ciṟu viṭayaṅkaḷ*, "little daily matters." A person setting out for work, for an important meeting, or for the town to make an important purchase, will stop by a Piḷḷaiyār shrine to break a cocoanut. Piḷḷaiyār also heals minor illnesses of children and of animals. When a child experiences *kiranti*, "skin eruptions," he is taken to the Ayurvedic physician (*pariyāri*) for a cooling oil treatment; in addition, a vow will be made to Piḷḷaiyār asking the deity to bathe the little child in his cooling ambience of grace. For a sick cow, the same procedure is followed.

To serve as an *ākama* temple patron, or *yajamāna*, is, in sum, thought to coax from the shrine a beautiful power (*aruṟcakti*, *aruḷ*, "divine grace," + *cakti*, "power"), one that ensures the health and increase (*palaṉ*) of the patron's enterprises, his rice crop, his children, and his livestock. This belief about the auspicious condition of the patron is very old in Hindu civilization. To trace its ancestry is, as will be seen, not only to grasp its antiquity but also to comprehend the character of Sudra domination.

I.2. The Status of the Patron of Vedic Rites

One of the most characteristic patterns of Hindu ritual is the role division between the priest, the Brahman repository of esoteric knowledge and ritual skill, and the patron or *yajamāna*, who pays for the rites and receives from them their principal benefits (Heesterman 1964:2). In the classical tradition of Gangetic Hinduism, access to the patron status was restricted to the twice-born (Kane 1974:II,I, 156ff). The exclusion of the Sudra from the rituals granting authority can be explained, in part, by the nature of the rituals themselves. To get the benefits of the rite, as for example in the Vedic sacrificial rite, the recipient of the benefits (the *yajamāna*) had to be purified in a ceremony called the *dīkṣā*. Those persons who were impure by birth could not undergo the *dīkṣā*; apparently one had to be fairly pure to begin with for the purification ritual to achieve its aim. Having received the *dīkṣā*, a person is said to have undergone a second birth, and therefore the top three *varṇas* are known as the "twice-born" (*dvija*). Once purified, the *yajamāna* was ready to receive into his subtle, twice-born body the vitality which was won out of the ritual. The rite involved the violent destruction of a victim, an animal, by strangulation; the death, as Hubert and Mauss saw so clearly, "left a sacred matter behind it" (1964:35), which was then communicated to the *yajamāna*. In the classical system, only the twice-born could possess the vitality won out of the sacrifice, and therefore only they could possess the land. Indeed, in North Indian villages today, landholding is confined to a considerable extent to twice-born castes, who call themselves *jajmān*-s, the Hindi word for the Sanskrit *yajamāna* (Gould 1964:31).

The notion that the ritual's patron wins vitality out of the rite is found in consecration ceremonies as well. The royal consecration ceremony (*abhiṣeka*), an elaborate *dīkṣā* (Heesterman 1978:11), invests the king with a "power-substance," as Gonda calls it, which is shown in the turgid swelling forth of "vegetative life and increase of possessions" (1969:6-8). The consecrated king's vitality endows him with progeny, grain, prosperity, strength, competence, good fortune, and good judgment; he is also insulated, as we have seen, from impurity (āśauca). Thus the Ksatriya, or ruler, although inferior to and dependent on the Brahman, emerges from the consecration ceremonies as the person best suited to wield dominion in this mundane and tainted world. With his vitality and his insulation from impurity, the ruler as consecrated in the abhiṣeka is indeed the person who should bear the responsibility of the world's fertility, such that the enchanting increase of progeny, cattle, harvests and happiness which occurs in the realm should be attributed to his power. The consecrated ruler truly brings the possession of the gods (śrī, "prosperity") to earth (Gonda 1969:6-9, 81)

The paradigmatic conception of the dīkṣā as a consecration rite, which infuses the nominee with a power of vitality is repeated in the Saṁskāra-s, the personal initiation rites that every Aryan householder undergoes. Perhaps the most important of these is the upanayana, the ritual rebirth, whic constitutes the initiation rite of a boy into Aryan society. There are, in total, about forty Saṁskāra-s. Commenting on the various English words available to translate the Sanskrit term, Pandey notes that "consecration," rather than "initiation," comes closest. Subsequent to the upanayana, the initiate is deemed to possess an "outward and visible sign of inward and spiritual grace," which is his power of vitality (Pandey 1969:15). The upanayana seeks, as do the Saṁskāra-s in general (as they are popularly understood), to remove hostile, negative forces from a person's life or body, and to attract favorable, health-giving influences, thereby ensuring the continual "gain of cattle, progeny, long life, prosperity, strength, and intellect" (Ibid., p. 29).

From the consecration rites flow adhikāra, "authority," in the specific sense of the "entitlement of the conferee" (Bharati 1965:187). Thus the consecration ceremonies are more than initiation rites; they not only bring the initiate back into contact with society, but also invest him with pow and in particular the power to bring about bounteous reproduction and increase of life. So far from merely advancing the initiate to another status, the *Saṁskāra*-s install him in an *office*--a position of recognized importance for the durability and coherence of the total social order (see Gluckman 1965). Invested as he is with the power of vitality, the twice-born householder produces a bounteous harvest, and he has as well the duty and privilege to share out this harvest in the form of gifts (*dāna*), especially to Brahmans. The office conferred on the twice-born initiate of Aryan society requires that he maintain the fertility of the earth, and share out its products with those in need.

In sum, the person on whose behalf Brahmans perform sacrifices emerges from the rites possessing vitality; he possesses what the gods possess (*śrī*, *viz*., fortune, welfare, fertility, progeny, rainfall, and the increase of everything). Since the essential qualities of agrarian life--"the essence of water and useful plants, any refreshing draught, a well-nourished condition, and generative power"--are expressly stated to be the manifestations of royal power, it is felt that the kingdom should be in the hands of a person properly installed, by ritual, in the office of authority (Gonda 1969:8). The Brahman's rituals are really rituals of installation, granting to the person for whose benefit they are performed (the *yajamāna*) the entitlement (*adhikāra*, "authority") to bring prosperity and fertility to a realm. Only Ksatriyas can so serve a kingdom, but any Aryan can rule a smaller realm of fertile earth. For this reason I think it inappropriate that we continue to speak of the land among Hindus as "a means of production" whose possession is a putative "secular ranking criterion." The land, in the Hindu view, is a fantastic thing, invested with vitality and reproductive potency only to the extent that it is governed by a virtuous person possessing the specific entitlement of the Brahman's rites. We should speak, instead, of the means of *re*production, whose fertility is above all else a religious matter.

I.3 The Jajmani System

These beliefs would still seem to be evident in the social organization of North India. Throughout the Gangetic Plains, the twice-born families who own land deem themselves jajmān-s, and claim high rank as the producers of food (Mandelbaum 1970:I, 161ff; Wiser 1936). While the Vedic sacrifices are no longer done, jajmān-s deem themselves great in that they possess, by virtue of the rituals that Brahmans perform on their behalf, the entitlement stemming from vitality. The status actually claimed by the jajmān well illustrates its essentially religious meaning. As is now well understood, land ownership per se, in the sense of outright ownership of the land, is not a characteristically Hindu idea; what the jajmān traditionally claimed is, rather, the authority (entitlement) to control the instruments of reproduction--land, livestock, seed stocks, manure, timber, capital, agricultural tools, and seed--without denying that other persons might have legitimate claims to work the land and to receive a share of the harvest. The yajamāna claims not so much to own the land as to possess a power--a power of vitality--that gives him the right to manage the process and the instruments of reproduction, which is a sacred matter.*

The traditional status of the jajmān family vis-à-vis the serving castes in North India illustrates, again, the religious foundation of traditional authority as it stems from the Vedic sacrificial paradigm. The jajmān's family seeks to retain a monopoly on the instruments of reproduction, which must not be possessed by the serving castes; the latter, in turn, must appeal to the jajmān family for food, and for the occasional loan of those instruments. Thus the servants provide the food-producing family with services that do not

---

*The most obvious claim of the yajamāna is to the instruments of agrarian reproduction, but it should be noted that the entire ideology of entitlement is phrased broadly enough to be relevant to mercantile endeavors, whose object is the increase of wealth.

require the power of vitality, such as the crafts (pottery, blacksmithery, and the like); furthermore, the lower of the service castes remove impurities from the jajmān's home, so that he can retain his claim to be pure enough to enter the ritual rebirth that occurs in the Brahman's rituals. In return, the servants are rewarded with compensations that are not, in themselves, reproducible; one cannot, for example, plant a plate of cooked rice. From the jajmān the servants receive residence sites, supplementary food, land for subsistence farming, food for livestock, timber, enough manure for subsistence farming, supplementary employment, credit, tools, draft animals on loan, funeral pyre plots, aid in litigation, and security in old age. The jajmān controls the reproducible resources; he lets them out to his subordinates in quantities just large enough to meet their needs, but not large enough to permit them to become masters of reproduction themselves. Only the jajmān may possess what may grow or increase, or facilitate growth or increase.

Now the jajmān status as it is understood in North India is restricted to the twice-born, and for precisely this reason it is not entirely accurate to say that there is a jajmān-style relation (the so-called jajmāni system) among the castes in South India, at least insofar as Sudra dominant castes prevail on the South Indian scene. The jajmāni system places at the pivotal center of intercaste relations a landholder who receives into his twice-born body the benefits won from the Brahman's rituals (and, it must be added, from the services of the low castes in purifying the jajmān's home). The Sudra's body, non-Aryan by birth, is not refined enough, so the classical texts imply, to receive the sacred substance of the victim directly, to possess, in consequence, the powers of vitality, or to produce food that may be given without blemish. Sudra domination does, however, have its postclassical rationale.

I.4. The Sudra Yajamāna and the Plan of the Temple

That rationale is provided by temple worship, with which Sudra domination has historically had its clearest association. Temples, a fairly late development in the Hindu tradition, have been seen by some authors as representing a radical departure from the Vedic religion of the early classical period (as epitomized by Vedic sacrifice), but Gonda disputes this assertion. In his view, temple worship reflects a development and an extension of the Vedic tradition, rather than constituting a radical departure from it (1965:17ff). With this view I am, to a certain extent, in agreement, but the rise of temple worship brought with it a social innovation that no doubt contributed to radical changes in the fabric of social relations. Temples permit Sudras to enjoy part of the twice-born *yajamāna*'s entitlement, because the temple, as is expressly stated in the temple-building texts, stands in the *yajamāna*-Brahman-God relation as the Sudra's twice-born body.

Like the Vedic sacrifice, the temple has its patron, the *yajamāna*, whose status is not an issue; there is no bar whatsoever for a Sudra's serving as a temple patron. Just as the Vedic sacrifice established a communication between the sacrificial victim and the purified body of the *yajamāna*, so too does the temple establish a communication. But here the communication is with the remainder, not of an actual sacrifice, but rather of a mythological sacrifice: the self-dismemberment of the primordial Man, Puruṣa, who created the universe by sacrificing himself. The spent, sacrificed body of Puruṣa is drawn on the prepared, purified ground of the temple's site, in the form of a *yantra*, a diagram representing--and at the same time, controlling--the power of Puruṣa. This body, though sacrificed, contains a remainder, a charged remainder of vitality which is like a seed. The temple building creates a communication between this vital seed and the temple patron, because the temple is at once the vital remainder and the *yajamāna*'s alter ego, his second body (Kramrisch 1976:52). A closer look at the plan of the temple reveals that its equation with a twice-born body is not merely an esoteric idea of the texts, but an essential principle of the temple's design.

At the very heart of the temple is said to be a "womb" (garbhagṛha), in which the vital "seed" of the remainder may come to flower into divine presence under controlled circumstances. The temple plan is of a body traced on the floor and the "womb"--mūlastānam in Tamil--is thought to represent the point between the eyes, a holy part of the body which can receive divine wisdom. The mūlastānam is a small chamber, preferably built of stone, and with a single door facing the east. The mūlastānam represents prakṛti, the universal Substance, into which the "seed" of Puruṣa, Spirit, will be planted; it is therefore a womb (hence its Sanskrit name, garbhagṛha, from garbha, "womb"). Over the mūlastānam is raised a golden or copper dome, which symbolizes the Sacred Mountain, Mount Meru. The mountain is thought to rise up from the womb-cave under it, thereby symbolizing the glorious rising up of divine grace. The mūlastānam with its dome thus represents the glorious results when puruṣa and prakṛti are in union, or in Saivite terms, the union of Śiva's transcendent spirit-body (aruvattirumēni) with its incarnate form (uruvattirumēni).

In front of the mūlastānam are the halls (maṇṭapam). The first of them, the arttamaṇṭapam, provides just enough space for the Brahman priest to perform the rituals of anointing, called apiṣēkam, and the waving of lights (tīpārāntanai). The second hallway, the mahāmaṇṭapam, is larger, but it is a less sacred space. The mūlastānam is hidden from view by a curtain (tiraiccīlai), which is thrown aside only when the waving of lamps is performed. A third hall, the pūcai maṇṭapam, is provided for the convenience of male worshippers who are kin of the temple donor; others must wait in the exterior hallway, the veḷimaṇṭapam, to worship.

Within the mūlastānam is the mūla mūrtti, the granite image of the shrine's chief deity. It is believed that the process of getting the deity to reside in the image is an extremely dangerous one, and that if anything goes wrong, the power which the temple attempts to capture could go out of control and cause great destruction. The story is told in Jaffna that, once long ago, a certain man was farming not far from the lagoon and saw some chaps row up in a boat and bury something on the seashore, departing afterwards in a big hurry. Later he went to dig it up, and found a huge cache of opium. He sold it, deciding to use part of the money for the glory of Śiva. First he thought of doing charity by digging a well for public use by the road, and as he was digging it out treasure was discovered. Now he was very rich, and he resolved that his good fortune being the grace of God, he would build the most beautiful temple that he could. He bought large tracts of palmyra land. But he was in a big hurry, and he did an unwise thing. Instead of hiring an architect, he got hold of a small temple and expanded it. He had a Śiva liṅkam made for the mūla mūrtti, but because he was ignorant he did not know that it was of the wrong proportions for the temple. Finally a temple architect was brought in to ascertain the proper place for certain subsidiary images. The temple owner was not there, but the architect had a look at the liṅkam. He saw right away that it was the wrong kind. The temple manager came back, and the architect said, "Don't put this in! If this liṅkam is worshipped here, the whole village will come to naught!"

The image itself, for all the injunctions surrounding its manufacture, is not really the seat of the deity's life and power. The yantirattakaṭu, an embossed copper plate, is the real seat of divine presence in the temple. It is kept under the granite image in the mūlastānam, and its installation, called kumpāpiṣēkam, gives divinity to the temple-body. The kumpāpiṣēkam is preceded by the "charging"

PLATE IV.

Brahman priests of a Jaffna _ākama_ temple performing a fire sacrifice (_hōma_).

of the *yantiram* with *mantiram*-s, the process being known as *citpirakāca āvakanam* ("the establishment of luminosity"), so that it acquires the brightness of thousands of radiant suns, glowing with the grace (*aruḷ*) of God. When the granite image has been seated on its radiantly powerful *yantiram*, the ritual of anointing (*makākumpāpiṣēkam*) takes place, by which the temple becomes suitable for worship. In the *makākumpāpiṣēkam*, two special *kumpam*-s, made from a precious metal, are lavishly decorated and then, by *mantiram*-s, the divine presence of Piḷḷaiyār and of the god of the granite image are invoked into them. The two *kumpam*-s are taken into the *mūlastānam*, and kept there while *yākam*, the fire-sacrifice, is performed in the *ōmakuṇṭam*, an octagonal firepit placed in the *pūcai maṇṭapam*, or outer hallway. The *kumpam*-s are then taken around in procession, accompanied by umbrellas, torches, and auspicious music; then the water in the *kumpam*-s, after a besmearing with sixteen pure, cooling, refreshing, and pleasing substances, is poured on the heads of the respective images (*apisēkam*). The *kumpāpisēkam*, or temple initiation rite, is identical in logic to the rites that establish the right to rule in the person of the king (Inden 1978).

The body of Puruṣa contains within it the gods, for it is from the body of Puruṣa that the gods issued in the primordial differentiation of the universe. Thus there are found around the temple, which is the earthbound form of Puruṣa, various subordinate shrines, the arrangement depending on which god serves as the chief deity. In Śiva temples, the Piḷḷaiyār shrine is always situated to the right rear of the *mūlastānam*, facing in the same direction as does the image of the chīef deity. On the left rear is found the shrine of Skanda (Tamil: *Kantacāmi*). To the right of the doorway is a shrine for Vairavar, the temple's guardian.

During the annual festivals, an image of the deity is sometimes taken in procession around the exterior of the temple. One such occasion is the "demon war" (*cūran pōr*), when people carry statues of the demon and an image of the deity, acting out their momentous battle. For such festivals the image of the deity used is not the *mūla mūrtti*, which once established may never be used, but rather a portable copper image. This image is kept in the *vacanta maṇṭapam*, the hallway of "springtime, of openness to the breeze," suggesting its accessibility to the people. None save the Brahman may pass beyond the *artta maṇṭapam*, but at the *vacanta maṇṭapam*, where the subsidiary image is stored, people may congregate freely. In a storage room called the *vākana cālai* the vehicles of the deity (*vākanam*) are stored along with the other statues and paraphernalia used for festivals.

Before the outer hallway of the temple, and on a platform jutting out into the interior courtyard, are situated (1) the till-box (*uṇṭiyal*), for gifts of cash; (2) the camphor burner (*karpūra caṭṭi*); (3) the flag pole (*koṭimaram*), on which the temple flag is hoisted before the festival begins; (4) the sacrificial altar (*palipīṭam*), where *naivettiyam* (food offerings) are presented; and (5) the *vākanam* or vehicle of the deity, which alone has sufficient devotion to the god to stand directly facing him along the *kōyilmaiyam* (temple axis, along which the deity's *aruḷ* reaches its zenith).

Every temple has its inner courtyard (*vīti*), which is used for circumnambulation. Around the temple is a stout wall, *curru matil*; the temple exterior is entirely bounded by streets. Outside the temple there is a well for purifying oneself before entering the shrine. At the larger temples, there may be a tank (*kēṇi*) or a pond (*kuḷam*) for bathing. There is a well for the priest's use, called the *tīrtta kiṇaru*. It is very small, and is exclusively for the Brahman priest. Likewise, only a Brahman temple priest may cook food in the temple kitchen (*maṭaippaḷḷi*).

The body of the temple should be kept pure and free from any "faults" (*kuṟṟam*-s), which include omissions in the ritual as well as impurities. Traditionally, Untouchables were forbidden to enter the shrine, although the sentiment is now fairly widespread that they may do so as long as they have had a bath and are wearing clean clothes. In actual practice, many Veḷḷāḷar-owned village *Ākama* temples in Jaffna remain closed to Untouchables even now, the leverage over the Untouchables being their client relationship to the temple owners. In the traditional framework, men and women of clean caste (as well as Europeans) could enter the temple freely to circumnambulate the inner courtyard, but only male relatives of the temple owner, as well as the owner himself, could enter the *pūcai maṇṭapam*. In the *makāmaṇṭapam* only the temple service castes, *viz.*, Paṇṭārams, Śaiva Kurukkaḷs, and Brahmans, are permitted, and only the Brahman temple priest may enter the inner sanctum.

Just as the temple (like the twice-born body of the Aryan) must be kept pure by keeping pollutants out of it, so too must the temple's embodied presence be consecrated and thereby invested with power. The rite of consecration, *kumpāpiṣēkam*, as discussed earlier, likens the god to a king and the rituals of the shrine further attest to this equation. Daily rites include the sixteen reverences due to a lord or king, presented in a rite called *upacarittal*, "treating with civility." These reverences include the offering of fumes (*tūpam*); the waving of lamps (*tīpam*); the offering of cooling foodstuffs including *amutu*, cooked rice, as well as fruit and milk (*naivettiyam*), and the presentation of betel and areca-nut (*tāmpūlam*), camphor (*karpuram*), wash water (*calam*), oil (*eṇṇey*), mirrors (*kaṇṇāṭi*), hair fans (*camarai*), umbrellas, flags, and textiles. It is hardly surprising, then, that the Tamil word for temple (*kōyil*) also means "palace" (Hart 1975:13).

That the temple stands for the twice-born body of the Aryan is clear enough from the temple's plans and rites.

It serves, moreover, a very clear role in Jaffna and throughout South India as the patron's purified body:

> The man who causes the temple to be built must be a man of inner virtues (wealth, power, and prestige). His virtues are incorporated into the temple by the act of taking as the basic unit of measurement a portion of the temple donor's body and using this unit in following ṣastric proportions for building a temple. Both his and the temple's virtues are held to radiate out to the inhabitants and the land and to affect the quality of both. All these qualities are thought to affect the quality of the products of the land, especially rice. The circuit is complete when a product of the land is both offered to the temple and consumed by the inhabitants (David 1976:497).

The connection between the temple patron and the temple itself is so close that it is thought to be dangerous. This identity is "felt in the living body of the donor," who may suffer or die if the temple is defiled (Kramrisch 1976:52). But so long as the temple is protected and all goes according to plan, the temple, by establishing the communication between the donor and the vital remainder of the sacrifice, wins for the donor the same vitality that was won out of the Vedic sacrifice. Thus, the Bṛhat Saṃhita advises, "let him who wishes to enter the worlds that are reached by [the Vedic] sacrificial offerings and the performance of religious obligations build a temple to the gods, by doing which he attains both the results of the sacrifice and the performance of religious obligations" (cited in Kramrisch 1976:139). Another text, the Silpa Prakāśa, a medieval temple building manual, asserts that the patron will, in this world, always have "peace, wealth, grain, and sons," which are precisely the objects of the Vedic sacrifice (Kaulācāra 1966:122).

Classical doctrine specifically permits Sudras to build temples. Temple building was one of several meritorious acts called pūrta-dharma, or the "building of wells, tanks, temples, parks, and distribution of food as works of charity" (Kane 1974:II, I, 157). Prior to the fourth century, when the temple worship tradition was little developed, this distinction probably did not appreciably alter the rank of the Sudra vis-à-vis the twice-born. And yet the classical texts admit to two kinds of Sudras: the *aniravasita śūdra* (the "not-excluded *śūdra*") and the *niravasita śūdra* ("the excluded *śūdra*," which is the *cāṇḍāla* or Untouchable) (Kane 1974:II,I, 121-22). The former were permitted to serve the higher *varṇas* and give gifts to them, but the latter--the Untouchables--were set apart and despised (*Ibid.*, p. 165ff). Despite the strong emphasis in classical doctrine on status as a matter of birth, it is nevertheless true that, as expressly stated, the distinction was not made on the grounds of birth alone, but rather on "the basis of the customs of the Sudra group in question and the profession followed by its members" (Basham 1954:143). It may be that *pūrta-dharma* was one of the customs that distinguished the *aniravasita śūdra*; in any case, the late- and post-classical development of temple worship was to have the radical effect of elevating the Sudra to a position rivaling that of the twice-born.

By providing Sudras with a twice-born body, one suitable for a person wishing legitimately to dominate others, temple worship invested them with the advantages of Ksatriyas with one exception: Sudras could not claim the throne.* The Sudra temple patron, now a *yajamāna* with an entitlement as glorious as that of the twice-born, claimed recognition as a master of men and of fertility. In one medieval inscription, Veḷḷāḷars described themselves as "sons of the earth goddess . . . who are light to all quarters . . . with the lands filled with coconut, jackfruit, mango groves,

---

*It is, therefore, a misrepresentation of the Dravidian tradition to suppose that Sudra dominant castes emulate the "royal" or Ksatriya style of domination. There is, on the contrary, a well-defined model of Sudra domination operating in the Dravidian system, a model whose rights and obligations are perfectly expressed in the temple-Sudra *yajamāna* relation.

plaintain, areca nut . . . [which are] increasing in numbers without any waning . . . with their fame spreading . . . with the plowshare as their god, with golden fertility . . . as their goal" (cited in Stein 1969:182). Authority and high rank, whether at the Sudra or royal level, was established by endowing temples, most often by setting aside a proportion of the harvest of certain lands for the temple's maintenance. The donors were to receive the first and best benefits of the rituals, which inspired them with the power of vitality, and insulated them from impurity.

Because their claimed status rests on the developed and extended premises of the highly valued religion of the Vedas, which constitute the fons et origo of all tradition and truth among all Hindus, Vellāḷars win a high position in the traditional, South Indian social structure. They are inferior, to be sure, to the Brahmans and to the Ksatriya king, but they are only slightly inferior to the latter. The Vellāḷar emerges from the temple with a clear mandate for rule (at least at the village level) and for high rank. Furthermore, it should now be clear why giving is constitutive of high rank, and why receiving and poverty are of low rank. The giver posseses the power of vitality, and with it entitlement and the means of reproduction; the receiver, possessing no power of vitality, is dependent and landless. To a considerable extent, the Vellāḷar status can be explained in these terms. Even the Sudra model of duty in the Śastra-s fits well enough into this rationale: the Sudra duty is to serve, and throughout the history of the Tamils, Vellāḷars have seen themselves as the servants of Brahmans and of all humanity. They view themselves as the great ones who, despite their close involvement with the world, create life and feed everyone (David 1976:185; Stein 1980:446). While the Vellāḷar's high rank is without question deemed inferior to that of the Brahmans, the exemplars of priestly purity, the Sudra achievement is sufficiently appealing in the Hindu context to win for them a rank surpassing that of persons who merely emulate the Brahmanical ideal.

Thus, when Veḷḷāḷars seem to flaunt their impure customs and their connection with the plow, they are in reality celebrating the majesty of their achievement. They have resolved the contradictory demands of the classical traditions, which demand that a man accumulate power, that he be pure and celibate, and yet that he father sons for the sake of the manes (pitir-s). Veḷḷāḷars combine power and worldliness, and in this respect they are like the great one (cāṉrōṉ) of ancient Tamil literature, a "great and noble man" who had "balanced the various contradictory demands" of ordered, agrarian life (Hart 1979:28).

II. The Frailty of the Veḷḷāḷar Achievement

II.1. The "Right-Side" versus "Left-Side" Distinction

The Veḷḷāḷar achievement as a Sudra yajamāna is, in the Hindu view, truly a great one, and we can now see the essential validity of the Veḷḷāḷars' claim that they are, in fact, arch defenders of the varṇāśrama dharma. Notwithstanding their Sudra status, the Veḷḷāḷars of southern India have replicated the esteemed role of the twice-born landholder, the defender of the holistic, Hindu social ideal. Indeed, the Veḷḷāḷars and their allies and subordinates in South India were often referred to in temple inscriptions as valaṅkai or "right-side" (Stein 1980:480f), a term almost universally redolent of moral conservatism, normative order, and concern for maintaining the status quo. Yet the Veḷḷāḷar achievement is by no means without its implicit frailty, by reference to which some persons in the system can legitimagely claim to reject the Veḷḷāḷars' idea of their rank.

Veḷḷāḷars disregard the niceties of purity restrictions in favor of the ideal of the wordly Sudra yajamāna, but by acknowledging the supremacy of Brahmans and the legitimacy of the varnāśrama dharma, they have already admitted, in principle, the supremacy of the purity and Sastric ideals. Throughout southern India, certain castes characteristically challenge Vellālar domination by emulating Brahmanical purity, or by claiming to be of higher varna rank than Vellālars. There appear to be three styles to this mode of rebellion: those of the peripheral warrior castes, the artisan castes, and the vegetarian farming castes.

The first type of entirely legitimate rebellion against Sudra authority is to claim Ksatriya status and to rival the claims of Sudra cultivators to preserve the varnāśrama dharma. In South India as well as in Sri Lanka this strategy has been pursued by groups attempting to control areas peripheral to the nuclear areas of agrarian civilization. In South India, the dry lands have long been dominated by the "warrior" castes like the Kallars and Maravars.* Firmly established in their peripheral homelands and jealous of their autonomy, these warlike castes resisted the political authority of the core agrarian areas, even though it was ever the ambition of the later South Indian kings (who styled themselves cakravarti-s, or comprehensive rulers) to incorporate the warrior castes into their realms. Nonetheless, these castes evidently found it more convenient to reproduce the Vellālar status when they tried to enter the social system of the irrigated, agrarian core areas. It is said throughout South India and in Jaffna, for instance, that "Kallars, Maravars, and Ahamudiyars, by slow degrees become Vellalas. Having become Vellalas, they call themselves Mudaliyar ['headmen']" (Béteille 1969:98).

The second style of legitimate rebellion, that of the artisans (the pancāla, or five artisan castes), is to claim

---

*It is tempting to suggest that Dumont's overemphasis on the Ksatriya ideal of domination stems from his having worked among the martial Kallars (1957).

descent from Visvakarma, the Brahman architect of the gods. To drive home the connection, members of these castes wear the sacred thread, eat a vegetarian diet, and emulate the Brahman style of religiosity. For all their efforts, however, the artisans do not win a high rank; everywhere, they are ranked below the more impure Veḷḷāḷars. Throughout the South, artisans claim to be "Brahmans of the purest water and highest degree," but everyone else agrees that they are "no such thing" (Mandelbaum 1970:II, 459). Nonetheless, Mandelbaum continues, this "unresolved controversy apparently was not a great impediment to the functioning of the local caste systems" (Ibid.).

This interpretation is surely correct, but it is also true that Veḷḷāḷars seem to have taken special pride in subjugating the artisans of an area to their will. Ever recalcitrant, artisans were for centuries the prime movers of the "left-side" (iṭaṅkai) division of castes, which opposed the right side and which, at least in historical times, quarreled and battled with the Veḷḷāḷars' allies (Stein 1980:196). In Jaffna, there is no evidence whatever of this type of conflict, for the Veḷḷāḷars' control over the artisan castes of the kuṭimai division was evidently very decisive. That control ended when the British courts of the late nineteenth century refused to recognize the legality of Veḷḷāḷar claims to kuṭimai services. Artisans in Jaffna today emphasize what David calls a "mercantile" orientation, disavowing the agrarian, Veḷḷāḷar-regulated network of jajmani relations (1976:194ff). Marketing their services in the towns and cities of the peninsula, the artisans make much of their independent status, refusing to perform any traditional kuṭimai service for traditional modes of compensation. They see themselves as beholden to no man. As their position was pointedly expressed to me, "If Veḷḷāḷars want our services, they come, pay the money, and go."

The reluctance of the Jaffna artisans to acquiesce in the matter of Veḷḷāḷar-regulated jajmani relations is by no means a modern phenomenon. As long ago as the twelfth century, artisans in South India appear to have escaped the oppression of the "right-side" castes by seeking royal intervention (Stein 1980:199). Moreover, artisans came to serve increasingly prestigious roles in the construction and ritual of urban temples. Pursuing economic opportunities in the impersonal marketplaces of towns and cities, the artisans did all they could to avoid becoming enmeshed in the jajmani relations sponsored by Veḷḷāḷar chieftains in the hinterland (Ibid., p. 480). Veḷḷāḷars, in sum, have traditionally faced a problem of incorporation with regard to artisans, for the very ideology that establishes the greatness of the Veḷḷāḷar also provides the artisan with a license for resisting Veḷḷāḷar authority.

Veḷḷāḷar tradition would appear to recognize this problem of incorporation, or so it would seem in this myth of Veḷḷāḷar origin:

> In ancient days, when the God Paramēsvaradu [Siva] and his consort the goddess Parvati Dēvi resided on the top of Kailāsa Parvata or mount of paradise, they one day retired to amuse themselves in private, and by chance Visvakarma, the architect of the Dēvatas or gods, intruded on their privacy, which enraged them, and they said to him that, since he had the audacity to intrude on their retirement, they would cause an enemy of his [the first Veḷḷāḷar] to be born in the Bhūlōka or earthly world, who should punish him for his temerity. Visvakarma requested that they would inform him in what part of Bhūlōka or earthly world he would be born, and further added that, if he knew the birth place, he would annihilate him with a single blow. The divine pair replied that the person would spring up into existence from the bowels of the earth on the banks of the Ganga river. On this, Visvakarma took his sword, mounted his aerial car, and flew through the regions of ether to the banks of the Ganga river, where he anxiously awaited the birth of his enemy. One day Visvakarma observed the ground to crack near him, and a kiritam or royal diadem appeared issuing out of the bowels of the

> earth, which Visvakarma mistook for being the head of his adversary, and made a cut at it with his sword, but only struck off the kiritam. In the meantime, the person came completely out of the earth, with a bald pate, holding in his hand a golden ploughshare, and his neck encircled with garlands of flowers. The angry Visvakarma instantly laid hold on him, when the Gods Brahma, Vishnu, and Siva, and the supporters of the eight corners of the universe, appeared in all their glory, and interceded for the earth-born personage, and said to Visvakarma though didst vow that thou wouldst annihilate him with a single blow, which vow thou hast not performed; therefore with what justice hast thou a second time laid violent hands on him? Since thou didst not succeed in the first attempt, it is but equitable that thou shouldst now spare him. At the intercession and remonstrance of the gods, Visvakarma quitted his hold and a peace was concluded between him and his enemy on the following stipulation, viz., that the pancha jāti, or five castes of silversmiths, carpenters, ironsmiths, stone-cutters, and braziers, who were the sons of Visvakarma, should be subservient to the earth-born person. The deities bestowed on the person these three names. First, Bhumi Pālakudu or saviour of the earth, because he was produced by her. Second, Ganga kulam or descendent of the river Ganga, by reason of having been brought forth on her banks. Third, Murdaka Pālakudu or protector of the plough, alluding to his being born with a ploughshare in his hand, and they likewise ordained that, as he had lost his diadem, he should not be eligible to sovereignty, but that he and his descendants should till the ground with this privilege, that a person of the caste should put the crown on the king's head at the coronation (Thurston 1909:VII, 362-64).

This tradition establishes at once that Veḷḷāḷars are Sudras, not Ksatriyas, and that they possess the right to rule over the five artisan castes. It appears that this caste origin myth attempts to clothe in the stories and personages of Gangetic mythology the circumstances by which Veḷḷāḷars first came to be, and so to invest those circumstances with legitimacy. Specifically, the tradition addresses precisely those aspects of the Veḷḷāḷar status that are ambiguous or problematic. This aim is a common one in traditions of its type. However satisfying the "resolution" of the problem of incorporation might have been for Veḷḷāḷars, there is no evidence that artisans were ever persuaded by it.

The third style of rebellion, also emphasizing purity, is that of the vegetarian farmers, who compete with Veḷḷāḷars for control of the land while attempting to gain the edge in ranking matters by maintaining zealously pure customs. In Jaffna, this strategy is carried on today by certain groups of Kaikkular weavers. Like the vegetarian Khatis of central India, the Jaffna Kaikkulars seek to score a point against the more impure, dominant caste by emulating the aloofness of Brahmans from the tainting world of agrarian interdependence. Kaikkular farmers do not maintain any _kuṭimakkaḷ_ (_jajmani_) relations at all, and their religious style is identical to that of the artisans. Yet, like the artisans, their claim to high rank is rejected by the consensus of informants. Veḷḷāḷars, unable to prohibit Kaikkulars from pursuing their ambitious lifestyle, simply ignore them.

Attempts to resist Veḷḷāḷar control by claiming superior purity have surely vexed Veḷḷāḷars, who believe that every caste should, ideally, submit to them. And yet these attempts, even when successful, have scarcely challenged Veḷḷāḷar control. For instance, the artisans and the Kaikkular together comprise only about four percent of Jaffna's population. Moreover, the services denied to Veḷḷāḷars by rebellious, client artisans may still be purchased in the marketplace. The greatest threat to Veḷḷāḷar power and privilege comes not from the artisans, but from the landless, _aṭimai_ Untouchables who, as their origin myths suggest, do not conceive of themselves as deserving their low status on grounds of ancestry. Relying as they do on Untouchable labor, Veḷḷāḷars have much to fear from the resolute and widespread Untouchable claim to a distinguished ancestry. Were it nothing more than a pathetic fabrication, this claim could be easily ignored by Veḷḷāḷar landlords. And yet in making it, the *aṭimai* Untouchables have no small support from the temple worship tradition, the very source of Veḷḷāḷar prestige. That tradition, it must be noted, was socially rather revolutionary in that it opened the ranks of the twice-born to impure persons. The corollary of this development was that impurity alone was no longer a sufficient rationale for defining someone as despised and landless.

Consider the implications of this drastic change. The point of Untouchable ritual services in the northern, classical system is to remove impurities from the homes of the high castes, for impurities are antithetical to their possession of vital power. Since their bodies must serve in the Brahman-*yajamāna* relation as the very vehicles of divinely granted vitality, the high castes possess legitimate rights to dominate others. Similarly, the low castes are felt to lack that right. But in South India, after the temple worship revolution, it was no longer necessary for the *yajamāna* to have a zealously purified body; the temple took over that function. Consequently, impurity came to lose its force as an effective rationale of low status. If even the impure could possess temples, why should anyone want to remain in his low status? And, as we have seen, Untouchables indeed regard themselves to be fallen Brahmans or Veḷḷāḷars, really deserving of high rank.

Untouchables throughout South India have never believed themselves to be low by birth. On the contrary, Par̲iayars deem themselves to be Brahmans, albeit "fallen" Brahmans who became associated with drums or beef through no fault of their own. Similarly, Paḷḷars deem themselves to be

---

*The persistence of this ranking ideology in North India is measured well by the fact that temple worship remains uncommon at the village level (Susan Wadley, personal communication).

"fallen" Vellālars, who became associated, again through no fault of their own, with landlessness and poverty. Of the two, the Paraiyar caste appears generally to be more successfully incorporated. Pariayars are priests of the lowest grade, but priests nonetheless, performing vital ritual functions. In Jaffna, for instance, the Hindus among Pariayars, a kutimai caste, deem themselves to perform a lowly but still essentual function (drumming) that they, and only they, can perform. This ideology is right in line with the holistic plan of the varnāśrama dharma, and therefore it is quite sensible that in South India, Vellālars would readily number Pariayars among their supporters in the "right-side" division. It is not the Paraiyars, but rather the "left-side" Untouchables--quintessentially, the Pallars--who pose a threat to Vellālar interests.

The contrast between the tractable "right-side" Paraiyars and the rebellious "left-side" Pallars is particularly evident in Jaffna.

> Pallas always shout, even when standing beside the person they are speaking to; they make no effort to look humble or smile ingratiatingly. Vellalas are often somewhat frightened by Pallas as fierce and noisy, probably drunken ruffians who must be severely repressed. The wild appearance of a young Palla man, with his hair sticking out in all directions, his violent gestures and loud voice, contrast markedly with the soft, polite speech and neat hair of the Paraiya, . . .and are felt to be uncivilized (Banks 1957:6).

Pallars, moreover, have long resisted Vellālar authority. Leach has suggested that unrest among South Indian Untouchables is an artifact of recent liberal legislation and of population increase (1960:6), but it is quite evident that "left-side" Untouchable rebelliousness precedes the nineteenth and twentieth century impact of the West. As early as the Chola times, there is evidence of low castes joining together against the "Brāhmanas Vellālans who hold the proprietary rights (kāni) over the lands" (Stein 1980:180).

Low caste Tamilians near seventeenth century Madras refused to concede their low status, and in contemporaneous Jaffna, the Dutch rulers were obliged to pass stern orders forbidding Untouchables to desert, carry weapons, or divest themselves of the imposed features (Banks 1957:441). Soon after the British acceded to the Dutch colonial possessions in Sri Lanka, they were likewise obliged (in 1806) to make it clear in an ordinance that

> all persons of the lower castes shall show to all persons of the higher caste such marks of respect as they are by ancient customs entitled to receive.. . . All questions that relate to those rights and privileges which subsist in the said provinces between higher castes [on the one hand] and particularly the Coviar, Nalavar and Pallar on the other shall be decided according to the said customs and usages of the provinces (cited in Arumainayagam 1976a:18).

On the whole, as this ordinance would suggest, it is the atimai castes (which, together with the artisans, correspond to the "left-side" castes of South India) that have resisted incorporation into the orbit of Vellālar domination.

The "right-side" Untouchables, epitomized by the Paraiyars, have historically tended to accept incorporation, for they were at least given a secure occupational niche. With an important duty to perform and a stable minimum income, the "right-side" or kutimai Untouchables have proven far more amenable to Vellālar domination, and in particular to the holistic social ideal of the varnāśrama dharma, than have the atimai Untouchables. These "left-side" Untouchables are not thought to possess any particular fitness for their role; for instance, Pallars have no monopoly on toddy-tapping since the job is done by Nalavars as well, and at one time was done by Cāntars. Their occupation, therefore, is hardly secure in the same sense as the Paraiyars' or the Barbers'. Neither is there any particular ritual service for which the atimai Untouchables are thought to have a special caste fitness.

It is hardly surprising that the _aṭimai_ Untouchables would resis incorporation into a social order that ostensibly promises security in exchange for the performance of a caste-ascribed duty.*

In sum, the artisans and Paḷḷars are, among Tamil castes, the left-side castes par excellence, and their equation should no longer seem surprising. Whatever other functions the right-side versus left-side distinction may have performed in South India, it is clear that the latter castes were those which posed a threat--real or imagined--to the holistic social order that Veḷḷāḷars and Brahmans were trying to create. The "left-side" castes could not be simply and unambiguously ranked; their place in the total scheme was consequently not so clearly fixed that mobility and high aspirations were out of the question.#
The frailty of Veḷḷāḷar authority stems, therefore, from ambiguities within the very ideological framework that makes Sudra domination possible.

---

*In a recent study of South Indian Untouchables, Moffatt (1979) found that Paṟaiyars tended to accept the beliefs that relegate them to the bottom of the caste hierarchy, and adduced from this fact that Indian Untouchables generally tend to accept their status rather than reject it. It is tempting to speculate how his conclusions might have differed had he studied the restive and rebellious Paḷḷars.

#The firm grip of Jaffna Veḷḷāḷars on the artisan castes in traditional Jaffna no doubt accounts for the lack of a clear-cut "right-side" versus "left-side" distinction there. With the artisans firmly under control, Veḷḷāḷars did not need to link them (and so stigmatize them) with the "stranger" or "aboriginal" castes (_aṭimai_); nor were the artisans free to engage in alliances with the enemies of Sudra domination.

II.2. The Political Role of the Imposed Features

The South Indian social formation could never have been integrated merely on the basis of its spoken ideology, the Gangetic tradition. As that tradition was realized in South India, it gave rise, not to a social formation in which everyone was persuaded to accept his caste rank and duty, but rather to one in which very many people did not. Only about eight percent of Jaffna's present population pursues caste-ascribed occupations because they believe in their fitness for them and find in them a secure economic niche. In the agrarian sphere, the indeterminacy of caste statuses is most pointed in the case of the Veḷḷāḷars and the *aṭimai* Untouchables, who comprise nearly seventy percent of the population. Yet Veḷḷāḷars possess a title, at least, to hold land, one issuing from their role as temple patrons.

Clearly, Vellalar domination is most pointedly threatened by the aspirations of *aṭimai* Untouchables, not to destroy the social system that oppresses them, but rather to realize their ambition to become Veḷḷāḷars, with whom Paḷḷars claim an ancient kinship. Becoming a Veḷḷāḷar involves assuming Veḷḷāḷar customs, becoming a temple patron, and gaining control over land. It is for precisely this reason that entire villages may be burnt down and people killed over so trivial an incident as a Paḷḷar cutting his hair or wearing a shoe. For Veḷḷāḷars, much is at stake. Without the imposed features,

> What would distinguish a Vellala from a Palla? There would be nothing to stop Pallas from behaving as Vellalas and calling themselves Vellalas . . . and within a short time probably becoming indistinguishable in all respects from Vellalas. Caste as it is at present would cease to exist and there would simply be larger numbers of endogamous groups all claiming to be equal to, or higher than others. . . . Once such a relativity of ranking was introduced, intermarriage would no doubt follow in time, as memory of which were or were not real

> Vellalas fell away, and the distribution of wealth changed (Banks 1957:415f).

That Vellālars are indeed aware of the peril posed to them is suggested by the following Jaffna Assistant Government Agent's report from the late nineteenth century:

> Great changes are going on in Jaffna native society, which are bitterly resented by the conservative part of the population. The (so called) 'low-castes' are becoming more rich, and having acquired property, most of them naturally decline to follow old customs, by which they were prohibited from wearing jewels, riding in carriages, using tom-toms for marriages, and other social functions . . . the Vellalas know that the next step in the progress . . . will be that of wearing jewelry and assuming Vellala customs (cited in Asumainayagam 1976b:21).

The imposed features, then, help to maintain Vellālar domination by demarcating in public just who is a "left" Untouchable, thus preventing--at least locally--mobility attempts like buying land or trying to marry into a Vellālar family. It would, therefore, be very easy to follow Dumont in viewing the imposed features as "symbols of subjection." Yet to do so would be to miss their religious value, and in so doing to ignore completely the essentially South Indian world view that underlies them. In the following chapter, it will be argued that for Tamil folk, the imposed features indeed possess a religious meaning: one so potent that, while their stigma is in essence only a temporary, local one, everyone--even Pallars--agrees that so long as they are applied, access to Vellālar rank is out of the question.

Chapter 4

THE RITUAL ORGANIZATION OF DISORDER

> . . . The jackal shrieks and howls; the owl's sad hoot is heard; the bittern whoops; dread goblin crowds and female ghouls that corpses eat with hair dishevelled fill the place. . . . Now the hunter leather-shod comes here with drum and curved bow.
>
> --Paṭṭiṉappālai, 319-31 (trans. by Chelliah 1962:45).

I. The Religious Meaning of the Imposed Features

I.1. Clues to the Status of the "Left" Untouchables

The spread of Gangetic culture into South India was no doubt facilitated by the postclassical rise of the temple worship tradition, which provided Dravidian Sudras with a high rank and a legitimate claim to rule other men. By the ninth century A.D., Brahmans and Veḷḷāḷars had established in the Tamil lands a social form that was genuinely in accordance with the holistic ideal of the varṇāśrama dharma, although its realization in the south among Sudras invested it with patterns of conflict absent in the domination of the twice-born. Despite the success of the Brahman-Veḷḷāḷar integration, it was nonetheless true that, as in Southeast Asia, highland and jungle areas were still the homes of non-peasant, tribal peoples (Stein 1980: 74ff). A major theme of South Indian literature was the fearfulness and violence of these peoples, who were said, for instance, to "shoot their arrows at poor and defenseless travellers, from whom they can rob nothing, only to feast their eyes on the quivering limbs of their victims" (Kanakasabhai 1966:42-43). An important clue to the status of the "left" Untouchables may be found in the aversion shown to these non-peasant folk, for it is from the ranks of the detested tribal peoples that the "left" Untouchables were, for centuries, recruited.

As the agrarian order of South Indian peasant society expanded, previously forested areas were cleared to make way for advanced agriculture. The inhabitants of these forested areas, if not driven off, were incorporated into the social framework--by force if necessary--as castes of the "left-side" (Stein 1980:182). That the "left" Untouchables were seen as persons coming from outside the system is suggested by the way Tamils regard the "right-side" Paṟaiyars, of whom it is said, "the Paṟaiyars are not of the left hand, they are Tamilians" (cited in Stein 1980: 209). In Jaffna, all of the *aṭimai* castes are viewed as "stranger" peoples, who for a variety of reasons--conquest, famine, and exile--were forced to come to Jaffna and submit to Veḷḷāḷar domination (David 1976:109ff; Banks 1960:66). Th word *aṭi* indeed connotes aboriginality and foreignness much more clearly than it suggests slavery in the sense of Roman law. Moreover, Untouchables are today called "original Dravidians," *āṭitirāviṭas*. Notwithstanding the fact that the "left" Untouchables are called "impure," their low status ca be better understood by examining the beliefs Tamils today maintain about aboriginal peoples.

I.2. The Sources of Autochthonous Disorder

Jaffna Hindus say that civilization became possible ages ago when the ancient Tamils discovered the rules (*muṟaikaḷ*) of ritual, the rules that made civilization's achievement possible. Prior to that time, they say, people led unhappy lives characterized by illness, sterility, fighting, and poverty. They suffered because they did not know how to protect themselves from the many supernatural powers that afflicted them. In the Tamil view, there are powers everywhere in this world capable of attacking people and ruining their lives. There are other powers, too, potentially helpful to people who know how to use the Tamil ritual design to save themselves, for through ignorance, a people is doomed. For Jaffna Tamils (and indeed for Tamils everywhere), this lowly state is symbolized by the Veddahs (Vēṭarkaḷ), the jungle people. Let us examine more closely the powers that can render an easygoing, unstructured (cummā) life impoverished and unhappy.

Snakes. Among the feared powers of the jungle are snakes, which can rob people of their fertility as well as kill them with their venom. Snakes are not thought dumb, but rather are considered highly sentient beings with enormous magical powers. Snakes (and, in particular, cobras or nallapampu) exist in the wilderness as a fearful and violent society, commanded by a chieftain, Nākatampiraṉ, the Lord of Snakes. Their very substance, thought to be distilled in an essential form in their blood and semen, is extremely dangerous to human life; it is believed that a snake's semen can kill merely by contact with the skin. It is said that sorcerers (mantiravāti-s) try to catch snakes' seminal emissions on a handkerchief, which then becomes a weapon.

The substance of snakes, as epitomized in their semen, is thought to cause sterility, madness, irascible behavior, and even death. Women are especially vulnerable to its power. It is thought in Jaffna that much mischief arises when young men, knowing of this vulnerability to the substances of disorder, try to inflict women with disorder so that no one else will want to marry them. Thus a man can get the woman he wants without competition and, in all likelihood, with a good dowry as compensation for her afflicted condition. A young man whose marriage proposal has been refused will try to inflict harm just out of spite. One family recounted this story:

> This fellow had been coming around freely (cummā) to chat and pass the time. We did not know he was after our daughter. Then, one day, he came when the parents were gone, and sat with our daughter for a while. He pulled out a handkerchief and touched her cheek with it, and left. She became very ill (tōsam). She was feverish and writhing around on the floor. We took her to the hospital. They told her it was all in her head. They gave her shock treatment, but that did not help. She has nāka tōsam (the affliction caused by snakes) and now nobody will want to marry her.

The beliefs about the affliction caused by snake semen coming into contact with a young woman show a more general conviction: the substance of wilderness beings is inimical to a woman's fertility, mental health, and capacity to enjoy a happy married life. We shall meet this principle in many guises, for "substance" is defined quite broadly. To touch or to eat disordering substances is the quickest way to appropriate disorder into one's system, where it causes a deep, afflicting disorder (tōṣam) of the body's natural harmony.

The affliction caused by snakes is said to consist of a disordering of the body's three humors (wind, bile, and phlegm), so that health is destroyed. The concept of bodily disorder stems from the Ayurvedic medical tradition, which posits the three humors and attributes ill health to imbalance among them such that one, while "excited" or "angry," predominates over the others. In popular Jaffna Hindu thinking, however, the three humors are reduced to a hot (cūṭu) versus cold (kuḷir) dichotomy. Thus, nāka tōṣam is thought to reveal itself in a condition of heat in the system. Heat is not measured by body temperature; it is, rather, a condition that manifests itself in irascibility, infertility, excessive or obsessive behavior, hard thinking, and disobedience. Excessive bodily heat can be produced by eating "hot" foods; however, the "heating" property of foods stems not from their temperature, but rather from their effect on the system. Ice cubes, for example, are considered "hot."

The symptoms of nāka tōṣam are symptoms associated in a general way, in Hindu thinking, with excessive body heat. They include a blackening or dark blotching of the face, caused by the accumulation there of poisons in the system; extreme thinness; frequent miscarriages, stillbirths, or complete sterility; dreams about snakes; and lustful fantasies. It is highly feared, for disorder completely destroys a woman's chance to bless her family with a salubrious power of vitality, which can radiate out only from a chaste woman who is protected from disorder. These symptoms can be induced, it is believed, merely by indulging in "hot" foods; if such is the case, it is cured by a highly "cooling" treatment supplied by the Ayurvedic physician. Indeed, whenever nāka tōṣam is suspected, that is the first option for treatment. However, if the treatment does not work, the conclusion is reached that the disorder is not a "natural" one (iyarkkai) resulting from a simple, temporary upset of the sys̄tem, but rather from a more deepseated mystical affliction caused by an attacking mystical being.

While touching or eating the substance of disorder is the quickest way to appropriate it, the mere sight or proximity of certain wilderness creatures, including snakes, is sufficient to induce the disorder. The intrusion of a snake into the house compound, or worse, into the house itself, is greatly feared; that in itself indicates the onset of nāka tōṣam. It is thought that, should a snake get into the rafters and pass over the body of a pregnant, sleeping woman, she will have a miscarriage. This misfortune occurs most commonly in the poorer homes, whose thatched roofs offer meager protection against the intrusion of snakes. Yet a snake found in the compound or in the house will not be killed; like all disordered beings of the wilderness, snakes are thought to have the power to curse (capam), and a snake's curse is especially feared. It can inflict sterility on the members of the killer's cantati or lineage, so that all of his work in this world comes to naught. Thus Hindus are very reluctant to kill snakes and to risk the feared curse.

It is also believed that nāka tōṣam can be caused by the malevolent influence of the two lunar nodes, Rāku and Kēṭu, of Hindu astrology. The nodes are "serpents," and when their malevolent aspect is exalted in a woman's horoscope she suffers all of the symptoms of nāka tōṣam. When it is discovered by as astrologer that the lunar nodes are at fault, the condition is properly known as kiraka tōṣam, the tōṣam of planets.

The *Tōṣam* of Wild Creatures. As the wilderness creatures par excellence, snakes possess the power to disorder and disharmonize a woman's system and rob her of her chastity and her fertility. This power is shared by certain other wild creatures, among them frogs (tērai), wild birds (paṭci), and large crows (periya kākkai). These are thought to possess the power to imperil a pregnancy or to afflict a small child. A woman must be protected from contact with these creatures if she is to bear a healthy child.

Omens (*Cakuṉam*). Birds are in general held to be inauspicious, and their calling out at certain times is though to be portentous. Owls (kūvai) are particularly regarded as harbingers of death when they call out near a house at midnight. In a sense, it is inaccurate to say that calling birds portend misfortune, for in a very real sense the very sound of a bird's call is misfortune, the very caus of it. The intrusion of this wilderness emanation, this sound of the jungle into one's life, is unpredictable and uncontrollable; there is little that can be done to defend oneself against it, save to destroy the creatures' habitats near the home.

Not all omens are portentous. The calling out of small crows (which are very numerous) may mean the impending arrival of guests, while the chirping of house lizards may mean good fortune. But crows and house lizards are common features on the domestic scene; what is feared is the jungle creature, whose very presence, sound, or touch is a source of disorder.

The Bad Sights (*Kūṭātamuḷiviyaḷam*). Just as the calling of a wild owl is in itself a source of tōṣam and misfortune, the bad sights are in themselves sources of illness and disorder. The bad sights are most dangerous at times of transition, especially when one is arising from bed or leaving the home. They may also occur in dreams.

The bad sights, which are listed in Table III, repeat the symbolism of omens. It is dangerous to see things which are peripheral to the full life of the great Veḷḷāḷar, just as it is dangerous to hear their sounds. The dangerous sights are things that suggest infertility (barren women, snakes); death (corpses, people polluted by death, widows, dead souls, black cloths, the direction south [which is the abode of the Lord of Death, Yama]); poverty (begging Brahmans, beggars in general, empty vessels); the presence of disordered supernatural power (present in iron and in sacrificial offerings, which absorb that power so that it can be disposed of); demons (which dwell in trees); wild animals; Untouchables (symbolized by brooms); and aboriginals (naked people without civility).

Ghosts and Spirits. The wilderness is primordially the repository of these beings, who despise and seek to destroy human happiness. Their career begins when, for some reason, a person is unable to get a decent funeral (cettu vīṭu), the "death house" rite. The purpose of the funeral

TABLE III

THE BAD SIGHTS (kūṭātamuḻiviyālam)

Bad Sights	Bad Symbols in Dreams
begging Brahmans	naked people
empty vessels	widows
brooms	dead souls
Untouchables	blackened bodies
beggars	forest animals
snakes	monkeys
cats	jackals
barren women	crows
blind people	black cloths
sorcerers	iron
impure people	sacrificial offerings
paraī drums	trees
corpses	the direction south

SOURCE: Field interviews in Chavakachcheri, Sri Lanka

is not only to console the bereaved, but also to speed the soul of the deceased on to the next world. Ideally, the soul should go on to the realm of the manes (pitir-s). The pitir-s are thought to maintain a fairly benign existence in the realm of Death (Yama), but they can only remain there so long as the family performs the proper funerary rites, the annual obsequies for the deceased in which they are offered balls of rice (piṇṭam) or rice meals (maṭai). These annual rites secure the continued vitality and happiness of the pitir-s, ethereal beings who bless the household with good fortune, prosperity, and health.

The funerary rites are designed to sever the bonds of the soul with this world, so that it may go on to the realm of the pitir-s and enjoy a fairly benign afterlife.

Thus, when the body is taken from the house compound to go to the crematorium, it is not taken out through the gate, but rather through a hole made for the purpose in the palm leaf fence surrounding the house. It is a one-way journey; there should be no return. After the body has been burnt, the ashes are thrown into the sea. The post-funerary rites are similarly intended to aid the soul on its journey, and to repudiate its attempts to get back to life.

The soul's desire to return to its life is deemed natural and normal; there is always some task that lies unfinished and some ambition which is unfulfilled. But to allow the soul to remain is not to do it a favor; indeed it is the duty of loving children of the deceased to see to it that the rites are done, so that the soul will not have to suffer a continued worldly existence as a disembodied ghost (āvi) and, finally, a vicious spirit (pēy).

That the pitir-s are supposed to retain a post-funerary consciousness and vitality contradicts the supposedly universal Hindu doctrine of metempsychosis, or reincarnation. On the one hand, the soul of the deceased is supposed to be reborn after death; on the other hand, the soul goes on to a permanent afterlife in the land of Yama. The contradiction bedeviled Hindu theologians, but it does not seem to disturb Jaffna Hindus. In fact, very little emphasis is placed on metempsychosis in Jaffna Hindu belief, although it is conceded to occur, being mentioned most often in mythological contexts. Most people want their children to perform the obsequies for them so that they can go to the realm of the pitir-s. Some people deny that there is an afterlife at all.

There is another option for the fate of the soul: absorption (mukti) into the cosmic body of Lord Śiva, as outlined in the Śaiva Siddhanta philosophical system, the formal theology of Jaffna Hindus. Few, however, desire such a goal. It is believed that, to attain mukti, one must have completely cut one's bonds with this world, so much so that one's whole family has died away. Rather, the best candidate for mukti is the person who has seen so much suffering--generally his own family's suffering--that he no longer wishes to live. Thus to desire mukti is to desire the destruction of one's family, and that is felt to be very unfair and unmeritorious, to say the least. Pictures of Śiva are never kept in a family's household shrine, for fear of the deadly consequences.

There are certain deaths for which the funeral is not thought capable of attaining its end. If a person dies with a great ambition or hunger (tirupti) for life, it is felt that the funeral's techniques of furthering the soul's journey are likely to be insufficient to overcome the magnetism of this world. A person who dies before his or her time is certain to desire continued life; so too is a man who had not fulfilled a deeply desired ambition a likely candidate for a ghost. For such persons a simple funeral may be held, but the rite may be given up altogether. The death of a young woman in childbirth is thought to ensure the terrestrial persistence of a spirit. Men and women in Jaffna agree that there is no hunger like that of a woman to see her first-born, and if it is denied her she will be unable to leave the world behind. Suicides and the youthful victims of violent accidents are similarly thought to retain their hunger for life. Most Jaffna suicides are connected with unrequited love affairs or depressions stemming from the rejection of friendship; the motive is not uncommonly agonistic, for the suicide seeks to punish the perceived tormentors with his or her death. The spirit of the suicide wishes to see the sad results of its act.

When a proper funeral is not done, the soul becomes a ghost (āvi), then a spirit (pēy). The āvi begins by staying around the house and vexing the family with loud noises and horrible, frightening dreams in which it tries to speak with them. But soon all this is forgotten, and all that is left is malice. The soul's desire to remain in life leads to a hatred for the living, for the ghost cannot actually enjoy anything or obtain satisfaction. Its spirit-body is defective, ridden with heat (c̄uṭu) and pain. It is eternally insatiable, and whatever good will it may have felt toward its old kinfolk disappears in a tide of envy (errical, "burning within") and hate (veṟuppu).

The ghost, consumed in the confusion generated by its hot anger, loses its intelligence, forgets its home, and wanders about looking for signs of human happiness to destroy. The nameless, confused, and malicious spirit hates beautiful young children; young, green shoots in the fields; happy young virgins with firm breasts; smiling wives dressed in beautiful saris; and houses which show prosperity. Hating all of these things, the spirit wishes also to crush them.

The malice of spirits is deepened by their need to appropriate the vitality of living things. Unlike the fortunate pitir-s who receive food from their descendants, ghosts and spirits do not receive regular offerings, and have to seek out vitality (uyir, "life") by arranging their own sacrifices. Indeed, spirits may kill to appropriate the vitality they need; alternatively, they may possess (piṭikkiṟatal) people, especially young girls, who are the most vulnerable to spirit attacks. Spirit possession is a greatly feared affliction, occuring when a spirit jumps onto a victim, causing an illness marked initially by difficulty in breathing, aches, numbness, dizziness, headaches, fevers, vomiting, shivering fits (pēy aṭṭam, the spirit dance), and insanity.

Spirit possession destroys a family's prosperity, happiness, and fertility, because it most commonly attacks the household's young women. The spirit causes the young woman to engage in immodest, indecorous, lustful, and disobedient behavior, all of which threaten her chastity and her reputation. A possessed woman may rush into the house during her period of menstrual pollution and touch the kitchen's pots, an act that pollutes them so much that they have to be destroyed. She may roll about on the ground moaning, or swoon with love for an unsuitable partner. Worst of all, she may be made permanently infertile. One villager related the following tale about his wife, Sarasvati:

> I have my house and I have a little land, and I have Sarasvati. But Sarasvati is childless. Her mother had been possessed when Sarasvati was yet in the womb. When the child was only four years old the possession started. She was taken to several temples but without any results. Finally she got married to me and I was able to help her. But still now and again she gets possessed. She has no child, although she is now twenty-nine.

Demons. The wilderness is the abode of countless demons of unaccountable origin. They are not, it should be emphasized, ghosts or spirits; they are inhuman beings of enormous power. They dwell in trees, bodies of water, open, deserted places; along boundaries, in groves, at ruins, and at road junctions. Demons, known generically as *muni*, are in their primordial state wholly and utterly opposed to human life. They are hot-headed, cruel, saturnine, bloodthirsty, and egotistical (*akaṅkāram*). Their presence is known by the fearful sight, at midnight, of a dull, burning glow in the distance; the sight alone is believed to cause vomiting or death.

Demons, like spirits, need vitality, which they appropriate by arranging their own sacrifices (*pali*). Demon-arranged sacrifices become known to people when there have been a number of uncanny, peculiar deaths in a vicinity, as for example, a number of violent, bloody accidents on a road beside a certain tree, or people falling repeatedly into a certain well. Confirmation of the demon's presence at such a spot could be as simple a matter as a person dropping dead suddenly, for no apparent reason, within a half-mile or so of the suspected locus of demonic power. The demons are completely heartless; they do not stop to appropriate the lives of their victims if they desire them. They do not bother to choose a person with few responsibilities, but afflict any person they can. They are random in their cruel, senseless attacks on the living, and it is believed that civilization cannot develop unless these saturnine beings are appeased by the violent death of a sacrificial victim.

The Feminine Disorder of Localities. Another disordered being of the primordial landscape is the disgusting female spirit Mū Tēvi. An abominable spirit who feeds on menstrual discharge and fecal matter, Mū Tēvi is attracted to the homes of *keṭṭavarkaḷ* (low-ranking people of filthy habits), and especially to women who live *cummā* (freely, without restriction). The possession of a person by Mū Tēvi may be distinguished from the possession of *pēy* because the affliction of the former causes a foul stench, prolonged menstruation, and an irascible ("hot") temperament. Mū Tēvi means "inauspicious goddess," and is said to be Lakṣmī's (Cī Tēvi's) sister, the latter being the very personification of chastity and good fortune.

In Tamil mythology, Mū Tēvi is thought to be the evil sister-in-law, rather than the sister, of a personified ideal of chaste feminity, and Jaffna Tamils maintain this account of her career as well as the one linking her with Lakṣmi. We have, in fact, already met Mū Tēvi in her guise as the sister-in-law of a good woman. The story of the Paḷḷar caste's origins, related in chapter two, appears to be a multiform of a South Indian myth about a good woman who seeks aid from her brother's wife, but is refused succor. In the Jaffna version, the good Paḷḷaṉ's younger brother, Veḷḷāḷan, was married to an irascible "bad woman," who refused them succor after Paḷḷan's house had been destroyed by a cyclone. In a South Indian myth, the *Nallataṅkāḷ Kaṭai* ("Story of Nallataṅkāḷ"), the good Nallataṅkāḷ seeks aid from her brother's evil wife Mūḷi ("Defective"); but when Mūḷi saw Nallataṅkāḷ coming with her seven hungry children, "she quickly hid all her valuables and bolted the doors to her house . . . she pretended to be asleep and would not even answer her cries." Nallataṅkāḷ threw her children and herself into a well; the children became *vaṉṉi* (jungle) trees and she became a goddess. Mūḷi's husband, Nallataṅkāḷ's brother, found out about his wife's treachery, and killed her; she was turned into a stone for all to deride.

In the *Nallataṅkāḷ Kaṭai*, Mūḷi is referred to with a standard epithet, *mūḷiyalaṅkari mūtevi cāṇṭali* ("she of the missing or defective ornaments, the evil woman of Untouchable caste") (Shulman 1980:256f). The word *mūḷi*, "defective," itself suggests a low-caste person who wears no ornament (*alaṅkāram*). Thus the Paḷḷar caste origin myth con-contains an especially ironic contrast, since it equates Veḷḷāḷaṉ's wife with an Untouchable woman; it was the good Paḷḷaṉ, not Veḷḷāḷan, who actually possessed the virtuous wife and deserved the high rank. This claim is "proven" in the myth because Paḷḷaṉ, with his virtuous wife, possessed many children, while Veḷḷāḷaṉ had only four. A woman's chastity renders her fertile, and brings prosperity to her family; conversely, a "bad woman" brings infertility and opprobrium.

A woman possessed by Mū Tēvi becomes like her; the disorder of the possession produces the "hot," irascible temperament that led Mūḷi to act badly. Thus a family cannot enjoy happiness, health, fertility, and dignity if women are exposed to the possession of Mū Tēvi; every precaution must be taken, as evidenced in the description of house-building rituals later in this chapter, to see that

Mū Tēvi cannot enter. The effect of the "bad woman" (koṭumpāvi) on the village as a whole is equally devastating; it is thought that, so long as there is a single "bad woman" in a village where rice is grown, the rains will not fall.

Localities--specifically, the bounded space of the village (kirāmam)--are also afflicted with the disordered presence of a more tractable spirit, the virgin--and therefore powerful--goddess of the type called Ammaṉ and Kāḷi. In their disordered, "hot" state, these goddesses are hardly distinguishable from the wholly evil Mū Tēvi; yet they can be appeased, controlled, tamed, and transformed in ritual, so long as the appropriate ritual technique (vēḷvi, "sacrifice" or kuḷirtti, "cooling") is known. Lacking that knowledge, people must suffer the afflictions Kāḷi and Ammaṉ visit on people: possessions, infectious ("hot") diseases, drought, and sterility.

Evil (*keṭuti*). It is thought to be in the nature of man that, if a family has somehow managed to escape the depradations of disorder enumerated above, their neighbors and kin will be inclined to hate them for it. Although the gods are beseeched to bestow abundance, experiences teach people that not all who try to attain wealth will succeed, for the good things of life are in short supply. Limited are jobs, protein, fruits, land, good marriages, money, connections, higher education, fertility, agrarian abundance, and happiness in family life. To be sure, not all good things are limited. Abundant are toddy, sun, well water, and most of all, the virtues of the palmyra palm. But when a poor person beholds a family that is blessed with many children, flourishing harvests, jobs, family harmony, and laughing, pretty women, these things may seem to have been achieved at the poor person's expense. In him, then, arises the desire to smash that happiness.

Envy (*errical*) is defined as a "burning within" which heats the system and leads to hot-headed confusion in which all scruples are lost. Envy and anger can also be produced accidentally, by eating too many "hot" foods, which in overheating the system lead to the "hot" disharmony. However derived, an envious person can harm a happy, prosperous one--especially a woman, since women are always deemed more vulnerable than men to supernatural powers--simply by an envious glance (kaṇṇūru, the "eye misfortune") or by speaking envious words of praise (nāvūru, the "tongue misfortune"). The eye and tongue misfortunes are especially feared when they emanate from keṭṭavarkaḷ, low-caste or aboriginal peoples, who are thought to be saturated with disordered power. Another option of the envious is to hire a sorcerer who can bring down a spirit on a man's wife.

The Gods. The inclusion of the gods in this list may be surprising, but apart from deities ordered by temple ritual, gods are believed very widely to pose a threat to the ordered, Veḷḷāḷar style of life. Consider, for instance, that Lord Śiva, despite his standing at the very apex of the Śaivite pantheon and as the epitome of the Śaivite religion, is a very unpopular object of worship in Jaffna. He is not represented in the lithographs that normally hang in every house's shrine room, and indeed, people hint that the sight of him is somewhat inauspicious. He is symbolized by the liṅka, which represented the enormous accumulated power of the antisocial yogi who has long performed austerities (tapas) and remained chaste. Śiva is thought very reluctant to involve himself in the world, preferring to haunt the seashore, that lonely place where the ashes of the dead are thrown into the water. His interests center on freeing the rare saintly seeker of any remaining bonds that tie him down to this world.

Few, however, are interested in that kind of liberation, since it involves the complete extinction of the ego-sense. Nearly every Hindu rejects this state as a proximate goal and moreover, the god is not seen as being interested in bestowing any boon that would help people cope with this life. "If you look at Śiva's devotees," I was told, "they all had miserable lives so they wanted to get away from existence. This is what Śiva does. I don't want mukti, I want to be reborn as a graduate teacher with multicolored saris." No one would dream of making a vow to Śiva, for it is feared that would insult him. One has to be careful in taking mundane matters to the gods; it is better, Hindus say, to start at the appropriate level, for Śiva has delegated authority to his sons and to other deities. "Śiva is like the Prime Minister;" it was said, "she appoints ministers so that she won't have to meddle with everyday affairs. If you try to get past the ministers, you may find yourself in a very dangerous situation."

Śiva is thought prepared to honor the wishes of anyone who wants to obtain mukti, or release, and towards that end will appear in theophanies to his devotees. Although he is not interested in helping people with mundane affairs, Śiva is thought to be very easily coerced by shows of devotion, especially those involving self-sacrifice and mutilation. One does not need to be especially deserving or of high caste to receive Śiva's grace; one only requires devotion. Among those who received mukti, according to the immensely popular Tamil hagiography, the Periya Purāṇam, were Untouchables and women; this is known to Jaffna Hindus, and they often cite the tale of Kaṇṇapar to show how little caste rank or purity matters to Śiva so long as there is devotion (nampikai). It is said that, long ago, there was a hunter named Tiṇṇaṉ, who used to sacrifice animals to the gods of the forest:

> One day, after chasing a wild boar, Tiṇṇaṉ came upon a linga on the hill of Kaḷatti. The moment he saw the linga he was filled with love for the god. He embraced the linga and kissed it; and then he hunted animals, cooked and chewed the meat, and, after spitting out whatever was without flavor, offered the rest to the god in a container of leaves. . . . A Brahman named Civakocaṉ used to serve the linga in the forest according to the proper rite. He was horrified when one day he found it polluted with meat and blood; he purified it and consecrated it anew, but each day he returned to find it once more renewed impure. For five days the Brahman and the hunter worshipped the god by turns, each in his own manner, until the priest could bear it no more and cried to Śiva. Śiva appeared to him in a dream and said, 'After the meat chewed and offered by Tiṇṇaṉ, the . . . [nectar] of the gods drunk in golden cups is like poison together with the bitter fruit of the neem.' To prove the hunter's devotion, Śiva devised a test. While the Brahman hid and watched, Tinnaṉ arrived to find the image of the god bleeding from the right eye. To stop the flow of blood, the hunter tore out his own eye and placed it on the linga. But then the left eye of the god began to bleed. The hunter placed his foot on the bleeding eye so he would be able to find the spot; then he began to scoop out his remaining eye as a gift to the god. Śiva stretched out his hand from the linga and stopped the devotee, who was ever after famous as Kaṇṇappar (from kaṇ, 'eye') (Shulman 1980:135).

Yet, I was told, "No one tells a tale of Śiva appearing these days, for there are no saints. No one would seek such a theophany; it would mean the end of the ego." In illustration, I was told that long ago, someone asked one of the great bhakti saints to prove Śiva's greatness by giving mukti to a bush. Before their eyes, the astonished onlookers watched as the bush slowly, slowly disappeared. Many believe this to be the fate of him who worships Śiva.

If Śiva has few devotees, it is nonetheless true that there are stories of his theophany here and there. In one Jaffna temple myth, the god appears as a bleeding liṅgam--

a common motif in temple origin myths generally--but the person who discovers the _liṅgam_ puts Piḷḷaiyār's (Śiva's son's) face on it instead. It is said that once there was a prominent Veḷḷāḷar, a Mudaliyar (headman), who as an act of charity helped to widen and deepen a tank (_kēṇi_) for the benefit of the village. The digging went well until one day a _liṅkam_ was encountered. The diggers were called Ōṭṭār, a special caste which in those days dug out ponds (_kēṇi_). One digger's mammoty [hoe] had struck it and made a gash on it. To their amazement, blood began to flow and ooze from this gash on the _liṅkam_. Everyone was very frightened, but the Mudaliyar took charge of the _liṅkam_ and built a temple there. He affixed to it the face (_mukavatakam_) of Piḷḷaiyār, and the temple came to be known as the Oṭṭankēṇi Piḷḷaiyār Temple. Now Piḷḷaiyār, whom we have already met, favors his patrons with material plenty. The Mudaliyar's heroic act transformed, therefore, a very dangerous situation into one helpful to the establishing of an ordered, prosperous life. Piḷḷaiyār, the god of the Oṭṭankēṇi temple and one of the most widely worshipped deities in Jaffna, is deeply beloved by Veḷḷāḷars. Indeed, it is sometimes said that Piḷḷaiyār is the _kula teyvam_ (tutelary deity) of the Veḷḷāḷar caste, for the god is thought to be interested in helping them to create wealth and abundance in this world.

Yet even Piḷḷaiyār has, in the wilderness, a far more violent and antisocial nature. Along the Jaffna-Kandy road south of Jaffna, there is an odd little Piḷḷaiyār shrine at Murukandy, a desolate spot in the jungles. Like the shrine of a demon, the Murukandy temple is nothing more than a small hut built at the base of an enormous tree, in which the god is believed to actually reside. Travelers on the Jaffna-Kandy road expect to stop at the shrine, where they must wash their feet, worship at the shrine, break a cocoanut, burn camphor, prayerfully circumambulate the temple, and make a _poṭṭu_ (sandalwood paste and vermilion powder) mark on the forehead, the latter as a token of the deity's grace. It is felt that, to ensure a safe journey through the jungles, Piḷḷaiyār must be propitiated and his assistance ensured. Otherwise he will himself see to it that the traveler's car is smashed up.

The murderous capacity of the primordial Piḷḷaiyār is shown in the following temple origin myth, from the Puṅkāṭi Piḷḷaiyār Temple, Kaccāy South, Jaffna. People in Kaccāy say that there was once a time when the area was all jungle, and only a few people were living out there. They had a small temple by the side of a puṅka tree [Pongamia glabra, "Indian Beech"]. But the Dutch came and said, "Show us your god." The priest replied, "Come next Friday and I'll show you my god." After the Dutch left the priest, realizing after some reflection how foolish his promise was, cast himself down on the ground and prayed to the god to help him out. On Saturday evening the god told him, "Get up, eat, and bathe. I'll get you out of this." The next Friday came, and the priest went to the temple and prepared the offerings. He was about to light the camphor. The priest was afraid, for the Dutch used to punish people for openly worshipping the gods. When the Dutch finally arrived, the priest was very terrified. The priest, with the Dutch watching, opened up the temple door and stammered out a mantiram (invocational verse). Suddenly a large noise was heard. Out of the puṅka tree came an elephant, which charged at the Dutch and killed them. The elephant stayed by the shrine for a while, and the priest would feed it with the offerings.

Śiva has two sons, Piḷḷaiyār and Skanda (Kantacāmi); the younger of the two, Kantacāmi, is sometimes called Murukaṉ. Now no Hindu would deny that Kantacāmi and Murukaṉ are one and the same deity, but the fact is that, in Jaffna Hinduism, the two facets of the god are treated as if they were completely separate deities. Kantacāmi is the exemplar of the Brahmanical tradition and all that is orthodox, while Murukaṉ epitomizes *bhakti*, or devotional religion. He exemplifies the adored god, the one chosen for worship (*iṣṭa teyvam*), who gives any boon to his worshippers so long as they love him with utterly unfaulted faith. Murukaṉ's headquarters are at the remarkable pilgrimage site Kataragama, which is located far to the south of Jaffna along the southeastern coast of the island. The site exemplifies the manifestations of a deity who is thought to have appeared on the scene due to his own volition (*tāntōnri teyvam*, "self-born god" or *tāṉāy vantu teyvam*, "self-arrived god"). The tale of Murukaṉ's birth is told in the *Kantapurāṇam*, another popular Jaffna text. It is said that, long ago a demon named Sūrapadma was greatly troubling the gods, and they went begging to Śiva to do something to stop the terror.

> They asked . . . [Śiva] for a son. Śiva sprouted six heads, and from the eye in the forehead of each of them a spark flew out, from their heat the worlds and the sea dried up, and Umā fled in terror, smashing her anklets in the process. Śiva told Agni and Vayu [the lords of fire and of wind] to take the sparks and deliver them to the Ganges; Vayu handed them to Agni, who threw them into the river. Desiccated by the fierce heat, the Ganges carried them on her head to Caraṿanam. From that pond Murukaṉ arose with one body, six heads, and twelve arms, floating on a lotus, in the form of an infant. The gods called the Kṛttikās (*Kārttikaitterivaimār*) [arrived] to nurse the child and, as they entered the water, they beheld six children instead of one; each took one to nurse. Śiva and Umā went to the pond; at Śiva's command, Umā embraced the six infants at the edge of the water, and they merged into one child with six heads and twelve arms. Milk flowed from the breasts of the goddess, and she collected it in a golden cup and fed it to her son (Shulman 1980:246f).

Murukaṉ, after a remarkable childhood in which he accomplished many prodigious feats, vanquished the demon, who appeared before him as a gigantic tree. The demon, split into two, became the god's vehicles, the cock and the peacock. In gratitude for his victory, the god Indra gave Murukaṉ his daughter, Teyvayāṉai.

But Murukaṉ was destined to have another wife, the second being a daughter, some say, of Viṣṇu. This girl, named Vaḷḷi, performed *tapas* (austerities) in the hope of winning Murukaṉ, and as a reward was given a birth as the daughter of a deer in the forest, the deer having been impregnated by the amorous glance of a sage. The deer, seeing that the baby was not of her kind, left her abandoned. Ceylonese myth has it that

> One day a Vedda-chief living in Parana, four miles off the present day Kataragama, while searching for wild yams found a small girl in the middle of the jungle.. . . The Vedda took the girl into his cave and adopted her, as his wife was childless. They called her Valli-amma or, in short, Valli, as she had been found among wild yam creepers (*valli*) and so she grew up.
>
> The messenger of the Gods, Narada, . . . came on his way through the three worlds into the area of Kataragama. There he met Valli-amma and was highly taken up by her gracefulness. He told Skanda [Kantacāmi] about her and he at once decided to go in search of Valli-amma. He did so in the disguise of a beggar who went towards the Vedda's cave to ask for food. Valli-amma was alone and she handed the old man some honey and yams. After he had eaten she asked him to go to the river nearby to quench his thirst. But the old man asked her to accompany him to which she eventually agreed. Then he confessed to her his love and asked her to become his wife. Indignant about his presumption, the girl decided to leave the unknown man at once. However at the same moment an elephant broke out of the jungle. It was Skanda's brother, the elephant headed Ganesha, whom Skanda had asked to hide himself in the jungle and to frighten the girl. The girl, frightened to death, asked for the old man's protection, whereupon he emphasized his love and extorted from her the promise of marriage. This had hardly happened when the elephant withdrew and the old man transformed himself into a young man. Marveling at the whole incident, Valli threw herself at his feet and asked his pardon, as she had at first treated

> him so rudely.. . . When the Vedda and his wife . . . returned to the cave, they didn't find the girl there any more. They searched for her with the help of other tribesmen in the surrounding jungle and eventually found her with Skanda, whose wife she had become. The Veddas tried to kill the seducer of the girl, but they did not succeed. Skanda was far stronger than they and in a short time killed a lot of people with his spear. Valli-amma was very enraged at this and decided to leave Skanda. The affair, however, took a favorable turn when Skanda called back to life all the Veddas he had killed. Peace was then restored and the young couple settled down on top of one of the neighboring hills (Wirz 1966:6f).

Murukaṉ's apparition at Kataragama has, then, an overtly sexual purpose. Nor is it the case that Vaḷḷi, at least in popular tradition, is really a proper bride for the god. The myths from the texts have it that Vaḷḷi is a reincarnated daughter of Viṣṇu, but in popular thought she is actually and expressly said to be the daughter of the Veddahs or to be of mixed Veddah-Sinhalese descent. Black in color and of low ancestry, Vaḷḷi's attraction for Murukaṉ shows in the Hindu mind that the gods, at least in their primordial form, are not at all concerned about the restrictions of caste, of purity, and of proximity to the afflicted that figure so strongly in ordinary social relations. Murukaṉ's behavior is, in a word, antinomian, for he takes Valli off and "marries her" (i.e., seduces her) without her parents' consent--an act totally out of keeping with the "rules" (*muṟai*) of social order.

Katarāgama (see Pfaffenberger 1979 and Wirz 1966) is thought to be an extremely dangerous and strange place, loaded with sacred power in its disordered form. Like the little shrines of demons, the temples are very small and plain structures built at the bases of enormous pipal trees. Murukaṉ's temple, called the *makākkōyil*, is actually a very small building, and anyone can enter it. The god is, however, kept behind a curtain, and only the high priests (who are Sinhalese) may enter. The priests, unlike their Brahman counterparts, do not chant any invocational verses (mantiram-s); indeed, it would be thought ridiculous to do so, for mantiram-s are intended to "invite" the deity (kuppīṭu) to take up a "seat" (piratiṣṭai) in a place. At Kataragama, the god is already seated, and by his own volition as well, so that to pronounce any mantiram-s would be tantamount to denying his immanence--a dangerous act indeed, for the god rewards lack of faith with swift and painful punishment.

Remote Kataragama is not the only theophany of Kantacāmi-Murukaṉ in the island. There are at least two in the Jaffna District. The oldest, Keerimalai on Jaffna's northern coast, is said to have been, long ago, a very powerful tīrttam (bath)--so powerful that, it is said, sins and deformities disappeared if one made a pilgrimage there. To this center came, long ago, a princess of the Chola kingdom, according to a tradition maintained in the Tamil chronicles of the Jaffna kingdom:

> She had been born with a horse's face, and greatly desired to get rid of it. She was otherwise a virgin of lightning beauty. She came to Keerimalai with her attendants, servants, and bodyguards, went down to the spring, and bathed. The miracle occurred and her horse-face disappeared. She then, having posted a guard all around, laid herself down to sleep on a delicate couch. But watching this miraculous spectacle was Katirgama, who had a lion's face, and despite the guards he suddenly entered the camp and carried the princess away to his palace at Katirgama. They lived there in great bliss. The princess gave birth to a beautiful son, Narasinha Raja, and later to a daughter. The son became King of Laṅkā (cited in Mootoothamby Pillai 1907:280f).

The identity of Katirgama, who is described as a king, seems to be somewhat confused. On the one hand, his name and residence indicate that he is none other than the Tamil god Murukaṉ; yet he is identified with Narasingha, an incarnation of Viṣṇu, by his lion's face. The Tamil

Chronicles would thus seem to display Sinhalese influence, for Sinhalese folk commonly regard the god of Kataragama (=Katirgama) as an incarnation of Viṣṇu. Sinhalese villagers tell this tale:

> There was a certain asuraya [demon], Brahma-asuraya by name, a very passionate man. One day he saw Umā Tēvi, Śiva's wife, and he desired her. He thought of a ruse to achieve his goal. He offered Śiva his services for twelve years. But one day Brahma-asuraya asked Śiva to teach him the mantra (incantation) that enabled the initiate to burn any person at once to ashes. Śiva put the spell on Brahma-asuraya's hand, but he had seen through the demon's intentions. Śiva ran away. Viṣṇu saw this, and transformed himself into a beautiful young woman and seated himself on a swing. When Brahma-asuraya came by, the demon at once forgot about Śiva and Umā Tēvi, and asked Viṣṇu to become his wife. 'Go first and talk the matter over with your wife,' Viṣṇu said, 'and ask her whether she has any objection to sharing her home with another woman.' Brahma-asuraya hurried home and got his wife's consent. But when he returned, Viṣṇu (in his female guise) was holding an infant. The demon was told, 'Go and ask your wife if she is willing to receive a woman with an infant in her house.' Brahma-asuraya again went home and received consent, but when he returned, the woman had a second infant. He was sent home to get consent, but on his return there were three infants. This happened again and again until Viṣṇu was sitting there with six children, and Brahma-asuraya was quite confused. Still he wanted to marry her. The woman demanded that he lay his hand upon his head and swear an oath that he was speaking the truth. Brahma-asuraya, forgetting his power, did so, and instantly burned himself to ashes. The woman on the swing had in the meantime developed six faces and twelve arms to deal with the six children, and so she became the six-faced Kataragama god (Wirz 1954:138ff).

In the Tamil tradition of India, the god of Kataragama is no incarnation of Viṣṇu, but rather a son of Śiva, as he is indeed believed to be in Jaffna today.

The second, more recent self-birth of Kantacāmi-Murukaṉ in the Jaffna District is at Tondaimannar on the northern coast, and it belongs to members of the fishing caste (Kaṟaiyar). It is said that, long ago, there was a fisherman. He caught fish in the little lagoon near Tondaimannar. He was plagued by just one problem. Sometimes, just as he was about to go to the stream to fish, a small boy would call him back. He could not see the boy, for the voice would come out of the wilderness. Each time this happened he was unable to catch any fish at all. Finally, one day the fisherman caught sight of the boy as he was called. He saw that the boy was playing with an elephant. He strode up to the boy and said, "Please don't call out to me in that way. It is inauspicious (to call someone back from a journey). I cannot catch any fish on those days." The boy replied, "Don't worry about it; come with me. I'll give you rice to eat." They went along into the jungle and came to a small hut. He was asked to fetch water and they went about preparing a pot of rice. But the boy said, "First we must offer pūcai (offerings of flowers and rice) to the god. You must go fetch banyan leaves." Having returned with the leaves, the boy said to the fisherman, "Please do the pūcai." The fisherman said, "I'm only a poo fisherman. I don't know how to do it." "It should be done after the fashion of the pūcai at Kataragama," the boy replied. "I've never been to Kataragama," the fisherman said. "Come then, we'll go," the boy said, and in an instan they stood before the shrine at Kataragama and the fisherma was able to observe the manner in which the priests do the pūcai. Suddenly they were back at Tondaimannar and the boy had disappeared. The fisherman did the pūcai just like he had seen it done at Kataragama, having tied a white cloth over his mouth. Later he went to tell everyone what had happened. They all said the boy must have been Murukaṉ, wh likes to appear as a youth. So they started the temple on the place where the boy played with the elephant. They called the temple Celvacannati Murukan Temple--the theophany (cannati) of the auspicious, young fellow (celvan).

For Vellālars in Jaffna, the propensity of the god Murukan to reveal himself to Veddah hunters, women, and Karaiyar fishermen, who are polluted or otherwise low status persons, demonstrates just how antinomian the primordial propensities of the god can be. Murukan, in his wilderness appearance at any rate, cannot serve as the foundation for social order; indeed, he is oblivious to it and destroys it.

I.3. The State of Nature

Exposed to all of the above sources of autochthonous disorder, the Veddahs (Vēṭarkaḷ)--despite their close connection with Lord Murukan--suffer poverty, afflictions, and unhappiness. Murukan does not help them to have happier lives. They are thought to hunt even now, living in the jungle and killing wild beasts, whereupon they savagely eat the meat without any decency. They are said to be unclean (cuttam illātu) and unkempt. They live a life without rules, without ritual, and without conventions (olaṅkumurai illāta vālkkai), celebrating no marriages and failing to seclude women. Their women possess no chastity. They know nothing about decorum, but go about naked; they are fools or bumpkins (kāṭṭu mirānti) in that they do not realize that they are themselves the cause of their low station in life. They have no protection at all against the disordering forces that abound in the wilderness, and as a result they are afflicted, enraged, disordered, stricken, blackened, rendered infertile and impoverished by disordered power.

It is felt that the Veddahs are very ignorant; they do not know anything of the rules (muraikaḷ) one must follow to lead a happy life. Jaffna Tamils say of the Veddahs, "They are fools of the jungle (kāṭṭu mirāṇṭikaḷ). They let their women go about freely (cummā) and later on they suffer for it." Afflicted and saturated with primordial and therefore disordering power, the fools of the jungle are riddled with the very opposite of the orthodox Hindu power of vitality. They are saturated with a negative power of disorder, so that they become, in Jaffna Tamil thinking, very dangerous indeed. The Veddahs, and anyone whose lifestyle resembles theirs, are deemed to be not only low by caste (*kuṟainta cāti*, "castes found wanting") but also thoroughly evil and dangerous (*keṭṭavarkaḷ*, "bad people"). Thus it is said of the Veddahs that they are not only impure by custom (which in itself is not a thorough justification for low rank), but also evil by saturation with disorder.

Jaffna Tamils feel that the Veddahs, lacking any knowledge of the ancient rules of civilization, are totally open to all kinds of affliction: the negative power of unchaste women, the malevolent aspect of planets, the vagaries of the calendrical cycle, possession by evil spirits, droughts sent by disordered goddesses, the play of the gods, and more. All of these afflictions are summed up under one term: *tōṣam* ("evil, disorder, imbalance of the humors of the body, fault, blemish, offence" are among the term's many meanings). The term is an important one in Ayurvedic medicine, in which tradition it refers to a condition of bodily disorder caused by an imbalance of the three bodily humors. Among the symptoms of *tōṣam*, which in popular usage refers to any trouble caused by sacred powers, are hot-headed anger; wild, boisterous behavior; confusion of mind; sterility or low fertility; bad luck, disasters, and setbacks; frenzied fits of possession and dancing; disobedience; and hateful envy. In such a condition, the ignorant folk of the jungle are hardly likely to be receptive to civilization's message. The affliction of the tribal folk thus renders them violent, dangerous, and intractable.

I.4. The Meaning of the Imposed Features

The meaning of the imposed features should now be plain to see. They are signs of wildness, of ignorance, or peripherality, of affliction, and of a lowliness that merits suppression. It is felt that the affliction of Naḷavars and Paḷḷars is so considerable that they should not try to pass themselves off as civilized; they are not civilized, nor could they be, and their behavior, in the Veḷḷāḷar view, confirms this point. Thus demarcated, the <u>aṭimai</u> Untouchable is exposed before the community in a guise that not only explains his low rank, but also provides a religious justification for the disabilities Veḷḷāḷars heap on him. By associating the <u>aṭimai</u> Untouchable with the "fools of the jungle," Veḷḷāḷars invest him with a deeply discrediting stigma, or an "attribute that makes him different from others in the category of persons available for him to be." He becomes a "less desirable person," one who is "quite thoroughly bad" and "dangerous," a "tainted, discounted" person (Goffman 1963:3ff). But the Veḷḷāḷar strategy in this regard is by no means a calculated or rational one. Veḷḷāḷars do not say, "Let's associate the Paḷḷars and Naḷavars with tribal folk, and thereby discredit their mobility aspirations." On the contrary, the peripherality of the <u>aṭimai</u> Untouchables is, for Veḷḷāḷars, an established fact once Untouchables imbibe the very source of disorder in the process of creating civilization. To insist on the imposed features is therefore, for many Veḷḷāḷars, a matter of religious commitment--the commitment possessed by those who would defend civilization against its enemies.

The fear with which the civil Tamil Hindu beholds the wilderness can be seen quite clearly in the rites associated with house-building in Jaffna. In describing the beings and forces which inspire this fear, I wish to stress that these beliefs are not merely anachronisms associated with some long-calcified ritual form, but rather beliefs of pressing, daily significance for everyone in this system.

II. The Confrontation with Wilderness

II.1. The Rationale of House Design

Jaffna Hindus expressly state that the religious goal of the rites connected with house-building is to convert the wilderness of the site into a special, ordered space suitable for an auspicious, good-caste woman (cumaṅkali) to dwell in. In a very real sense, the founding of a house is similar to the construction of a temple; many of the same rites and precautions are used for both structures. Just as the temple is a sealed space, set off from the death and disorder which surrounds it, so too is the house supposed to serve as an ordered space for a woman. Within its confines, protected from the disordering forces which surround the house, a woman's generative power as a personification of Śrī (Cī Tēvi) reaches its height; she becomes very fertile, and conceives. Just as the inner sanctum of the temple contains a protected womb (the garbhagṛha or mūlastānam) which conceives the deity, so too does the house quite literally contain a protected womb: that of the Veḷḷāḷar's chaste wife, who dwells happily and conceives many sons.

II.2. House Design and Female Chastity

The traditional Veḷḷāḷar home in Jaffna is designed with a central atrium (nāṟcār), which affords fresh air and sunshine for the women of the home. Prior to the mid-twentieth century, women of high caste standing were not permitted to leave the house except under extraordinary conditions; thus, they needed the atrium. Indeed, the whole interior of the home (vīṭu) was and is considered to be a refuge for women, where they may preserve their chastity. A carpentry contractor explained, "strangers are never received inside the home. Who knows what vices we admit as guests into our home? A man who visits without some legitimate purpose [cummā] is probably after my wife or daughter. Only blood kin [iratta contakkārar] may be admitted to the interior of the house." Most houses have an exterior verandah or a specially built reception room, called a talaivācal in which visitors can be entertained. The kitchen, kucini, is set apart from the house, preferably toards the rear of the compound, so that women will not be visible from the talivācal. In sum, every possible step is taken to seclude women, not the least of which is a stout fence of plaited cocoanut leaves, often reinforced with barbed wire.

The compound itself is kept scrupulously clean. Tennant's description of village houses in the Vanni, south of Jaffna, still describes the compounds of Hindus in Jaffna: "each house is built in a well-fenced compound, from which all grass and weeds are removed, and the white sand raked every morning, so clean that it looks almost like a flagged courtyard" (1860:513f). No plant is permitted to grow within the carefully cleaned compound, since any growth might harbor snakes, which can rob a woman of her health and fertility. The house stands as a refuge, into which no stranger may penetrate. The house is the very opposite of the jungle, in that it is organized, clean, orderly, and designed to serve only the purposes of people.

II.3. Considerations in Planning the Home's Location

When a Hindu family decides to construct a new house on a previously unoccupied site, the astrologer (cāttiri) is asked to visit the lot and decide on the auspicious place (maṅkula iṭam) for the house. The astrologer brings along a palmyra leaf manuscript (eṭṭupputtakam) which is said to contain ancient knowledge regarding the astrological aspects of house placement. Upon arriving, the astrologer requires two facts from the owner of the lot: the exact size of the house compound (kāṇi), and the lunar asterism (naṭcattiram) corresponding to the birth of the woman who is to become the center of the household. He takes this information into account when making his calculations.

Aside from the formal astrological judgment made by the astrologer, several other important considerations enter into the selection of a construction site within a compound. First, no house would be built directly to the east of a temple. It is a common belief among Jaffna Hindus that the occupants of such a house would sicken or die. As they explain it, the inner shrine (m̄ulast̄aṉam) of a Hindu temple is built of stone with a single door facing towards the east. This orientation is thought to focus the deity's "grace-force" (aruṟcakti) along an axis called the "temple center" (kōyilmaiyam). The emanations of the deity, thus concentrated, are said to be inimical to human life; no person could long survive exposure to this axis of power. The temple center's force is dangerous for a considerable distance. Generally, a street leads east from the temple, but no structure is built at the end of this avenue, which is called caṉṉati ("presence"). When asked about this custom, informants stated that households, particularly those with several women in them, produce "faults" (kuṟṟam) which are offensive to Hindu deities, who therefore punish the offenders. It is thus that only the vehicle (vākaṉam) of the deity, sufficiently pure and devoted to withstand the power and grace of the deity at all times, faces the inner shrine door.

Second, no house should be constructed so that the shadow of another family's house falls upon it. This is said to be an omen (cakuṉam) that the neighboring house will surpass the new household. It is sometimes said that all persons are ultimately in competition with one another, and that the prudent person does not dismiss the idea that neighbors, and even close kin, harbor a wish for his humiliation. A neighbor would not fail to note the shadow of his house falling across the newer structure; this situation is not merely ominous, it is dangerous. The neighbor might be encouraged by such an omen to give vent to his malicious envy (errical) by hiring a mantiravāti (sorcerer) to perform cuniyam (a word meaning, literally, "nothing, a waste or emptiness" in common usage, cuniyam brings to mind the secret rites by which a sorcerer calls down a spirit, or pēy, to possess and wither his victims).

Third, the house must face towards an auspicious direction. East is preferred; north is satisfactory. The directions of the compass are the provenance of emanations associated with certain cosmic forces of the compass, which are personified as deities, or with the planets (Table IV). The house is oriented to catch the positive emanations of the north and of the west, which is to say, the influences that encourage (for the planetary deities) right religion, education, right fatherhood, right motherhood, and right marriage. For the regents of the compass, the encouraging influences are wealth, water, light, and fire. Note that the excluded influences comprise not only the evil ones of infertility, decrease, and conflict, but also the influences that guarantee the fertility of the earth (influences that are irrelevant to home life).

Fourth, the house compound must be surrounded with an opaque fence of plaited cocoanut palm leaves. During construction, the fence facing the lane along which people may pass must be especially high; some construction screens are ten feet tall. These provide some protection against the tongue and eye misfortunes, nāvūru and kaṇṇūru, respectively. Envious comments from passers-by on the street are to be particularly dreaded since, as one informant stressed, "We don't know who is going to be walking by out there." People of low rank (keṭṭavarkaḷ) have a special capacity for nāvūru.

Few would omit these considerations in house construction. They are reinforced by no small dread of the consequences of omission as well as by fear of ridicule. Leaving aside the former for a moment, it should be noted that Hindus believe that friends, kin and neighbors alike stand ready to taunt the slightest neglect of custom, particularly those pertaining to the household. One building contractor told me, "Should a man neglect to erect a high fence along the lane in front of the house he is building, passers-by will not fail to call out loudly to the owner and make preposterous suggestions regarding revisions to the construction plans." Some would walk through a house compound, even at the cost of wasted steps, just to deride a man who neglects to build a stout fence.

The consequences of error or carelessness in house construction are thought to be grave. Informants agree that family life is certain to be characterized by squabbles, illness, misfortune, and infertility should the location of the house fail to receive careful treatment. The measures discussed up to this point are designed to protect the house, and its women in particular, from negative emanations originating outside the house compound. When the house is placed away from the temple axis, the "faults" produced by the women of the household will not offend the temple deity. When no omen or sign of weakness is presented to neighbors and passers-by, the chance is diminished that some person will attempt to destroy the household's women through sorcery. Finally, when the house is properly situated and oriented, the women who live in it are protected from the tōṣam (malefic influence) of the lunar modes, rāku and kētu, which cause infertility.

When a family experiences undue difficulty which is not eased by visits to temples, Ayurvedic physicians, or Western doctors, they may ascribe their trouble to house placement errors. In such cases, a shaman who undertakes trance (kalai) may be invited to visit the house. I encountered two houses (out of a research population of 252 households) which were diagnosed by shamans as dangerous. One of these families had just built a house when they experienced a nunber of illnesses and accidents; when the shaman came by, he went into kalai and the deity announced that they would have to tear it down and start over

TABLE IV

THE COSMIC FORCES OF THE FOUR DIRECTIONS

Direction	Cosmic Force	Mystical Impact
North	Viyālan (Jupiter)	Right religion
	Kuperan (Wealth)	Prosperity
Northeast	Putan (Mercury)	Education
	Īsana (Water)	Water
East	Velli (Venus)	Right marriage
	Indra (Sun)	Light
Center	Cūriyan (Sun)	Right fatherhood
Southeast	Cantiran (Moon)	Right motherhood
	Agni (Fire)	Fire (hearth)
South	Cevvāy (Mars)	Conflict
	Yama (Death)	Death
Southwest	Rāku (Serpent)	Infertility
	Niruti (Earth)	Agricultural productivity
West	Cani (Saturn)	Decrease; infertility
	Varuna (Rain)	Rain
Northwest	Kētu (Serpent)	Infertility
	Vayu (Wind)	Winds

SOURCE: Field interviews in Chavakachcheri, Sri Lanka.

again. They said that they intended to do so.

For most families, the preliminary cautions described to this point are sufficient to protect them from dangerous forces arising outside the compound. Further ritual is required to protect the family from dangers contained within the compound itself; these rituals are performed, at least traditionally, by the men of the Taccar (Carpenter) caste who undertake the construction of the house.

II.4. Laying the Foundation

The first step in the construction of a home is to dig the foundation down to a depth of six feet. "This is done to ensure that no human remains are under the house," the Taccar said. "During twenty years of house construction, I have never found any human remains, but the whole idea of building would probably be given up if we made such a discovery." Ghosts (āvi) which hover near the place where they lived as people are more dangerous than spirits (pēy). Pēy have forgotten their identities and the ways to their old homes, and so they are easily chased away and dispelled by the various tricks intended for this purpose. Spirits which remember the way home cannot be so dispelled.

The digging commences in the southwestern corner, for that is the abode of a demon (cūran), a cruel personage able to inflict people with tōṣam-s (troubles). By digging first in his corner, it is felt that the demon will be well pleased. A ritual follows, not with the intention of dispelling the demon of the southwestern corner, but rather of making him pure and holy; this is done by burying a conch shell in the southwestern corner of the foundation, containing very pure items. This ritual removes all of the "fault that the earth possesses.

When the digging is completed, the conch shell containing "new foundation items" (nāl attirapārapporuṭkaḷ) is placed in the southwestern corner of the foundation trench, These items consist of aimpon, the five metals (gold, silve iron, lead, copper); nāvarattinakkarkaḷ, the nine gems, eac of which is sacred to one of the planetary deities; aintuma the five kinds of earth; a lotus bulb; cow's milk; and a flower. These are stuffed into a conch shell, which is inserted into the foundation by an auspicious, well-marriec and lucky elder male of the family which is to inhabit the house. The nine grains (nāvataniyam), one for each of the planetary deities, are then scattered about.

II.5. Occupying the New Home

An auspicious day is selected for the rite called vīṭu kuṭi pukutal or "the family entering the house." According to the Carpenter, the Taccar caste alone has the right (urimai) to perform the ritual, although many families prefer to hire a Saiva Kurukkaḷ (non-Brahman priest). To circumvent this, the Taccar may instruct the workmen to leave some small, but difficult, job unfinished until he has secured assent to perform the rite.

The Taccar undertakes much of the ritual alone in the largest room of the new house. The first step is to set up a kumpam for Piḷḷaiyār in the southwest corner. A kumpam is a brass vessel containing water, milk, and a few coins; a cocoanut is set on top of the pot, so that several mango leaves are made to stand upright. The vessel, thus decorated, may serve as a temporary manifestation place for mystical beings. Kumpam-s are probably the most commonly used item in Jaffna ritual. Six other kumpam-s are set up for the deities selected to attend.

Having prepared the kumpam-s, the Taccar sets three stones on the floor to support a large earthenware pot. He builds a fire, and boils a mixture of water and milk. When the milk boils over, the direction towards which the milk spills is believed to indicate the future of the household. If it spills towards the east, all is well; other directions indicate problems to come. Should the pot break in the midst of the boiling, a calamity is indicated. The Taccar claimed that he takes steps to assure that the pot is level. Generally, he said, the prognosis is auspicious. He pours "raw rice" (paccai arici) into the boiling solution. When cooked, the rice is offered on plantain leaves to the deities which are assembled in their kumpam-s. This ritual is called poṅkal (boiling milk-rice) and is one of the most common elements of household and temple ritual in Jaffna.

Next, the Taccar hangs framed lithographs facing towards the east; among the deities generally included are Lakṣmī, Sarasvati, Piḷḷaiyār, and Murukaṉ. Śiva is never pictured in such a context, since it is believed that he has no interest in assisting a householder. The Taccar places auspicious objects, such as flowers, salt, turmeric powder, rice, jewels and cocoanuts before the cuvāmi paṭams (pictures of the deities). A large plantain leaf is laid out on the floor and spread with paddy. At this point, the Taccar calls for the family to enter the house. Among those attending are the "close kin" or bilateral kindreds (kiṭṭiya contakkārar) of the man and woman who are to become the chief occupants of the house.

During the construction, the Taccar will have omitted several tiles near the ridge beam, leaving therefore a large hole in the roof. An older male who has sons steps forward, takes up a mixture of rice, vermilion powder (kuṅkamum), and turmeric and throws it up and through the opening in the roof. While doing so, he shouts, "Mū Tēvi, go! Cī Tēvi, come!"

An auspicious, lucky couple is invited to step forward to stand on the paddy before the images of the gods. The Taccar gives them an offering of holy ash, vermilion powder, and sandalwood paste; these are applied to make a spot (poṭṭu) on the forehead signifying attendance at an auspicious ritual. The Taccar presents the house key in a cocoanut shell to the couple standing upon the rice; they accept it with cupped hands. The couple then gives the Taccar cantōṣam: presents which express satisfaction. These include a vēṭṭi (a man's white dresscloth), a shawl, and a small amount of cash. The auspicious couple then presents the key to the man who is to become the head of the household; he in turn hands it to his wife, saying, "The house is yours. You try the key."

Meanwhile, the Taccar slashes open an ash pumpkin (n̄irruppucaikkay) and smears it with vermilion powder. This rite is a substitute for blood sacrifice (vēḷvi), which has come under attack by Hindu reformers. Slashing open a pumpkin is generally called narapali, which means, quite unambiguously, human sacrifice. The vermilion powder stands for blood here, as it does in the ritual segment in which rice, turmeric and vermilion are thrown through the hole in the roof. The intention of these actions is to draw spirits away from the house; it is said that once lured away, the spirits will become confused and get lost. Such rituals, which involve a real or a metaphorical blood lure, are collectively called cānti (a rite which cools and pacifies).

The Taccar picks up the ash pumpkin, portions of the other offerings, and a young cocoanut. He departs with these items and goes to a four-way junction, where he dumps them on the ground. The spirits have been tricked: having followed, and consumed the offerings, they are unable to return to the new home. They might stay at the junction and afflict passersby, especially any foolish enough to touch the cānti offerings.

Having disposed of any spirits, the Taccar returns to the house; however, he cannot enter, for he has acquired a "fault" by performing the cānti. This state is remedied by a quick bath, after which he is given a new dresscloth and allowed to resume his tasks. The Taccar takes a post and an unsightly gourd to the southwestern corner of the compound. He drives the post into the ground and sets the gourd upon it; the gourd is thought to catch the eye of people walking along the lane, and thus conceals the beauty of the new house. The next step is to remove the high wall of plaited cocoanut leaves which has stood along the lane during construction. Next, the Carpenter climbs onto the roof to replace the tiles which were set aside to provide an exit for Mū Tēvi. He drapes a white cloth over the ridge beam, to frighten away owls, which are said to fear the color white. No owl should alight on the roof during the first days of occupancy, for such an event would constitute an omen (cakunam) of impending death. The Taccar descends, collects the rice and cocoanuts used as offerings for the kumpam-s, and departs.

When these steps have been carefully followed, a family feels relatively secure that the women of the household have been protected against forces inimical to their health, happiness, and fertility. However, no home is complete without a well, and sinking a well exposes a family to new dangers. The water of the prospective well is thought to have a life (uyir). It is a malevolent spirit which will be offended by the drilling; therefore, one additional rite must be performed.

II.6. Cutting a Well

The cāttiri (astrologer) must decide on the proper location of the new well, which is generally located on the north side of the house within the compound. Once the cāttiri has selected the spot, an auspicious day in the dry season is selected for the rite called kiṇāru veṭṭa toṭaṅkutal ("starting the well-cutting"). On the spot where the well is to be sunk, the owner of the house places a kumpam and a ball of cow dung; these represent the deity Piḷḷaiyār. The head of the household breaks a cocoanut, and the work begins.

The craftsmen do not belong to any specific caste, although it is said that many persons belonging to the fishing castes are taking up this occupation. The work begins with mammoties in the soft sand. Soon, stone is reached; in some parts of Jaffna, the crews must blast through the stone to reach the abundant ground water.

When the craftsmen reach water, they set down their tools and call for the home owner. As soon as possible, a rite called kiṇarruppoṅkal is performed. The "well poṅkal" is identical to the poṅkal performed in the new house by the Taccar, but it is performed by the owner of the house, at the bottom of the well. Narapali, the metaphorical sacrifice, is frequently omitted in favor of vēḷvi, the blood sacrifice, for the well-spirit is greatly feared. One informant told me, "Malevolent spirits demand lives when they are offended. A well-spirit has the means to take them if it is not placated. Failure to give a life [that is, perform vēḷvi] will insure that uncanny accidents will occur --someone will fall into the well and drown." If people are very careful and manage to avoid this fate, crows, dogs, or rats will fall in, causing the home owner to go to frequent expense to purify the well by having it pumped out.

Therefore, few omit the sacrifice at the sinking of a well. If the family has an aṭimai Untouchable servant, he performs the sacrifice of a chicken on the Veḷḷāḷar's behalf. The rite involves the decapitation and offering of the chicken, and giving the offerings to the Untouchable. Veḷḷāḷars say about such offerings, "What has been offered to the gods we will eat. But these offerings have been made to evil (tōṣam)." The offerings contain the substance of the demonic force which, having partaken of them, has left behind its saliva (eccil), so that when the Untouchables carry offerings away and eat them, they become riddled with evil themselves.

III. The Pre-Aryan Substratum

III.1. The Origins of the Concept of Disorder

The low status of the "left" Untouchables, presented in terms of impurity, is incomprehensible unless we pay close attention to the ritual forms in which that low status is organized and sustained. In the rites of home construction, it is quite clear that the opprobrium of the aṭimai Untouchable derives from his having imbibed the very source of disorder, so that it comes to afflict him on the deepest physiological level. In that state he becomes identical to the Vēṭarkaḷ, the ignorant fools of the jungle, the anti-social tribal folk who must be severly repressed. The disordered condition, incidentally, is shared among all Untouchables, but the stigma of exteriority or peripherality is not a little moderated in the case of the kuṭimai Untouchables, who combine their disordered condition with a positive, helpful set of ritual duties in the Veḷḷāḷar home.

It is possible to find a Gangetic antecedent for the hatred and scorn shown to the equated non-peasant peoples and aṭimai Untouchables. In the Śāstra-s, the most despised people of all were the tribal mleccas, those who were opposed to the Vedic social order. And yet, without denying the influence of this idea in South India, it is quite clear that the most direct antecendent of the disorder concept is to be found, not in the Gangetic tradition, but in the earliest stratum of Tamil literature.

That ancient Tamilnadu had a distinctive cultural tradition, one that probably arose with at least some degree of independence from the Gangetic or northern tradition, is a point few scholars recognized until very recently. The Dravidian tradition of the south has been persistently assumed to have been a primitive, aboriginal one that gave way before the advance of civilization. The Dravidian religion was supposed to be a "primitive animism" (Elmore 1915:8ff), or a belief in the worldly persistence of souls and ghosts. A bloody sacrificial religion of "fear and superstition" (Whitehead 1916:153), its traditions were maintained only in "confused [but 'limitless'] legends" which lack any "interesting systems of philosophy" (Elmore 1915:4).

The discovery of the ancient Tamil literary tradition, the poems of the so-called "Academy" (Caṅkam) era (circa first to third centuries A.D.), has done much to alter that impression. We are indeed fortunate that the texts survived at all. During the nineteenth century, while British Orientalists were proclaiming that the ancient Gangetic tradition was the *fons et origo* of all that was once great about India, the ancient Tamil texts remained unpublished and forgotten. They might have been lost forever had not V. V. Swaminathaier (1855-1942) devoted his life to finding them and preserving them, undergoing much hardship in the process (Hart 1975:viii).

The poems, thought by Hart to have been composed by illiterate, itenerant, low status bards called *pāṇaṉ* (circa first to third centuries A.D.), were later written down by learned poets of high status called *pulavaṉ* (circa eighth century A.D.). The two themes of the poems concern matters relevant to daily life: love and heroism (*akam* and *puṟam*). While the *pulavaṉ* poets were, according to most sources active fairly late (circa eighth to fourteenth centuries A.D.), tradition and other sources indicate that the poems themselves may date back to the second century A.D., and they are thought by some scholars to inform us about the social life, customs, and beliefs among Tamils prior to the full incorporation of the south into the Gangetic tradition.

What is evident from the texts is that they show a distinctively Tamil tradition, one that was only marginally influenced by the Gangetic tradition. Sanskrit words are "few and far between" (*Ibid.*, p. 11; cf. Nilakanta Sastri 1966:22). According to Hart, the *Caṅkam* texts, with their very minimal ties to the Gangetic tradition, reveal that the religion and world view of the ancient Tamils was a tradition almost diametrically opposed to that of the Aryan, Sanskritic North.

III.2. Religious Concepts in the Caṅkam Texts

The Aryan tradition, it is generally agreed, is oriented to a notion of the divine as a numinous, transcendent realm, one that is "wholly Other" (cf. Otto 1958:

25ff; Kingsley 1977:3). The gods dwell in a divine realm and there possess everlasting life (<u>śrī</u>). The problems for Hindu theology, then, are (1) to explain why most people are here on earth afflicted by death and suffering, and (2) to devise a means for contacting the gods and obtaining their blessings. O'Flaherty (1976) has dealt with the problems of theodicy in the Gangetic tradition, and many scholars have commented on the communication channel created by the Vedic sacrifice, which was (according to Renou) a portable affair: "sacrifice took place on a specially prepared piece of ground, but the same spot was not necessarily used again for subsequent ceremonies" (1953:33-34). The site of the sacrifice was the <u>axis mundi</u>, but the <u>axis mundi</u> was, nonetheless, wherever the sacrifice was.

Now the ancient Tamil religion and world view did <u>not</u> assert an order of mystical reality that was "wholly Other." On the contrary, according to Hart (1975), the ancient Tamils believed that the essential nature of the sacred was its immanence, or full saturation throughout the persons, places and objects of this life. The sacred showed itself in anything that could be associated with disorder, for the power of the sacred was capricious, showing itself in the "increase of entropy" and especially in disease and death. This is certainly a rather negative notion of the sacred, but the ancient Tamils drew from it a positive implication: If the capricious loci of sacred power were only surrounded with some other force that could control it, then the deadly, life-negating power could be neutralized and even put to good use. Sacred power thus has two states: a primordial state in which it is capricious and antithetical to social order, and an ordered state in which it has been controlled and has thereby become advantageous. The transformation was effected by surrounding the locus of sacred power with order, its antithesis. Sacred power was ordered by ritual, and particularly by music (that is, ordered sound). Yet those who performed the ordering did not win a high rank, but rather a low and despised one, for their efforts. The low castes of ancient Tamilnadu were indeed involved closely with music: they were lutenists (Pāṉaṉs), drummers (Tuṭiyaṉs and Paṟaiyars), and dancers (Vēlaṉs). They were said to be of distinct "descent groups" (kuṭi), and were deemed to be "low-born" (ilicinaṉ). They were thought to be saturated with the very disorder that they controlled. The low ones played music for the great ones (cāṉṟōṉ), whose homes were in consequence made wholesome and auspicious. But the low ones themselves became afflicted with disorder, so much so that they could not grow rice themselves. Furthermore, they were not associated with rice lands but rather with the desolate wilderness, where sacred power in its primordial state abounds. The low ones were indeed thought to be saturated with disordered power, and so they were thought dangerous to the extreme.

Many were the loci of sacred power, especially in the wilderness. With its diseased vegetation, its enraged beasts, its impoverished tribes, and other dangers, the wilderness no doubt epitomized the peril posed by primordial, disordered power. The wilderness was the abode of most deities, who afflicted and terrified people, and who demanded bloody sacrifices, ecstatic dances, and absolute obedience. The offerings set out for the gods of the wilderness were evidently very dangerous after the gods had partaken of them; if they were eaten by someone afterwards, that person would become feverish and shake like one possessed.

Power was not, however, found exclusively in the wilderness. Among Tamils ancient and modern, women were and are deemed to be both charged with sacred power and especially vulnerable to it (Hart 1973). They had to be surrounded with order to control their own power and also to be protected from afflicting sources of it outside the home. Chastity (kaṟpu) was thought essential to maintaining a woman's power in its ordered state. A woman had to remain chaste until she married, and when she married, she had to accept the man her parents chose for her. So long as she remained chaste, that is to say, surrounded with carefully controlled and ordered social relations, her power did for her husband and family just what the temple does: it imbued them with the power of vitality. A woman's chastity was deemed essential to her own fertility as well as to that of her husband's fields. But if she became unchaste, either through premarital sex or adultery, she brought disease, destruction, and poverty to her family (Hart 1974:39).

The ancient Tamil beliefs about the nature of sacred power would seem to be epitomized in the notions about the status of the king. Like that of a woman, the power of the king was ambivalent and vulnerable. If it was ordered, his kingdom flourished; the rains fell copiously, and everywhere there was life and an increase of life. If it was disordered, his kingdom would "suffer drought or be taken by enemies" (Hart 1975:87). Yet the power of the king, unlike that of a woman, was not dependent on his remaining chaste and secluded. On the contrary, his power was contained by his chaste wife, his drum, and his tree, and presumably radiated out to him from these sources. The drum (*muracu*) was certainly more than a musical instrument; like the Golden Stool of the Ashanti, to possess it was to possess the kingship. The tree (*kāvalmaram* or *kaṭimaram*, "guarded tree") was thought to constitute an *axis mundi*, so that if it were cut down by the king's foes, the king's power would be destroyed. To vanquish the king, it was necessary to take his drum and cut down his tree.

So long as the king's "power base"--his wife, his drum, and his tree--remained ordered, he was himself immune to any disorder consequent on impurity or propinquity to death, Thus could the king express his affection for the Untouchable bards (*pāṇaṉ*) who praised him. One bard, lamenting the death of the king Atiyamāṉ, recalls, "With his hand fragrant with orange blossoms he would stroke my head, which stank of flesh.. . . Where is my lord who loved me?" (cited in Hart 1975:125). The gore and mortality of the battlefield likewise posed no threat to the king's power; indeed, the battlefield was a source of additional power. In the aftermath of a victory, the king would cook the corpses of the vanquished for a grisly sacrifice, which led to much rejoicing among bloodthirsty demons. From the sacrifice issued even more power. "Thus the poems describe over and over the metamorphosis of the gruesome objects of battle into beautiful or productive things associated with peace, especially things connected with agriculture" (*Ibid.*, p. 32). The king's protected base of power rendered him immune to pollution or affliction, just as the low one's disorder rendered him open and vulnerable to all attacking forces, especially the intrusive possession-trances of the gods.

III.3. The Persistence of Ancient Tamil Notions

The objection may be raised that the *Caṅkam* poems, being a courtly, literary tradition, cannot be used to win any understanding of actual daily life and beliefs in ancient Tamil culture. Without doubt the method is very perilous, yet the validity of Hart's interpretation seems to be amply demonstrated by the persistence of precisely the notions he elucidates in contemporary Tamil social life.

Let us first consider the themes of divine immanence and localization. The post-classical temple tradition, issuing as it does from the classical tradition, posits the transcendence of the gods and also the idea that the shrine can be built anywhere so long as the soil has been properly prepared and other precautions have been taken. A ritual of consecration causes the divine presence to take root in the shrine's "womb." But in Tamil mythology, it is clear that the consecration of a spot by building a temple on it "merely reflects a preexisting relationship between the god and the site. A divine power is felt to be present naturally on the spot" (Shulman 1980:48). For Tamils, the significance of the temple is not that it creates a divine space where none existed before (as the texts would have it), but rather that it imposes order on a capricious theophany:

> At the center of the temple lies a focus of violent power . . . [but] this power is circumscribed by the temple walls and located within a ritually ordered universe. The inner sanctum --the garbhagrha, the "womb" where the deity is conceived anew--is not alone as a symbol of bounded power in the shrine; the tree with its roots sunk in the nether world, and the temple tank, which draws its water from the realm of primordial chaos, are part of the same pattern of chaos subdued by order. The strict limits applied to the sacred force detach the shrine from the surrounding, less ordered sphere, which is saturated with impurity and evil--in contrast with the pure, harmonious realm within the temple walls.. . . the sacred power is controlled, and in this way made auspicious and accessible to the pilgrim.. . . the shrine is power preserved intact and made useful through limitation (Ibid., p. 26).

This Tamil interpretation of divine immanence and localization shows the persistence not only of these ancient themes, but also of the notions of disorder and order. The temple's power is auspicious because it is ordered; yet the myths also show that the site's autochthonous power was fearful, disordered, and capricious. The autochthonous god is violent; if displeased, he kills anyone who does not bow down to him, but then if asked, he brings them back to life. The god shows no concern whatever for the needs of an orderly society: he bestows kingdoms on Untouchables, acquittals on murderers, salvation on the undeserving (Pfaffenberger 1979:265ff). He might for the most unaccountable reasons bestow blessings, but equally mysteriously, he may suddenly withdraw them. It is felt that society could not exist if the autochthonous sites of divine immanence were left disordered; civilization begins when the temples are built to control the sites. The only sites left in their autochthonous condition are situated away from social order, deep in the wilderness, and they have small, open structures rather than ordering temple buildings.

Ancient Tamil notions of low status would also appear to be widespread among contemporary Tamils. Untouchability is, to be sure, conceptualized in terms of impurity, but it has already been noted that for the aṭimai Untouchables, impurity alone does not appear to fully explain their low status. In a very real sense this is true of all Untouchables. If pollution in the strict classical sense--the stigma arising from the contact with organic waste and with death--really determines Untouchability, then Washermen, who wash menstrual cloths, the paragon of impurity, must certainly be Untouchable. But in Jaffna, they are not. Yet Paṟaiyars are, and as if this were not mysterious, Dumont (1981:54) simply notes that their "drums skins [are] . . . of course impure." Without denying that Untouchables are deemed impure and held low on grounds of impurity, it is also true that they acquire an even deeper stigma--that of disorder (tōṣam)--through their ritual roles.

The ritual roles of Jaffna castes are summarized in Appendix II. Note that Carpenters and Washermen acquire impurity as a consequence of their roles, and that disorder as well is a consequence of Untouchable ritual roles. Untouchables serve as priests in controlling disorderly loci of evil powers, and also consume the afflicted food that has been offered to those powers. The latter act appears to be constitutive of Untouchability throughout South India. In Tanjore, the entrails of the sacrificial victim are hung around the Sudra priest's neck, and after the procession the entrails are mixed with curry and rice, offered to evil spirits, and then "eaten by . . . low-caste people" (Whitehead 1916:114). Untouchables perform the sacrifices at such rites throughout South India, and if the offering is made to a particularly low and vicious deity or spirit, it is they who consume the offerings. To be sure, not all sacrificial offerings are consumed exclusively by Untouchables; at many rites the sacrificial animals are eaten by Vellālars and even by the village headman (e.g., Whitehead 1916:102f). Whether or not the act of consuming the sacrificial offerings is stigmatizing depends, as the Jaffna evidence shows, on the status of the being to which it has been offered. If the god is ordered, the offerings (even if they are of flesh) may be consumed without lowering one's status. If the god or spirit is disorered, however, the offerings take on the substance of that disorder, and to consume them is to become disordered. If the disorder is not divine (that is, bhakti) but evil (deadly and intractable), the disordered person is also evil.

The contemporary expression of this old Tamil idea shows how effectively the Tamil and classical traditions have been syncretized. In the northern, classical tradition, to take food from the higher castes is an act constitutive of low status. It is tantamount to eating someone's leftovers, which have been polluted by saliva (eccil). To eat someone's leftovers is to say, in effect, "I am so low that, relative to you, your spittle is pure enough for me to eat" (Babb 1975:53ff). Throughout India, the low castes take food from the higher ones, and this act symbolizes (and indeed creates or reaffirms) the low castes' polluted status. But it would be very wrong to reduce the Tamil ritual transactions to the pollution idea of food transactions. It is true to a certain extent that Untouchables "take food" from Vellālars after they perform some ritual service on the Vellālars' behalf. But they derive from this act not only pollution; when they imbibe what has been offered to evil, they imbibe its disordering substance and its disordering power.

Contemporary Tamil culture also shows the persistence of ancient Tamil beliefs about the power of women (Wadley 1980). Notions about a woman's ambivalent sacred power, which can bring either prosperity or destruction, comprise an important theme of contemporary Tamil religion, folklore, and literature. Like an unmarried virgin, the goddess Mariyammaṉ is thought to possess two facets: she can bring drought, infertility, and disease, but if she is ritually ordered she brings rain, fertility, and health (Beck 1969: 561). In folklore, women are placed at the center of life; a female is taken as the first principle in Tamil creation tales, and it is believed that women's power underlies everything. A chaste woman whose power is "controlled and well managed" brings her husband "good luck" and "blessings"; on the contrary, a woman who is righteously angered can cause "impoverishment and even death" (Beck 1974:7ff). An unchaste woman also causes death. In the contemporary Malayali novel Chemeen, for instance, a fisherman named Palani dies in a storm at sea as his wife, the cause of his misfortune, embraces her lover back on the shore (Hart 1975: 101f).

I shall mention only briefly beliefs that show the persistence of ancient Tamil beliefs about the king, the great lord whose "power base" was his ordered wife, drum, and tree. The kings of Jaffna made much of the chastity of their wives, and indeed it was felt that a man could not rule unless he was properly married to a chaste queen (Pieris 1914:II, 122). Among the Sinhalese, beliefs surprisingly reminiscent of the Tamil notions about the drum and tree came to focus on the Sacred Tooth Relic (Daḷadā). Ownership of the Tooth was, by the twelfth century A.D., "an indispensable possession of the country's legitimate ruler" (Seneviratne 1978:17). Warfare and rebellion in medieval Ceylon seemed to focus on capturing the king's wives and the Tooth, his power base (Raghavan n.d.:33).

The relevance of these beliefs did not expire on the termination of kingship. The role of the Tamil king was emulated by all who wished the epithet "the great one" (*cāṉṟōṉ*), the one who possesses an ordered power base. The great one, like the king, was immune to pollution and to the intrusive possession of evil spirits. This is precisely the belief that underlies the Veḷḷāḷar status in Jaffna today. Veḷḷāḷars are not thought to be easily polluted; pollutions that are very degrading to Untouchables are of little consequence to Veḷḷāḷars. Thus all sources would seem to agree that Paṟaiyars are polluted by their drum skins, while no one would say a Veḷḷāḷar is polluted by putting on a belt or by wearing shoes. Furthermore, it is thought extraordinary for a Veḷḷāḷar to be successfully attacked by an evil spirit. Untouchables, however, lack this ordered power base and the immunities, largely because Veḷḷāḷars do not permit Untoucable women the appearance of chastity. Lacking chastity, Untouchables--both men and women--are like the defeated king of the *Caṅkam* poems, whose tree was cut down and whose drum was stolen. It is a potent metaphor of defeat.

Chapter 5

THE RITUAL DESIGN OF SUDRA DOMINATION

> Siva is the god of the Brahmans, Madhava of the Ksatriyas, Brahman of the Vaisyas, and the village gods [grāmadēvatās] of the Sudras.
>
> --*Āgamasmrtisāra*, cited in Oppert (1978:450).

I. The Achievement of Order

The Tamil tradition posits an autochthonous landscape dotted with loci of disordered power, both demonic and divine. In Jaffna, tales about the origins of settlement (see Casie Chetty 1847-1848; Anonymous 1827) invariably stress that the peninsula was once a desolate wilderness. There was a disordered theophany, that of Murukan̲, at Keerimalai, and everywhere groves of trees were infested with vicious, intractable demons. The Tamil chronicles of Jaffna hold that civilization began in the peninsula only after a Brahman-staffed, ordering temple was built near the site of the theophany, at Maviddapuram; royal insignia were bestowed on the king by Viṣṇu's avatars; and women of great chastity were sent from India.

These ordering acts are, Jaffna Hindus believe, constitutive of civilization's great achievement, at least in its inception. They show a resolute dedication of great leaders to the creation of order, both in its religious and its social sense. Order is achieved only when a great Sudra chieftain, through the aegis of the king's protective rule, the Brahman's temple, and the chastity of his wife, commits himself to lend his personal virtue to the landscape. But this task could not be completed if the autochthonous, demonic disorder of the landscape were left untouched. Civilization is achieved only when the staid and formal ākama rites are wedded to an architectonic ritual process involving ecstatic trances and violent sacrifices. From the Tamil viewpoint, there is no distinction at all between what some would see as, on the one hand, Brahmanical, Sanskritic, or "transcendental" rituals, and on the other hand, low-caste, non-Sanskritic, or "pragmatic" rituals (cf. Mandelbaum 1966; Pfaffenberger 1980). They are all part of a single ritual design, whose purpose is to create the very foundation of social order and dignified life.

The achievement of order requires, then, a wide variety of ritual forms, all of which are singular in their aim: just as the ākama temple focuses on the temple patron and his lineage (cantati) a salubrious energy (aruḷ), so too do the other rituals focus on Veḷḷāḷar families an ambience of vitality and increase (palaṉ), thereby justifying their claim to monopolize the instruments of reproduction. These rituals, the rituals of Sudra domination, begin with the winning of the Veḷḷāḷar home out of the wilderness. They require a violent confrontation with the demon of the well, which can be appeased only by offering it a life (that of a chicken or a goat). The sacrifice is performed on the Veḷḷāḷar's behalf by his Untouchable servant, who removes the afflicted offerings and eats them. Thus the Untouchable loses any claim he might have made to the land, and the Veḷḷāḷar gains a power base. The home has been constructed to suit the special needs of his wife; it is like a temple, built to protect her and to order her power (cakti).

To sustain the power base of the home, it is essential to confront the disorder in the locality and in the fields. The disorder of the locality is feminine: the goddess (Ammaṉ) of the village must be ordered or she will inflict drought and disease upon it. The disorder of the fields is predominantly, though not exclusively, masculine. Like the demons of the well, many of the disordered personalities of the field cannot be ordered unless placated with violent, bloody sacrifices, out of which issues the bounty of the harvest. To complete the ordering of the home, the village, and the fields, the Veḷḷāḷar lord commits a portion of his wealth to a Brahman-staffed temple, which seals and completes the power base of the patron.

The rituals of Sudra domination thus invest Veḷḷāḷars with feminine power, the coveted benefit of "increase," and the salubrious grace of the gods. They entitle Veḷḷāḷars to possess the means of reproduction, but the rituals are not perceived to be selfish in their intent. On the contrary, they install Veḷḷāḷars in an office that is felt to be essential to the prosperity of all. The fertility of the earth is deemed a very precarious matter, and the Veḷḷāḷar achievement is a noble one. It is perceived and validated in the flourishing green carpet of young rice shoots, in the even welling forth of gentle rains, in the abundance of the harvest, and in the generosity of the Veḷḷāḷar's gracious gifts. And it is a publicly known achievement, for it is the noble Veḷḷāḷar, the grower and giver of rice, who appears before the shrine with his copious gift of milk-rice and who, after the rites are completed, receives the first fruits (and the benefits) of the now-consecrated substance. In awe of him, those who cannot give are shamed by their poverty. Thus Navaḻi has it: "correctly stated, there are on the earth only two castes: those who give in consonance with an unerring moral code are noble; those who give not, are low" (cited in Somasundaram Pillai 1959:263).

The village rituals of Sudra domination, which will be explored in this chapter, illustrate vividly the geographical and familial limitations of the Sudra entitlement. The aim of Sudra domination is to establish civilization by confronting and transforming the autochthonous powers of a locality, and to enter into a deeply somatic relationship with them. Just as the temple owner is physically tied to the temple (so that if the temple is defiled he is subject to a profound threat), so too do the autochthonous powers of the landscape come to possess a profound tie to the Veḷḷāḷar and his kinsmen. These powers are local in provenance and in influence, and their ties with men are limited in genealogical spread. One generally finds, at the local deities' annual festival, seven to nine men who are members of a kindred (contakkārar, "relations"), and who bear a mystical tie (toṭarpu, "connection")--often made manifest by possession (kalai)--with the deity. It is to them and their close kin that the benefits of the deity, always localized in scope, accrue.

II. The Ritual Regulation of Feminine Power

II.1. Banishing the Evil Woman (Mū Tēvi)

In his daring, heroic confrontation with the disordered beings that afflict the natural landscape, the Veḷḷāḷar, active in and committed to this life, rejects and banishes Mū Tēvi, the Evil Woman (chapter four, I.2). The construction of a properly built home and the resolute seclusion of his wives and daughters is decisive in denying Mū Tēvi that which she seeks: the filth and disorder issuing from a life lived freely, without restraint (cummā). Mū Tēvi must be banished; there is no prospect of gain issuing from merely propitiating her. She must be driven to the wilderness and scorned, like Mūḷi, who was turned into a stone for travelers to deride.

The banishing of disordered beings to the wilderness is a theme that suffuses Tamil myth and ritual. The wilderness is thought to be the repository of countless male and female spirits (pēy), often resident in the substance of wilderness trees, and existing in exile from the ordered, moral boundaries of civilization. The following tale exemplifies the process by which female spirits arise.

In the *Vanni* jungles to the south of Jaffna, it was the custom, during the nineteenth century, for a man traveling along the road to deposit a stick under a *nāval* tree, while a woman traveling along the road would pick up one of the sticks and throw it away. To explain this custom, a Hindu said that

> Once upon a time a woman ran away from her husband, and while on her journey sank exhausted on this road. A man pitying her condition lifted her on his shoulder and carried her along. A second traveler, in his surprise and contempt at seeing a woman in such a position, put out his tongue at her, which action the woman interpreted as an offer to carry her on his tongue, and she at once proceeded to accept it. The first traveler, annoyed at her ingratitude, left her and departed, the second also decamped, and the woman perished miserably. The heaping up of sticks upon the spot where she died marks the males' disapproval of the conduct of the faithless wife. The women's surreptitious removal . . . shows womanly sympathy with an erring sister (Lewis 1920:176).

Lacking a proper funeral, the life of an unchaste and scorned woman persists in this world as a tortured spirit (*pēy*), driven by its hatred for the young women who have what the spirit has lost. The spirit wants to smash the happiness of young, chaste girls, and on that account is judged wholly malevolent, and useless to humanity. Since she lacks chastity (*karpu*) she lacks power (*cakti*) as well. She can never be reconciled with men, and the achievement of civilization is deemed dependent on the ability of men to keep her out of the village.

It is believed that no village can prosper unless every woman in it is chaste. If, for example, the rains should fail, it will be said that Mū Tēvi has managed to arrogate herself into the village, and she must be expelled.

> Under the cover of darkness, the villagers place a woman's effigy upon a crudely constructed cart, and a few men dressed as women, will follow the cart, crying aloud and beating their breasts. In this way they will pass through the village, carrying torches and reciting the following

couplet: 'Won't the evil woman [kotumpāvi] die? Won't we have fresh rain?' (Cartman 1957:174).

The effigy and cart are taken to the cremation ground and burned, and it is expected that the rains will soon begin.

II.2. Appeasing the Chaste Suicides

Mū Tēvi must be banished, but there are other feminine spirits, those of girls (unlike Mū Tēvi's female pēy) who died with the full power of their chastity (karpu) intact. The life of a deceased, chaste girl does not become a vexed, disordered spirit; the power of chastity is such that her spirit will possess consciousness and with it, the ability to do good. Nonetheless, the spirit of a chaste woman is angry at men, believing that they let her down; and she will do no good until these men bow down before her. It is said in South India that one day a Paraiyar came to a Brahman village and, having disguised himself, managed to get himself married to the daughter of a blind accountant, a Brahman by caste. But the faithful bride began to suspect her husband's low caste origins, and when one day her suspicions were confirmed, she burned herself alive. She reappeared in the midst of the village as a goddess, informed the villagers that they had "done her great wrong by marrying her to a Pariah, and that she would ruin them all." The villagers managed to appease her by promising to behead her Paraiyar husband, and bring him before her as a sacrificial offering. The husband was reborn as a buffalo, it is said, and since that time her offerings have been beheaded buffalo (Whitehead 1916:119-21).

In Jaffna, the tale is told of the fifty-nine Kaṇṇimār or Naccimār, the chaste wives of the Vaṉṉiyār chieftains (Anonymous 1827:51ff). The Vaṉṉiyār, it is said, were great warriors who served the King of Madurai. That king heard tales of the jungles of northern Lanka, noting with horror that these jungles, called the Vaṉṉi, were ruled by giant demons. As did the Nāyakkar Kings of the period generally (Hudson 1978:111ff), the Lord of Madurai wished to bring justice not only to the fertile rice-lands, but also to the jungles and dry lands, and towards this end he dispatched the courageous Vaṉṉiyār to Lanka. They did battle with the evil demons, but they were defeated and all but six died in battle. Of the six remaining, five elected to return to their wives in Madurai, but their boat sank in a horrible storm and they drowned. Never hearing a word of any of these events, the Vaṉṉiyārs' wives in Madurai pined for them:

> A certain person one day, mounted on his horse, passed through the [Madurai] street they lived in, which they seeing, grieved at it, and determined to quit the place and to go to Ceylon, for which purposes they sent for the navigator . . . who accordingly conveyed them in ships to Ceylon.. . . at Jaffnapatnam . . . the Wannia [Vaṉṉiyār] women [were] informed . . . of the death of all their chiefs, except one.. . . As soon as the Wannia women heard this, they being grieved and sorrowful for the loss of their husbands, proceeded to Sellechy, and throwing themselves upon the fire made for the purpose, perished there, except the . . . [one]. the wives of the Wannias who burnt themselves . . . became [the deities] cannimar and natchimar (Anonymous 1827:55-56, 66-67, 79).

In a multiform of this myth, it is said that the King of Madurai once went to war with the King of Lanka, and finally sent word back to his palace in Madurai that his sixty wives should come join him. They set off for Lanka in the company of the king's most trusted regiment of warriors, the sixty Nampis. In one version, the boat is attacked by the king's enemies, and the queens, fearing rape, drowned themselves. The Nampis, knowing their failure, followed suit. The suicides became the Kaṉṉimār and Naccimār. In another version, the queens killed themselves, not because the boat was attacked, but because they began to suspect the Nampis of having kidnapped them under false pretences. The Nampis escaped to Lanka, intermarried with Cāṇṭārs to disguise themselves, and became Naḷavars.

The Kaṉṉimār and Naccimār, angry at the men who let them down, want those men to bow down before them, and to give them a life (uyir) to sustain their spirit existence. Blood sacrifice is judged to be obligatory at most of their shrines, the deities preferring a goat or a chicken. Failing that, they will rain down punishing depradations--illnesses, crop failures, drought, and spirit illnesses--on the people living near the tree in which they dwell. They bring few benefits besides the cessation of punishment.

The angry goddesses make their desires known to men by inflicting an illness on them or on a member of their family, and then seizing a body (kalai, "incarnation") that they might speak through the person's mouth. The deity warns that, unless the demanded offerings are given, she will punish not only the man and his immediate, nuclear family, but all of his "close-kin" (kiṭṭiya contakkārar, a bilateral group). It is thus the obligation of this entire group to participate in her propitiation, which they must undertake to save themselves from doom.

It is this bilateral kindred, and not the agnatic cantati that comprises the propitiation group for all temple purposes, except ākama temple worship. In the patrilineally oriented, formal kinship theory of classical Hinduism, the cantati is an essentially agnatic group; membership is owing to birth, but girls lose their membership when they marry, Thus the cantati consists of a group of agnates, their wives, and their unmarried daughters. Like the classical sapinda, the cantati is said to consist of people sharing one body (orē oṭampu), and it is seven generations in depth. The latter point requires some qualification. Jaffna Tamils are rarely able to trace their ancestry back beyond two or three generations; a man knows the names of his father, his father's father, and his father's father's father, which indeed he must recite at the annual obsequies for the ancestral shades. Beyond this the name of the ascendant paternal ancestors are generally unknown. Nonethless the *cantati* is figured by counting three generations up, ego's own generation, and three generations down (for a man has, at least potentially, a son, a son's son, and a son's son's son). When reckoning membership in the non-*ākama* pollution group, however, Jaffna Tamils state that the "close-kin" constitute "one body." When an angry goddess or demon afflicts a man, it is not just his *cantati*, but his whole bilateral kindred that shares the obligation (and, it should be added, the benefit as well).

II.3. The Dark, Autochthonous Virgin

Quite often an angry, afflicting goddess is identified with the textual deity Kāḷi, although Jaffna Hindus are explicit in stating that the name "Kāḷi" is nothing more than a category (*inam*) to be applied to millions of autochthonous spirits of unknown (and probably unknowable) origin. In point of fact the nomenclature of feminine power in Jaffna is extremely confused. Many Jaffna Hindus insist, for instance, that Kāḷi is properly known as Kāḷiyammaṉ, suffixing to her name the categorical term for "village goddess" (*kirāma teyvaṅkaḷ*, e.g., Ammaṉ). Yet, when asked whether Kāḷi is indeed one of the Ammaṉ goddesses, the Tamil Hindu answer is invariably negative. Compounding the confusion is the fact that, here and there in Jaffna, a wealthy man has built up his Kāḷi shrine into a very dignified structure indeed, and in these cases the style of worship is indistinguishable from that of the Ammaṉ goddesses. The case of Kāḷi raises an important point in the analysis of the Hindu "pantheon" in Jaffna: there really is no such thing. The identity of a god or goddess is substantially less important than the specific ritual transformation to which he or she has been subjected. The presence of an autochthonous power at a site entails no more, initially, than a range of potential ritual strategies which men may utilize in the service of civilization. To say of a power, "That is Naccimār" is to say, in effect, "Here is a power which men must appease, but we may expect from it little practical gain." To say of a power, "That is Kāḷi," usually suggests an angry goddess, dark in color and sullen in temperament, who demands appeasement, bloody sacrifices, and ecstatic rites, in exchange for which she will provide the men who house her with certain benefits--especially agrarian fertility. It would take a prodigious investment indeed to so mollify Kāḷi that she behaved as meekly, modestly, and motherly as the Ammaṉ goddess, but--so goes Jaffna thinking--it can be done.

There is not a single deity in the roster of divine identities in Jaffna that lacks, at least in popular thinking, some textual source. Often the link of village god and textual mythology is rather vague: for instance, the lowly and bloodthirsty Aiyaṉār, whom we shall encounter later in this chapter, is often said to be a manifestation of Śiva's anger. Kāḷi's mythology, however, has been interpreted in Jaffna to sum up very precisely the etiology of her sullen personality. It is said that there once was a demon (cūran) who was troubling the gods. They wanted some relief, and so they came begging to Śiva. Śiva said, "What can I do? I have given this demon life with the promise that no male would destroy him." Umā Tēvi (Śiva's consort) said, "I will destroy him." Śiva said, "No, that is impossible. If you shed one drop of his blood, one thousand demons will spring up from it." So Umā Tēvi fasted for ten days to get power to create some being to defeat the demon. On the seventh day of the fast, the demon came to know about her plans, and tried to interfere with the meditation. He took hold of her shoulder, and tried to disturb her. So Umā Tēvi got furious and out of her anger was born Kāḷi. Kāḷi was born a dark-colored, angry-faced virgin of very great power. Kāḷi said, "What shall I do?" Umā Tēvi replied, "I'll kill this demon, and you drink up all the blood so that none of it falls on the ground." On the ninth day Umā Tēvi and Kāḷi went to battle, and after Umā Tēvi killed the demon, Kāḷi drank up all the blood. But then Kāḷi became drunk with the blood and started to destroy the universe. The gods went begging to Śiva again and said, "Help us. Kāḷi is destroying the universe." Śiva replied, "I'll subdue her," but it wasn't so easy. Finally Śiva decided he would have to kill her, and lifted up his leg to kill her by crushing. But Kāḷi herself lifted up her leg, and in so doing showed her vagina. Śiva said, "Chi! Kāḷi, go away!" This hurt Kāḷi much worse than any blow could have, and ever since that time she has hated pretty girls. Kāḷi, like the Naccimār and Annamār, now resides in the life of a tree, waiting for a pretty girl to pass unawares. The angry goddess, unable to restrain her envy, strikes her down with a vexing illness, manifest in aches, pains, and fever and unresponsive to medical treatment. A girl, especially when dressed up nicely, will take a circuitous route rather than risk a confrontation with Kāḷi.

The presence of the dark and brooding Kāḷi in an area is thought to be revealed when someone falls down possessed, and the goddess speaks through his or her mouth, demanding of men that she be given offerings and shelter. Often the possession (kalai) occurs after a man has been walking in a jungle or a desolate area. Once established, the bond is scrutinized by the goddess and she demands proper treatment if she fells she is being treated unfairly. One villager kept his Kāḷi in a small mud shrine, but in 1945 the man married, and he had to complete a house for his family. So he made plans to complete it, and bought a load of concrete. That night his mother was struck down by possession (kalai) and the goddess spoke, saying, "It is wrong of you to build a house when I am still living in an open mud shrine, exposed to the elements." The possession was very violent --the man's mother was rolling around on the floor and shouting. He said, "All right, I'll start on your temple the next day, just let my mother go." She was satisfied at that, and the next day the concrete was transferred over to the temple compound. Since then Kāḷi has been very helpful to him and to his close kin.

So long as Kāḷi is housed properly and given what she demands, the fertility of the earth is assured, because Kāḷi with her immense power is able to control a retinue of spirits (pariyalaṅkaḷ). These innumerable spirits envy and detest the green, growing shoots in the fields, and with to destroy them; but Kāḷi can restrain them, and her own power is felt to radiate fertility to the fields. When she is pleased, it is thought that she guards the fields, and seeks to enhance the harvest. The Kāḷi of the Kāḷi Kōyil in the village Kaccāy, for instance, is said to be very partial to the shareholders of the temple (five closely related families). At harvest time, the people who own fields adjacent to the shareholders' wait until they have harvested, for it has been found that should the neighbors harvest first, Kāḷi will blow a great part of the grain into the shareholders' fields. This has happened, it is said, several times in the past few years.

Just as the ākama temple patron wins out of his generosity a salubrious and auspicious ambience (aruḷ) of increase (palaṉ), so too do the keepers of Kāḷi--to the extent that they house her well--derive the benefit of agricultural increase. Moreover, as will be seen in section II.6, the benefit, like that of the ākama shrine, is vested in the hands of the temple shareholders by means of a public ritual (vaḷarntuppoṅkal or "large pot of milk-rice"). Underlying both the "Sanskritic" rites of the Brahman's temple and the "non-Sanskritic" rites of the Kāḷi shrine there is, then, a single principle of relationship between men and the gods: the patrons of the ritual are linked to the deity by what must be seen (as Hindus see them) as essentially corporeal bonds. In the ākama shrine. the link is established in temple contruction as the yajamāna's measurements are incorporated into the temple; the temple comes to stand as his "twice-born" body, and all members of his lineage (cantati) share the benefits. In the Kāḷi temple, the pūcāri bears the incarnation (kalai) of the deity, as indeed may any member of the pūcāri's bilateral kindred (contakkārar) who collectively experience the benefits.

To be sure, there are important differences between the worship of Kāḷi and of ākama deities. The benefit of the ākama deities accrues to a small, sharply defined kinship group, whose patrilineality contradicts the essentially bilateral nature of kinship in the Jaffna system. Kāḷi's benefits, by contrast, attach to a much wider and far more vaguely defined kinship group, which can (and does) include persons whose actual genealogical relationship is unknown. Ākama worship tends, in short, to be divisive, in that it establishes the high status of specific lineages, and juxtaposes them to lineages bereft of temple patrons. Kāḷi worship, however--and this is true of all the non-Brahmanical forms of goddess and demon worship--is integrative, tending to unite groups of cooperative and intermarrying kinsmen.

The aim of the ākama rite, furthermore, is to enclose within a bounded, purified, and above all else, ordered space the devastating and amoral power of the autochthonous god. The emphasis all along is, in a word, dignity. The god who would grant heaven to Untouchables is treated like a king; he is given, for instance, the sixteen reverences due to a king (upacarital) and so becomes one, benevolently dispensing grace to his devoted subjects. The aim of the Kāḷi rite is, as will be seen, expiatory. Men must atone for the wrongs they have done to the goddess; she demands of them that they give up something: the concrete bought to complete the house, a red and black chicken, a handsome young goat. So far from emphasizing order and purity, the rites of Kāḷi show a conviction that the benefits must be won through sacrifice, which is often violent and bloody.

But the existence of these differences should not blind us to the unity underlying the ritual design of Sudra domination. Each ritual which the Veḷḷāḷar patronizes is a key component of a total process, the culmination of which is the establishment on earth of that which the gods possess, viz., śrī, everlasting life and abundance. Whether "Brahmanical" or "non-Brahmanical," each step of the total ritual process is intended to invest in Veḷḷāḷar hands the benefit which legitimates the Sudra cultivating caste's claim to control the instruments of agrarian reproduction. And from them emerges, as well, the low status of the aṭimai or "left-side" Untouchable, whose deep affliction justifies no less effectively his poverty and landlessness.

II.4. The Village Goddess

Some in Jaffna say that the Kaṉṉimār are none other than the Eḻu Kaṉṉimār, the Seven Sisters, who are widely known in South Indian folklore and ritual. But it is more commonly said that the Seven Sisters are not the spirits of the sixty or fifty-nine deceased virgins, but rather varieties of the goddess. A virgin like Kāḷi, the Ammaṉ goddess is unlike her more saturnine counterpart due to her more pacific temperament. While Kāḷi is hot-tempered and accustomed to drinking blood, Ammaṉ is by nature a simple, mild, and chaste creature, whose power (cakti) must, nonetheless, be regulated by men. She must be treated, in essence, just the way a good Veḷḷāḷar girl is treated: dressed in a modest sari, secluded within an ordered structure, and kept away from the evils of the wilderness. She must be given the foods that suit her temperament, and also guarantee it: "cool" foods such as milk-rice and plantains, which tone down her system and render quiescent her spirit. Indeed, the rites for Ammaṉ are known generally as kuḷirtti ("cooling, refreshing offerings").

That the goddess Ammaṉ is more pleasant by temperament than Kāḷi should not blind us to the danger she is felt to represent. If men fail to house and "cool" her, she will, like a simple Veḷḷāḷar girl tricked into unchastity, rain down devastation on the families bound to her. And the connection (toṭarpu) between deity and patrons is here more general and hence more threatening to the total welfare. While the goddess has her Veḷḷāḷar patrons, she is identified with the very substance of space which the village occupies; all who live within it are at once obliged to care for her, and subject to depradation if they fail in their charge.

One of the more popular Ammaṉ goddesses in Jaffna is Kaṇṇakiyammaṉ, the deified Kaṇṇaki of the Tamil epic, the *Cilappatikāram*. Shulman summarizes the plot:

> Kovalaṉ was married to the beautiful Kaṇṇaki, but he spent all his wealth on the daṅcing-girl Mātavi. After a quarrel with Mātavi, Kovalaṉ returned penniless to his wife. Together they set out for Maturai, where Kovalaṉ hoped to sell Kaṇṇaki's anklet.. . . A goldsmith who had stolen a similar anklet belonging to the Pāṇṭiya queen accused Kovalaṉ of the theft; the Pāṇṭiya king believed his false testimony and ordered Kovalaṉ's execution. Kaṇṇaki, learning of his death, came to the court of the king and proved his innocence. The king died of grief at the injustice he had committed. Then the furious Kaṇṇaki tore off her left breast and hurled it at the ancient city of Maturai [Madurai] , and the city was destroyed by fire (1980:196).

The textual source for the worship of Kaṇṇaki would seem to suggest that she is scarcely distinguishable from the virgin suicides. She is wronged, and from her death issues an apotheosized goddess, who is angry. And yet, Jaffna Hindus identify Kaṇṇaki very explicitly and consistently with the seven Ammaṉs, although it is sometimes said that she is the lowest and the darkest of them. In practice, Kaṇṇaki is worshipped in precisely the same way as is the Ammaṉ goddess par excellence, Muttumāriyammaṉ, the goddess of smallpox and of rain, and the two are confused. Both Kaṇṇakiyammaṉ and Muttumāriyammaṉ are, for example, thought to have the power of bestow "pearls" (muttu, i.e., pox) on those whom they disfavor, and both possess one thousand eyes hidden beneath their hair.

The shrines of both goddesses arise from theophanies, in which the goddesses have revealed themselves (tānāka urpattiyātal). Of Kaṇṇaki's travels there is a tale widely known among Jaffna Hindus. After burning down Madurai,

> Kaṇṇakai, having found the mutilated parts of her husband's body, stitched them together with needle and thread and gave him life again by [the power of] her own virtue. Kovalan, on reviving, asked, "Is it Madavi or Kaṇṇakai who stands by?" Madavi was Kovalan's concubine, and Kaṇṇakai was greatly angered, for although she had given Kovalan his life, he had insulted her by placing his concubine's name before her own. Kaṇṇakai then changed into a five-headed serpent and slid away southwards from Madurai, crossing over to Jaffna in North Ceylon (Cartman 1957:77).

One of the spots at which she revealed herself along the way was Kaccāy, which at the time was a jungle frequented only by cowherds. They were astounded one day to see a great lady being carried on a palanquin. They went to see, but the woman, an old lady, asked one of them to comb her hair. One of the boys complied, but when he did, he saw that on her scalp were one thousand eyes. She then asked the boys to light a lamp for her every Monday and Friday at Kaccāy, and ever since then it has been done.

Some say that Kaṇṇaki made the trip to die, but others link the journey with the story of Maṇimēkalai, the daughter of Kaṇṇaki's husband in union with the courtesan. After Kaṇṇaki's husband's death, the little girl, Maṇimēkalai, was sent to live with the courtesan, who out of grief became a Buddhist nun. But Maṇimēkalai was very beautiful and longed for a husband. One day, she chanced to meet a young prince, and to protect her from herself, the goddess Kaṇṇaki whisked her away for a time to the Jaffna Peninsula, which was completely deserted. It was at that time that the cowherds ran into Kaṇṇaki, some say.

Kaṇṇaki continued traveling, it is said, until she reached Vaṟṟappalai, on the northeastern coast.

> When she arrived . . . she saw a man engaged in ploughing, and asked him for a drink of water. He left the plough and went to fetch it. On returning he missed his plough; the visitor had turned it into a margosa tree, the plough having been of that wood. The tree is still shown near the temple (Lewis 1920:180).

Muttumāriyammaṉ and Kaṇṇaki are scarcely distinguished by Jaffna Hindus, save that Muttumāri, although a manifestation of Śiva's consort Umā Tēvi, is thought to have been raised in a Paṟaiyar household. This tradition seems to recall the South Indian origin myth of Mariyammaṉ:

> Mariyammaṉ, the mother of Parasurāma and the wife of the sage Jamadagni, was so chaste that she could carry water in a ball without any container. One day she admired the reflection of a Gandharva (a celestial musician) as he flew over the water she was carrying; because of this lapse in her virtue, she lost her power and the water flowed away. Jamadagni, seeing her wet and without the ball of water, made her confess to her fault; then he ordered Parasurāma to cut off her head. Parasurāma took his mother into the wilderness; there she met a Paṟaiya woman and, longing for sympathy, embraced her. Parasurāma cut off both their heads together and returned to his father. In return for his obedience his father promised to fulfill any wish, and Parasurāma asked that his mother be revived. The father sent Parasurāma to accomplish this by sprinkling water on his mother and striking her with a cane. In his haste he put his mother's head on the body of the Paṟaiya woman and vice-versa, and brought both of them back to life. The woman with the Brahmin head and Paṟaiya body was worshipped as Mariyammaṉ, while the woman with Paṟaiya head and Brahmin body became the goddess Ellamman (Shulman 1980:264-65).

The dual nature of Mariyammaṉ, who is at once Brahman and Paṟaiyar, reflects the two facets of the goddess in village worship. On the one hand, she poses a threat like the impure Paṟaiyar; on the other, she promises the dignity won out of purity, which is symbolized by the Brahman. The two aspects of her nature suggest her malleability. If she is not treated properly, her nature will be like that of the Paraiyar; but if she is treated properly, she becomes like a chaste, high-caste woman--one of great power, for she is deemed to be a virgin.

Both Kaṇṇikiyammaṉ and Muttumāriyammaṉ demand to be treated properly. If either one strikes a man down with a feverish illness, she will say, "Alas, for I wander from place to place homeless, with no protection. Give me a home." Thus the people must build a temple for the goddess, giving her "cooling, refreshing offerings," pacifying her nature so that she becomes placid and beneficent (cāntam). She brings rain and good health to the villagers, and does not again inflict infectious, feverish diseases upon them. She equips herself with a retinue of spirits (pariyalaṅkaḷ), whom she bends to her will to guard the village from evil.

II.5. The Veḷḷāḷar Lord and His Bonds with Feminine Power

The god Murukaṉ has two wives, Teyvayāṉai, his heavenly, chaste, and very Brahmanical consort, and Vaḷḷiyammaṉ, his lover, whom he met at Kataragama one day while hunting. Teyvayāṉai, like the Ammaṉ-s, is thought to be golden in color, while Vaḷḷi, a girl raised by the Veddahs, is (like Kāḷi) deemed to be lustful and dark. Murukaṉ benefits from both of them. From his wife he receives the salubrious energy (cakti) that is generated from chastity, while from Vaḷḷi he receives the generative energy of the fertile soil; to unite with her, as Tamil mythology suggests, is to "merge for a moment with the dark and life-giving soil." The dark Vaḷḷi is a "child of the soil, born in a pit in the ground . . . ," and her connections with the soil are reinforced at points throughout the myth: "[when she is first encountered by the god Murukaṉ] she sits on a raised platform in the millet fields, guarding the ripening crop:

her food is all in its natural state, fresh and uncooked--honey, fruits, millet, the milk of a wild cow, and the valli root from which she derives her name" (Shulman 1980: 281-82).

Like Murukan, the traditional Vellālar lord would maintain his wife's chastity, but in the outbuildings of his home would be found a dark Pallar or Nalavar girl, his concubine. So too is the pattern repeated in ritual: the worship of the golden, chaste Amman is ever conjoined in Vellālar ritual activities with the cult of the dark Kāli. From both he receives benefits appropriate to a master of reproduction. Just as the lineage of the ākama temple owner receives benefits (palan) and specific entitlement (mariyātai) to the management of agrarian reproduction, so too does the Vellālar's family benefit from his patronage of both a Kāli and an Amman temple. But here it is not the lineage, but rather the patron's bilateral kindred who benefit (and are obliged to serve in the ritual).

The Vellālar who is first contacted by the deity becomes her medium, the channel through which she will speak to the people, admonishing them to treat her well, and helping them with their problems. The priest is obliged to present the deity with a large pot of milk-rice (valarntup-poṅkal, literally "grown milk-rice") at her annual festival. The deity also chooses others of the kindred--up to nine persons--who are similarly obliged. Both ritual offices--that of pūcāri (priest) and valarntukkāran (pot-giver)--devolve bilaterally upon the death or incapacity of the holder of an office. Sometimes it is not known exactly who among the many eligible kin of the deceased should occupy the office. In such a case, the deity will nominate someone through the conferral of a possession. I was present at a ritual in which the medium seized the valarntu pot from the hands of an elderly pot-giver, saying, "You are finished; you will die this year, and will no longer be able to present this pot." The medium gave the pot to the man's sister's son. The man in fact died some months later.

The pot-givers at a Kāḷi or Amman̲ temple, the valarṇtukkārarkaḷ, are known as those who hold shares (paṅku) in the temple, and everyone knows that the deity is most partial to them. Generally, the shareholders are a tightly-knit group of intermarrying and otherwise cooperative kinsmen, and the deity (through the medium's words and actions) shows a keen interest in the solidarity of the group. Invested with her power (cakti), they are known as big men in the village; they are patrons, not only of the goddess, but of their poorer relations and of the low castes.

II.6. The Ritual Maintenance of Feminine Power

The Veḷḷāḷar landholders of the village typically maintain a Kāḷi shrine and an Amman̲ shrine in addition to their Brahman-staffed ākama temple. The rites at the Kāḷi shrine are intended to appease the goddess, whose demand for shelter and for offerings has been issued to a specific group of kinsmen (the bilateral kindred of the temple owner). The rites are also aimed at producing tangible benefits for these kinsmen. The focus is always on the family, and the rites emphasize the idea of solidarity among those who attend; they have no impact on the rest of the village except insofar as the threat posed by a potentially malevolent, autochthonous spirit has been neutralized, thus granting the temple shareholders a bounteous harvest.

A *Vaḷarṇtuppoṅkal* for Kāḷi. Kāḷi shrines are hardly imposing affairs; most commonly, they are made of plaited cocoanut leaves built up around a concrete floor in rectangular form. Situated at the base of a tree in which the goddess is deemed to dwell, the shrine is left deserted throughout most of the year. The temple compound usually contains a well and is surrounded by a cocoanut frond fence. People fear the place, for a dark and dangerous power dwells there, brooding and sullen.

It is only at the deity's annual festival that the shrines are scenes of great activity. Throughout Jaffna's villages, little Kāḷi temples, situated at the base of *illuppai* trees (*Madhuca longifolia*), are the site of a ritual called *vaḷarntuppoṅkal* ("large pots of milk-rice"), undertaken yearly on the new moon day (*āmavācai*) of the Tamil month *Āṇi* (June-July). Informants cited several factors for the choice of this day. By mid-June, gardens have been harvested, nights are warm, and the fruit which is used for offerings is plentiful and cheap. Any enterprise which begins on the new moon day is bound to gather momentum and success as the moon waxes. It is said that a year is actually a day for the gods; they are asleep until January, when they awake; just before *Āṭi* (July-August), their powers reach a peak, and they are ready to take up their weapons and help people with their problems. At one Kāḷi shrine, it is believed that *āṇi āmavācai* is the day when the priest's grandfather first received the trance possession of the deity. It is said that Kāḷi came to him in a dream, and told him, "I am residing in the *illuppai* tree nearby and desire to have offerings. Failing that I shall inflict illness upon you and your kin."

The man chosen to be the first priest founded the temple to protect himself and his "close kin" from the deity. Since they have fulfilled their part of the bargain, the deity, in turn, is expected to provide certain benefits. But the rites must be done properly, with real evidence of generosity and commitment. Most of all, the kindred of the *pūcāri* must be united in service to the deity. The *pūcāri* at this little Kāḷi temple was Karthigesu, the temple founder's grandson. It was, in 1975, his duty to present the first *vaḷarntu* pot, to communicate mystically with the deity in his role as the medium through whose mouth the deity may speak, and to see to it that all of his kin--the bilateral kindred centering on him--cooperate in pleasing the deity. The second pot was to be presented by Kanagamoorthy, who owns the land on which the temple stands. Informants were unsure of his relationship to Karthigesu, but it is said they are members of the same cantati (patrilineage). The third pot was supposed to be presented by Thambirajah, a wealthy merchant living in Jaffna Town. Thambirajah is only distantly related to Karthigesu, and they belong to different cantati-s. However, the merchant is a very desirable kinsman; he is said to be quite rich and he owns a car. Karthigesu is very much interested in keeping up close ties with this man, but in this year he declined to present the pot. Instead he handed it over to his daughter's husband, Nagarajah, who dwells with his daughter in the priest's village.

Thambirajah's disavowal of vaḷarntukkāraṉ duties was something of a slight to the prestige of the temple, and may even have served as a prelude to a split in the family. The office should technically devolve only upon the death or incapacity of its holder; therefore, handing over the pot to his son-in-law in the prime of life indicated either his disinterest in the temple or his plan to draw away from Karthigesu's family. In the description of the seance we shall see how the deity, speaking through the hardly disinterested Karthigesu, chose to deal with this troublesome situation.

At noon of the poṅkal day, the little temple is decorated with cocoanut leaves plaited into various shapes and strung on cords stretched across the compound. A white cloth is hung over the rafters of the shrine to catch any lizard droppings that might fall onto the ceremonial objects. The decorations, like the cooking of the offerings, must be done by men only; women are not allowed within the temple. The "close-kin" of the medium are expected to contribute the supplies needed for the rite. These supplies--rice, fruit, cocoanuts, betel, areca-nut, camphor, pots, and brass oil lamps--are brought in throughout the afternoon and stored inside the temple building.

At dusk, the Paṟaiyar drummers arrive, and, as only they can do, begin to beat out a rhythm which announces the beginning of the ceremonies. The supplies are removed from the temple and stored in a special shed (pantam) about about fifteen yards away from the shrine. The temple floor is washed. Stones are arranged for cooking a variety of fried oil cakes, which will constitute the chief "heating" offerings to be given to the goddess in the maṭai ("funerary offerings").

At about 10 p.m., the medium waves burning camphor in front of the trident and recites mantiram-s, magical formulas intended to invoke the presence of the deity. He then goes to the pantam, where all the provisions have been stored, and waves the camphor again. The Paṟaiyar drummers then switch their rhythm to the one intended to bring forth the kalai of Kāḷi; almost immediately, the medium becomes possessed. He appears to be unsteady on his feet; he hyperventilates and sweats. Reaching inside the pantam, he seizes one of the large ceramic pots (vaḷarntu) and brings it to the temple door. At this point the drums stop beating and the medium loses his trance. Males of his "close-kin" group bring the rest of the supplies from the pantam and preparation of the foods begins in earnest. The goddess will be offered the meal called maṭai , offerings which are placed out in the home for the ancestral manes (pitir-s) once a year. The offering of maṭai to Kāḷi shows the dedication of the people to maintaining the Kāḷi-spirit just as they would maintain the spirits of their deceased kinsmen. At many other Kāḷi temples, including most of those owned by Veḷḷāḷars, the goddess is maintained not only by offering maṭai, but also by giving her the life (uyir) --and hence the vitality--of a sacrificed chicken or goat. In recent years, the practice of sacrifice has come under much criticism from Śaivite reformers, and, as in this case, many educated Hindus have abandoned the practice, save in those cases (such as house construction) where it is deemed indispensable.

Having finished the preparation of the *maṭai* offerings, the men set them out on four plantain leaves within the temple. First betel leaves are placed upon them; sliced areca-nut is sprinkled on these. On top of the betel leaves a cocoanut is placed, which is then decorated with flowers. Hence there are four mats, four cocoanuts, and four separate offerings. The first is offered to Piḷḷaiyār, and the medium recites a brief invocation, which invites the deity to reside in the cocoanut. The second arrangement is for Kantacāmi, the third is for Vairavar, and the fourth is for Kāḷi. Though she is the chief deity of the shrine, her offerings can only be presented after the males have received theirs.

Next to be brought in are the fruits (plantains, jak, mangos, and limes) and the fried cakes (*murukkukal*, "gram cakes"; *mōtokam*, "rice cakes"; and *vaṭai*, "flour cakes"). During the presentation of the *maṭai*, the milk-rice which has been cooking on hearths adjacent to the temple building becomes tender; a small portion is placed on the *maṭai* mats and offered to the deity. Prior to this time, the door to the temple has been covered by a curtain, for no one must watch the deity consume the offerings lest their envy result in supernatural damage to the goddess by means of *nāvūru*, the "evil eye-tongue"). The curtain is now removed, since the deity has finished "eating" her offerings

The trident is now decorated with a garland of red flowers and strung oil-cakes. The assembled worshippers stand on either side of the temple door, forming two parallel rows perpendicular to the entrance. The men stand on the deity's right and the women on her left. The medium, who is by now the only person in the shrine, waves camphor in front of the trident and recites *mantiram*-s. The deity's picture, which is hung above the trident, is decorated with white and yellow flowers. One of the medium's relations steps forward to sing a *tēvaram*, or Śaivite devotional hymn. Just as the *tēvaram* ends, the

Paraiyars begin playing the Kāḷi invocation fortissimo. Immediately, the medium becomes possessed.

At this point, the deity, having been worshipped and fed, has enough power (cakti) to speak through the medium. In the vaḷarntupponkal which I attended, the medium then emerged from the shrine and confronted the double row of worshippers arranged on either side of the temple doors. He strode forcefully up to Thambirajah (who had handed over his pot to his son-in-law), and whacked him very solidly on the head with the flat of his palm, saying, "This blow is due to you for your failure to provide vaḷarntu." Turning to Kanagaratnam, he asked for a new brass lamp for the temple. He spoke as well to me, saying, "I wish you well." At the time, I was in the company of another anthropologist who had paid me a short visit, and to him was given a peculiar set of instructions: "You are to proceed to your home where you are required to construct a shrine just like this one, and offer vaḷarntu there. Failing that, you must attend this ceremony again and offer vaḷarntu or else ill fortune will result." Next, he approached a kinsman who had given many donations to the shrine over the past year. He said, "You have had to bear the pain of sickness and this has not been unknown to me. Your faithfulness is not without reward. Visit this temple daily and your illness will disappear."

After such pronouncements are made, the medium returns to the shrine and emerges with a large, curved knife. This is handed to a male kinsman. At the temple door, the man slices a cocoanut in two, and hands the knife back to the medium. The worshippers follow with several cocoanuts; these are set out in front of the still-possessed medium every ten feet. On each cocoanut a portion of the maṭai is sprinkled along with a little vermilion powder, which represents blood. The medium stops at each cocoanut and slices it in two, until the party finally reaches the road junction about seventy-five yards from the temple gate. At this junction the remainder of the maṭai offerings are dropped along with a little more vermilion powder; the last cocoanut is chopped in two and the party hastens back to the temple. Before entering, however, they must wash their hands and feet, as they have acquired a "fault" (kuṟṟam) from this ritual sequence. The goal of the cocoanut-chopping rite is to dispel any spirits that might be tempted to reside around the temple or attack the worshippers. They are lured away, with the metaphorical blood offerings, to a junction where it is believed they will lose their way. A round of hand-clapping signals the end of the rituals; the milk-rice is passed around, and all consume the "pure" offerings. The maṭai that has been offered to the spirits is charged with affliction, and is therefore not eaten; Veḷḷāḷars will require their Untouchable clients to eat these offerings.

A *Vaḷarntupponkal* for Ammaṉ. Just as the rites of the dark, angry Kāḷi are identified with a specific group of kinsmen, so too are the rites of the Ammaṉ goddesses identified with a specific social space: in this case, the entire village. While the Kāḷi rituals help to reinforce social solidarity within the caste, the Ammaṉ rites, despite their focus on the Veḷḷāḷar pot-givers, achieve a holistic and interdependent organization among the many castes of the village.

The village Ammaṉ temple is responsible not only for keeping the village "cool" (e.g., with rain, breezes, and health) collectively, but also for maintaining the "coolness" of individuals within the village. Should anyone become ill with a feverish disease thought to stem from excess heat in the body, the implication is that the afflicted person, and his or her family, must be at odds with the deity. Upon contracting such an illness, it is necessary to make a vow (nērtti) to the deity, promising to reward her with some pleasing act if only she will withdraw the illness. The vow fulfillment (nērttikkaṭan) must be presented at the deity's annual festival.

Among the diseases attributed to excess "heat" are the infectious diseases, torru nōykaḷ. These include "sore eyes" (kaṇṇōy, a very common ailment); measles (cinnamuttu); chicken pox (pokkuḷippaṉ); and mumps (kūvaikkaṭṭu). A child who has any of these disorders is not taken to the hospital, since these are felt to be the retribution of Ammaṉ and so must run their course. The purpose of the Ammaṉ rites is, however, to try to avoid these depradations of heat. The rites intend to house the goddess, to "cool" her with pacifying, cooling offerings, and to make her chaste. In them, the villagers express their deeply shared conviction that every caste must contribute to the goddess's transformation, for the prosperity and health of all in the village depend on the rite's success. Yet the lion's share of the benefits falls to the Veḷḷāḷar patrons of the rite, who receive from it a special and public honor as presenters of gifts to the deity.

The most elaborate annual ceremony at the Ammaṉ shrines of Jaffna occurs in the Tamil month Vaikāci (May-June), on the vicākam nakṣattiram, on or near the full moon night. The rites occupy a full day and night, and involve all of the castes and many of the temples of the village. The Ammaṉ temple rituals indeed constitute the village ceremony par excellence, in that each aspect of the ritual performance emphasizes the careful articulation of the various castes and temples in the area. The rite described here occured at the Kaṇṇikiyammaṉ Temple in Kaccāy South, a village not far from Chavakachcheri in the southeastern region (Tenmaradchi) of Jaffna.

Activity begins on the day prior to the festival, when the kinfolk of the temple owners, as well as those who have made vows to perform temple service (toṇṭu) begin to prepare the grounds for the festival. All the temples must be cleaned, temporary shelters must be erected for the convenience of worshippers, the grounds must be cleaned, offerings must be prepared, cocoanuts must be gathered, and rice must be collected for the *poṅkal* (milk-rice) ceremony.

In the wealthier villages of the central peninsula, these tasks were formerly handed out to the *kuṭimakkaḷ* (jajmani) subordinates of the Veḷḷāḷar temple owner. Although the Kaccāy Ammaṉ temple is owned by Veḷḷāḷars, they lack the requisite political and economic sanctions to force neighboring wards of *kuṭimakkaḷ* castes (i.e., Kōviyars, Barbers, Naḷavars, and Paṟaiyars) to perform their traditional services. Nevertheless, representatives of these castes can indeed be found on the temple grounds performing duties that correspond to their traditional occupations. Kōviyars assist with the cooking and Naḷavars clean the outer grounds, as well as climb palm trees to gather the needed cocoanuts. When asked why they were doing these tasks, these persons responded that they were fulfilling vows to perform temple service (*toṇṭu*), and that their service was for the benefit of the deity rather than for the glory of the Veḷḷāḷars. It seems clear that these village ritual institutions are strong factors in the persistence of some vestige of the former system of *jajmani* caste relationships. Kōviyars in Kaccāy refuse to perform any kind of service for Veḷḷāḷars, yet they do not object to acting out their traditional occupations at an Ammaṉ shrine.

Early the next morning there is an elaborate *pūcai*, after which the preparations within the temple begin in earnest. Garland-makers (Paṇṭārams), Cooks (Kōviyars), and Veḷḷāḷars work together within the temple building to prepare the offerings and decorations. Most of the rice is cooked in seven very large pots, called *vaḷarntu* (lit., "grown"). When the rice is cooked, these large ceramic pots are taken to a specially built hut (*pantam*) several hundred yards to the southwest of the temple. Later, they will be carried in procession to the temple for the *poṅkal* ritual, in which the milk-rice is given to the deity and then eaten as piracātam (consecrated offerings) by the assembled crowds.

Preparations begin at mid-morning for the pāl kāvaṭi āṭṭam ("shoulder-pole dance"). Kāvaṭi-s are elaborately decorated wooden arches which are carried on the shoulders in fulfillment of a vow. The arched structure has a small pot of milk tied to it. Any person who wishes to fulfill a vow by carrying the arch must arrange beforehand for a rental, which includes the services of an aṇṇāvi, or "teacher." The "teacher" begins his duties at the Nākatampiraṉ shrine not far from the goddess temple; he inserts hooks through two parallel folds in the dancer's neck and back. During this painful ordeal, the dancer is expected not to move or show any feelings whatsoever. Once the last hook has been inserted into the flesh, ropes are attached to the needlelike skewers. The dancer picks up his kāvaṭi and, to the accompaniment of Paṟaiyar drummers, begins his dance towards the temple ground. The aṇṇāvi holds the "reins" or ropes. The dance consists of a number of wheeling movements which seem to tug very hard at the tautly held rope.

When the dancers arrive at the exterior courtyard of the temple, the Paṟaiyars change the meter and rhythm of their drumming. The new beat is an invocation for Kaṇṇaki, who is invited to possess the dancers. Almost instantly, most of the kāvaṭi dancers become possessed. They hyperventilate, shake, and eventually throw off their arches and writhe senseless on the ground. The "teacher" then rushes forward to hold the possessed man tightly until he regains his senses and balance. Once this is accomplished, the dancer picks up his arch and the dance resumes.

As the dances go on, more kāvaṭi dancers arrive in procession from the wards of Cāṇṭars, Naḷavars, and Kōviyars located within the village of Kaccāy or nearby. They join the procession of dancers, who circumambulate the shrine three times prior to returning to the Nākatampiraṉ temple for a rest.

Possession is deemed to mark the deity's acceptance of the vow fulfillment. It is also a potent generator of faith (*nampikai*). Villagers point out that the presence of trance-dancers indicates that very many people have gotten satisfaction out of their worship. Furthermore, the goddess indicates her pleasure at the offerings and vow-fulfillments by conferring *kalai* on the dancers, so it is certain that she is really resident at the shrine and is interested in the villagers' mundane problems.

Thus far two modes of fulfilling vows have been mentioned: *toṇṭu*, "temple service," and *kāvaṭi āṭṭam*, "shoulder-pole dance." These may be performed only by men of good caste. Women may fulfill vows by carrying a *cempu* (brass pot) filled with milk and margosa leaves (both "cooling" substances) upon their heads. Occasionally, women undertake mortification by inserting silver needles into their arms and shoulders, as do men. Aside from these modes of fulfilling vows, one may also: 1) burn several rupees' worth of camphor before the temple; 2) perform *aṭi aḻittu kumpṭitutal* (worship by going around the temple backwards, "eating each footprint"); 3) roll around the temple (*aṅkappiratiṭṭai*); 4) arrange for a special *pūcai*; 5) arrange for alms to be given to the poor (*tānam*); 6) bear the expenses of a festival day (*tiruviḻā ceytal*); 7) purchase articles for the temple; 8) make rice soup (*nīr kanci*) or rice gruel (*nīr cōru*) for the goddess; 9) make a lamp out of oil-soaked flour (*mā viḷākku*); 10) break cocoanuts in great numbers (*teṅkay aṭittal*); or 11) build a shelter for the devotees (*maṭam kaṭṭutal*). When all the vows have been fulfilled, *aṉatāṉam* (alms), consisting of milk-rice, rice gruel, and rice soup, are distributed to those in attendance.

After nightfall, the drummers, *pūcāri*, and some fifty to sixty observers go in procession to the *pantam* where the *vaḷarntu* pots have been stored. The pots are removed

PLATE V.

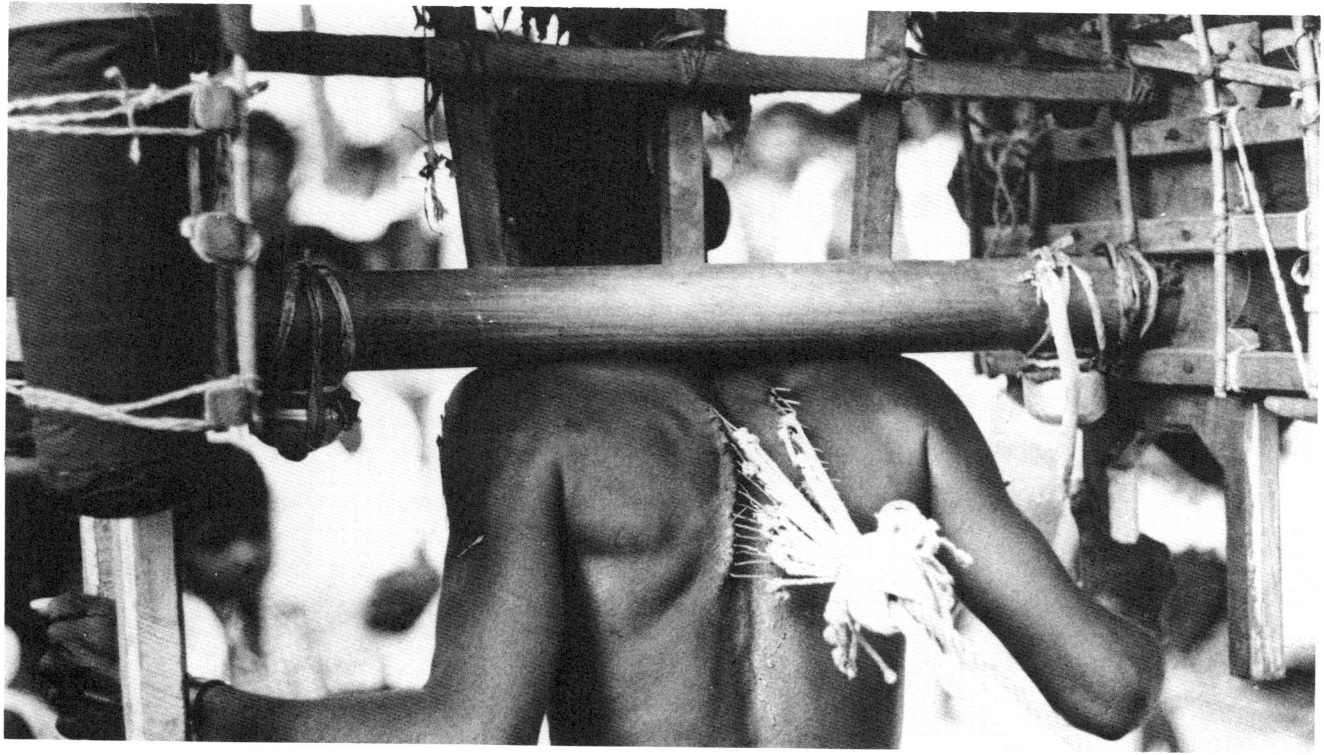

<u>Kāvaṭi</u> vow-fulfillment (<u>nērttikkaṭan</u>) at an Ammaṉ shrine in Jaffna.

from the hut and, as the valarntukkārar-s take up their pots, the Paraiyars play an invocational meter and most of the pot bearers become possessed. Torches are lit and the procession begins to move towards the temple, stopping at other shrines along the route. Having made the rounds to the various temples in the village, the procession moves on to the Amman temple where the big event, the valarntu poṅkal, takes place. The donors bring the valarntu pots to the temple door, and each is offered in succession to the goddess by the priest. The milk-rice, taken out once again by the pot-givers, is then eaten by the assembled worshippers, and the rites draw to their conclusion. After the end of the specifically religious events, there is very often a dramatic or musical performance on a stage built especially for that purpose not far from the temple.

II.7. The Greatness of the Pot-Giver (*Valarntukkāran*)

In the rites addressed to the feminine disorder inherent in localities, Vellālars demonstrate their willingness to give lavishly in support of ordering rites: those that expel disordered spirits, pacify the anger of the virgin goddess, and maintain (for the benefit of the whole village) the auspicious power of the Amman goddesses. From these rites the villagers gain knowledge of the spirit realm that surrounds them; they gain help in combating the attacks of spirits as well, and treatment for diseases. The rites are, moreover, of considerable significance in defining the solidarity of the caste and the moral space of the village, within which the holistic ideal of cooperating, interdependent castes is strongly shared and prominent. Few dispute the legitimacy of these values or the beliefs underlying the rites--even emancipated low caste folk willingly honor their traditional duties--so that when the Vellālar patron emerges from the shrine to distribute the consecrated milk-rice, he is judged great indeed for his generous act, which is tantamount to preserving the ideal of the varṇāśrama dharma.

III. The Ritual Confrontation of Demons

III.1. Demons in the State of Nature

Male demons (muni, generically, or in more literary language, cūran), are part of the autochthonous disorder of the primordial landscape. Since demons are thought to reside in the sites on which Veḷḷāḷars plans to construct houses, they must be appeased before construction can begin. It is something more than a pun to say that the controlling of demonic power is the very foundation of social order, for placing the "new foundation items" in a ditch is thought to placate one of the demons of the compass, thus securing his blessings for the family. The propitiation of demons--expelling the intractable ones and transforming the useful ones--is as important to the creation of order in the village as it is to that of the home.

Among Jaffna Tamils, demons are felt to be present in disordered, primordial localities. They are found along roadways and boundaries, in jungles and bodies of water, in deserted groves of trees and empty, open spaces, and at ruins. They are most often thought to dwell in large, old trees (particularly the aracu or bo tree [Ficus religiosa]). A stone at the base of a tree marks the demon's presence within the substance of the tree itself, a living substance that the demon has appropriated to sustain its own shadowy existence.

The notion of wilderness-dwelling demons who have appropriated a tree for a residence is an old and characteristic theme of Tamil literature. The Caṅkam poems, for example, mention a "terror-inflicting god" of the bo tree (Hart 1975:25). In the Tamil version of the Skanda Purāṇam, the Kantapurāṇam of Kacciyappacivacariyar (a popular Jaffna text), the demon cūr (not the Vedic asura, but rather an indigenous Tamil spirit of the wilderness whose name means "cruelty" or "fear"), takes the form of a mango tree in his battle with the god Murukan̲. The huge tree, situated in the middle of the ocean, threatens to block out all light and destroy all life (Shulman 1980:32).

Places infested with demonic power are thought to be exceedingly dangerous. The spots are safe enough during the auspicious morning hours, when the cosmic forces are strong and protective, but people avoid them during the "awkward times" (ekkaccakkamāna̲ nēram)--dawn, noon, the afternoon hours in general, but especially dusk, and midnight--when these cosmic forces are in transition from one regime to another and consequently weak. It is at these times that demons are most likely to be abroad.

In their primordial state, demons are wholly opposed to human life: hot-headed, cruel, saturnine, and egotistical beings (akaṅkāram), demons may make a person ill for a very long time, sometimes permanently, by afflicting him with possession (piṭikkirātal). Demons may also arrange their own sacrifices, and it is believed that a hungry demon will take the lives of innocent passers-by, chosen in a random fashion by the capricious mun̲i.

The impact of disordered, demonic power on human life is utterly destructive, useless and terrifying, and this is amply confirmed by the uncanny incarnations (kalai) that demons sometimes make. During the nineteenth century in Pooneryn, a wilderness area south of the Jaffna Peninsula, there was a demon thought to inflict dumbness, so that "any one sitting moodily and showing little inclination to talk" was said to be possessed by him (Lewis 1980: 5). Modern Jaffna belief echoes this tradition. Of one tree-dwelling demon and his unfortunate vehicle the following tale is told. A cook named Sittar, it is said, used to work at a school in Jaffna. On occasion, at midnight, he would sense that a mun̲i was strolling by on the road, and he would rise up without a word and go out to a bo tree. He would return later, his hair dishevelled and his body coated with mud, without the slightest idea of where he had been or what had happened to him. He was overheated from the *kalai*, and a cold shower was needed to put him back to normal; the *kalai* did not seem to do him, nor anyone else, the slightest good.

Other tales of the demons' disordered incarnations emphasize their more fearful qualities. In Chavakachcheri there is a Paṟaiyar, it is said, who on occasion gets the *kalai* (possession) of the demon Cuṭalai Vairavar. All of a sudden he would be found missing from his home in the middle of the night, and his family knew that he was at the crematorium, which is very dangerous and greatly feared at midnight. Having obtained the *kalai* of Cuṭalai Vairavar, he would return to the village, beating a small drum (*kuṭukuṭupai*). He would stop at the gate of some person of high caste, and drum; the family members would go up to the gate, frightened. And the Paṟaiyar would tell them that one of them would die.

Civilization cannot proceed and flourish so long as the demonic power of localities remains disordered. The demons of trees, of bodies of water, of the directions, and of the earth must be expelled, or else tamed and appeased; there can be no prosperity where demonic power rages unfettered. The devastation wrought be demons is described generically as *kuṟai*, "want, deficiency, poverty," the word being the same as that describing the low castes (i.e., *kuṟainta cāti*, the deficient caste, the caste found wanting). The great ones who desire to raise themselves above the lowly fate of the wilderness folk must endeavor, therefore, to control demonic power.

Demons are thought to vary considerably in their susceptibility to control, and in consequence a particular eruption of demonic powers cannot be treated until it is discovered just what sort of demon is causing the trouble. At the lowest level of the demonic pantheon is the wholly evil muni, a nameless, dumb, and fearful spirit whose cult serves no good whatever; no benefit can issue from propitiation of muni-s, who are appeased only out of fear. Hindus says, "Muni-s can do no good for man. It is rather that man must do good for the muni-s, by giving them the life they demand." Muni-s infest forest groves, but they are also to be found along boundaries and roadways. They represent an evil essence of the wilderness, one that prevents human beings from leading a happy, healthy life free from restrictions. Where muni-s are found to exist, they must be offered a life, or else they will take a life; there are few people who take lightly the tales of punishments inflicted by muni-s on villages that fail to appease them.

Spirits (pēy), both male and female, are another type (inam) of intractable power. Before the coming of civilization, is is said, people did not realize the precautions necessary to keep the spirit of the deaceased from remaining around and vexing them. Thus they left behind, as a legacy of their savagery, millions of spirits. The pēy, robbed forever of their vitality and sundered from the ambrosia of divine grace, detest the living, especially the signs of vitality and prosperity. Though spirits can be expelled from the home (which serves as a fortress against them), the field cannot be walled; they are open to attack, and consequently, the achievements of civilization may come to naught in a general, spirit-wrought famine (kurai).

In common with all loci of autochthonous disorder, the field-spirits (kuḷi) are capricious. Although they hate prosperity, they may favor a man who propitiates them by offering bloody sacrifices; but they do not favor him by blessing him with vitality, but rather by robbing his neighbors' fields. The kuḷi-s bring ruin and anger to the village:

> The kuli-s [like Kāḷi] are supposed to be mischievous, and to favor, or disfavor, the farmer according as they are propitiated by him or not.

> They will remove paddy from a neighboring floor to the one favored by them, from high to low land, from east to west, and to leeward, but not to windward. Accordingly, a man will not thresh on the same day as his neighbor, if the latter's threshing-floor is to the southwest of his. He is angry if his neighbor, with a threshing-floor thus favorably situated with respect to his, begins to thresh his paddy at the same time as he does. The neighbor, on the other hand, congratulates himself on the prospective assistance of the kuli-s, who will pilfer the paddy from the other man, and bring it to him threshing-floor; and seizes the opportunity to propitiate them, and so begins his threshing under the most favorable conditions (Lewis 1884:315-16).

These beliefs illustrate a general principle about demonic forces: they wish to move with the aid of other cosmological forces. They attack at times of weakness, aided by the winds and moving in inauspicious directions.

Muṉi-s, pēy, and kuḷi-s cannot, it is generally believed, he made helpful to humankind; they are too full of hate and disorder. Sorcerers (mantiravātikaḷ) may control them to harm others just as one farmer may employ them to rob his beighbor, but they bring no prosperity or vitality to men. Still, there are certain demons whose autochthonous state is indistinguishable from that of muṉi-s but who can, once transformed in ritual, aid humankind, principally by restraining the demons of the field. Dwelling in large old trees, these demons guard the flourishing fields so long as they are propitiated, usually with bloody offerings, cigars, arrack, cocoanuts, betel leaves, areca nut, and camphor. They are, unlike muṉi-s, given names, often those of gods known from the sacred scriptures or of godlings believed to be descended from the scriptural gods.

Aiyaṉār, it is said, issued from the hand of Śiva when the great lord, desiring to copulate with the beautiful Mokini (Cī Tēvi), issued forth semen, and some of it fell on his hand. The result was a being, Kaiyanar (from kai, "hand"), who has come to be known as Aiyaṉār. Another tale about the origin of this being holds that he is none other than Śiva himself in a rather lowly moment of his career: It is said that one day the baleful, dangerous Caṉi (Saturn) was chasing Śiva, and out of fear Śiva ran into a washerman's house and crawled into one of the big cauldrons in which the washermen boil clothes. Śiva hid himself, crying, "Aiyō, aiyō" ("Oh no, oh no") very softly. The washermen came back and heard this and, looking in, they saw Śiva, and so they saw Śiva in fear (aiyam); afraid, they said "Aiya!" ("Sir!"). And that is how Aiyaṉār got his name.

Vairavar, as Jaffna Hindus tell the story, issued from Śiva's anger. Thus, like Piḷḷaiyār or Murukaṉ he is a son of Śiva; however, these unintentional creations of Śiva's --Aiyaṉār included--are "rough gods" (kurañca teyvam), as Hindus like to say. They are by nature disordered and angry (koṭūramāna). On that account, it is said, Śiva never allows these lowly "sons" to sit on his lap. This tale aside, it is believed that there are many different Vairavars, of various grades of excellence. Lowest, and most demoniacal, are Cuṭalai Vairavar ("Crematorium Vairavar"), Kuttu Vairavar ("Aches Vairavar," who inflicts pains in the muscles of those he possesses), and Kāṭṭu Vairavar ("Jungle Vairavar"). Of a slightly less antisocial nature, but still to be feared, is Naraciṅka Vairavar ("Lion Vairavar"); and fully estimable is the Vairavar who serves as the guardian deity for Brahmanical shrines, Ñāṉa Vairavar ("Wise Vairavar").

Aṇṇamār, it is said, are the spirits of sixty Paḷḷar horsemen who joined the Vaṉṉiyar women on their funeral pyre; alternatively, they are the ghosts of the soldiers who killed themselves after the queens they were guarding slew themselves for fear of rape (see section II.2). Remembering their martial origins, they are fond of being given stout sticks, like warriors' clubs.

Kaṭṭavarāyar ("He whose coming was awaited") is thought to be the son who was greatly desired by the virgin goddess, Māriyammaṉ. It is said that even though she so desired a son, Śiva would not permit her to make love to anyone, and so she remained a virgin and resolved to adopt a son. She got one of the Aṇṇamār to make love to a deer, but this took a long time; finally Kaṭṭuvarāyar was born, and she adopted him for her own. When it came time for him to marry, he fell in love with a beatiful washer girl, but Māriyammaṉ would not hear of their marriage. To this day Kaṭṭavarāyar has refused to marry anyone, and he has a surly, resentful nature.

Perumpaṭai ("The Great Army") is a category (inam) of countless godlings, the ghosts of deceased and defeated soldiers. Like spirits, the Perumpaṭai died long ago, and rather dishonorably, so that they do not remember much of their former identities or even their names. They need to be presented with life (uyir) in sacrifices in order to survive. Unlike spirits, they retain very dimly the desire to serve, for they were once good soldiers. If treated properly they can be put to good use, but there are many times when their shrine is so dangerous that none dare approach it.

III.2. Ritual Strategies for Controlling Demonic Power

Expulsion. Intractable demons are expelled from the space to be ordered by offering them a life, or at least blood, and then disposing of the offerings in a spatially or socially peripheral zone: a road junction, a crematorium, or the bodies of Untouchables. Examples of this strategy have already been mentioned. During house-building rituals, for example, rice "bloodied" with vermilion powder is offered to Mū Tēvi, and then the infested rice is thrown up through a hole in the roof; similarly, in funerals, the corpse is removed from the house compound through a hole in the fence. When such holes are covered, the spirit cannot get back. Other offerings made to evil are dropped at crematories or road junctions; it is believed that in the latter case, the spirits will be confused at the multiplicity of pathways and thus unable to find their way back. A Vellālar with Untouchable clients will insist that the clients eat the offerings, thus confirming their lowly, afflicted state.

Appeasement. Some demonic personages, very evil by nature, need not be removed as long as they are appeased. Many muni are in this category, along with the lower forms of the godlings. The object of appeasement is not to obtain any benefit, but merely to stop the demon's deadly activity of appropriating his own sacrifices. One such case of appeasement is found in the village Urumpirai, where there is a greatly feared shrine of the god Kattavarayar.

The temple is the scene of an annual, marathon sacrifice, lasting up to ten hours, at which hundreds of goats and chickens are sacrificed. Unless the blood sacrifice is performed, the deity of the shrine (who is considered particularly vindictive) is feared to cause a great number of mysterious, fatal accidents, especially along the very busy road on which the shrine is located. If placated by the sacrifice, however, he will at least reduce the number of lives that he takes.

The ceremonies begin with a short invocation to Pillaiyār, who is asked not to disrupt the proceedings; after the invocation the door to the textual god Pillaiyār's shrine is shut, for he cannot bear the sight of what is to follow. Soon afterwards the "head goat" (talaikkitāy) is sacrificed. This goat, which has been provided by the temple owner, must be a particularly excellent specimen; profusely adorned with garlands, it is led around the temple in procession to the accompaniment of Paraiyar drumming. At this point the Nalavar medium, deep in trance, emerges from the inner shrine bearing a large, curved knife; he hands it over to the "cutters" (vettukkāran), who have fortified their courage with arrack. The goat is led to the cutters, who stand in front of the temple. It is believed that the "head goat" knows and accepts its fate, and willingly submits to it, even to the point of marching directly to the sacrificial spot and, facing the deity, sticking its neck out. Some assistance is generally needed, however, and the sacrificial technique requires three men: the first holds the goat's rear legs, the second holds its head with a rope held tautly around its neck, and the third severs the head with the curved knife. Hundreds of goats are dispatched in this fashion, so that a large pool of blood collects on the spot. The knife is washed and returned to the temple, and the goat meat is sold to dealers. In addition, each person who has fulfilled a vow must pay the temple owner Rs. 5/-, so the rites are very lucrative to those associated with the shrine. By afternoon the place is deserted, but the bloody pool left behind is said to be highly pleasing to the deity.

Apotheosis. All spirits, most muṉi-s, and the lower godlings are best approached by the rites of expulsion or appeasement. But certain godlings can be made ordered, and can then actually help humankind. They begin their careers, nonetheless, by causing affliction, suffering, and death like the lower demons. Long ago in Kaccāy, it is said, a certain Vairavar was causing terrible hardship. At this time, Kaccāy was only lightly settled, and the jungles were right on the edges of the village, containing the ferocious Vairavar. Some people died of disease inflicted by Vairavar, and the people were in a panic. They went crying to Kaṇṇakiyammaṉ, who said, "The trouble is that you won't give Vairavar a poṅkal offering. Without this he is unhappy and only does harm. You should make him a little shrine, just at the corner of mine," the goddess said. By bringing these godlings into contact with the ordered space of a benevolent deity, and by offering them pleasing, nourishing, and dignified foods, they can be made helpful.

Often the events by which the godling comes to be associated with an ordering deity, and thereby comes to serve the village, are uncanny. Once, long ago, it is said, there was a Veḷḷāḷar named Kuppaiyar. He had a great desire to visit Kataragama, the great pilgrimage center of the god Murukan̲, far to the south, and finally he got a friend of his to go with him on the long and dangerous pilgrimage. It took many months for them to reach Kataragama, traveling as they did on foot. They worshipped at the jungle shrine, and then it was time to return home again to Kaccāy. But Kuppaiyar said, "I shall stay here for the rest of my life. I shall not return to the village." His friend returned alone.

But Lord Murukan̲ appeared to Kuppaiyar in a dream and said, "You must return to your village, my child." Kuppaiyar fasted and prayed, saying, "I shall never leave you." Lord Murukan̲ appeared again in the guise of a Brahman, who gave him a parcel of food and told him that they would go to Kaccāy together. To this Kuppaiyar agreed. They started out on their journey, and they were accompanied by a monkey and a dog. After many long weeks of travel, they arrived at the shore of the Kaccāy lagoon, and suddenly the Brahman disappeared. Exhausted, Kuppaiyar fell down to the ground and dreamed of Lord Murukan̲, who told him, "Go to see the village headman and tell him that the villagers are to build a Vairavar shrine. The shrine will be my residence here, by which you will commemorate your journey. You have traveled with Vairavar and Hanuman, so it is they who will be worshipped." When he woke up, the monkey (Hanuman) and the dog (Vairavar's vehicle) had also disappeared.

With the assistance of the gods, the demonic forces immanent in the primordial wilderness can be put to good use. Among the benefits of this ordering process are: First, the demon will cease his frightening activities. Second, the god will protect the village, roaming its boundaries with the retinue of spirits which he controls. Third, the god will ensure the fertility of the fields by protecting the young shoots from spirits, who would otherwise destroy the harvest. Fourth, he will inflict his incarnated, conscious presence on his priest, who is called a _pūcāri_ and who is always a non-Brahman. In _kalai_, the deity will help diagnose various spirit illnesses afflicting people in the village, for he is an expert in the doings of the feared spirit world. Fifth, the god will grant to those who support him with offerings a special benefit (_pirayōcaṉam_, "usefulness") in return for their generosity and their faith in him. Finally, people who have troubles of the sort the god can address--spirit illnesses, problems with litigation, attacks by sorcerers--can make a vow to the god; if the problem goes away, they must then fulfill the vow by undertaking some act of austerity at the god's annual festival.

The ordered demon is very much like a great Sudra, just as a disordered one is like the _aṭimai_ Untouchable. By nature, demons and Veḷḷāḷars are disordered and impure. It is only be being located in order--the ordered space (_kōlam_) of the home and temple--that they achieve greatness. That order is achieved, for demons as well as Veḷḷāḷars, by bringing them within the ordering purview of chaste females and of the gods. The temple of the ordered demon is built within the power sphere of the village goddess, and contains images or stones representing the goddess as well as the great, textual deities. In this ordering context, the demon achieves greatness, just as the Veḷḷāḷar does thanks to his chaste wife and to the _ākama_ deities.

The rites of the ordered demon reveal quite clearly the link of ordered demon and great Veḷḷāḷar. The rites are called _maṉāvalakkōlam_, "ordering of the bridegroom." Repeating the symbols and rituals of the Śaivite Veḷḷāḷar wedding, in which the Veḷḷāḷar groom appears in an honored, auspicious state, the ordered demon is portrayed as an auspicious demigod whose original, natural flaws have been nullified by his immersion in order. For the demigod, as for the Vel̤l̤ālar, impurity is simply irrelevant; both may eat meat and go abroad fearlessly, as long as their ordering base is maintained.

The *manāvalakkōlam* of Vairavar occurs in the month *Āṉi* on the night of the full moon, and takes up a full day and night. In the morning, preparations begin early at the temple, which is located within the power-sapce (*koyil-maiyam*) of the adjacent Ammaṉ shrine. The temple is cleaned, sprinkled with turmeric water, and smeared with fresh cow dung within the inner shrine. A Brahman priest, a Panṭāram garland-maker, a Washerman, the temple owner's Pal̤l̤ar client, Nattuvar and Paṟaiyar drummers arrive, and preparations begin in earnest. The image of the deity, represented by a trident, is dressed up with a garland, and the other images (Pil̤l̤aiyar, Murukaṉ, and Ammaṉ), receive similar treatment. Within the temple are normally housed two very lowly godlings, Kāṭṭavarāyar and Aṇṇamār, represented by stones; these godlings are deemed very dangerous, and one of the central facets of Vairavar's protection is his control of these malevolent beings. The two stones are taken outside of the temple, and put in small sheds by the side of trees in the courtyard. The Washerman ties white cloths around the shed, and hangs more from the rafters of the temple. The Pal̤l̤ar busies himself collecting cocoanuts for the rites and cleaning up the temple courtyard.

When the images have been suitably prepared, the Brahman priest performs a *pūcai* for the god Pil̤l̤aiyār, whose blessing is sought for the ritual. He then departs, taking with him his cash gift, his cocoanuts, and his uncooked rice in a big bag slung over his shoulder. By this time six campfires have been raised adjacent to the temple, and the six big pots (*vaḷarntu*) are placed on them to boil. They will contain milk-rice, which is ordinarily deemed a cooling offering, but ash pumpkin is added to it; this is the extremely "heating" vegetable used in the metaphorical human sacrifice of the house construction rituals. In the afternoon, the food is finished, and the big pots are taken to a storage area about fifty feet from the shrine.

In the late afternoon, vow-fulfillment takes place. As the Paṟaiyars drum, a few men dance before the shrine with their kāvaṭi-s; several women wear nail shoes and carry kumpam-s of milk. The dancers and drummers circumnambulate the temple three times, stopping before the shrine to dance as the āṇṇāvi-s keep a tight rein on the ropes. A few little boys carry miniature kāvaṭi-s, but without any mortification; they dance a few steps away from the men, imitating the simple step.

After nightfall, the drummers, the pūcāri, and the six pot-presenters assemble at the spot where the pots are stored; the Paṟaiyars begin to drum, and the pūcāri soon shows that he is in kalai by quivering and jumping up and down. The vaḷarntukkāran-s pick up their pots, and the group moves in procession to the temple. There the pots are emptied onto mats, thus making a maṭai as one would for the dead; some of the food is taken into the temple and presented to the god. The pūcāri, still in kalai, comes out of the temple and confronts the worshippers, who are gathered at the door of the shrine. At this time he may comment on any illnesses the worshippers may have experienced; the cause is usually attributed to sorcery undertaken by enemies, and more worship at the shrine is prescribed.

Later a big bonfire is raised, and firewalking ensues when the fire has burnt itself down to a very hot bed of embers. Paṟaiyars drum, and the firewalkers, most of whom are fulfilling vows, wait until the trance takes them before jumping onto the coals. No one seems to be injured by the firewalking, although the coals are very hot; Hindus say the god protects them, as long as they have faith in his power.

III.3. The Demonic Division of Labor

All three ritual strategies--expulsion, appeasement, and apotheosis--are required in the battle against demonic depradation (kuṟai), a point made architecturally by a remarkable shrine complex near Chavakachcheri. The complex, located in Kaccāy North, consists of three separate shrines made of plaited cocoanut palm leaves. The complex is known as the Kaccāy Aiyanār Temple, although there are actually three deities worshipped: Aiyanār, Aṇṇamār, and Piḷḷaiyār. The Piḷḷaiyār and Aiyanār shrines are owned by Veḷḷāḷars, and a Veḷḷāḷar priest (pūcāri) performs the rites at them. The Aṇṇamār shrine is owned by the Veḷḷāḷars' clients, who are Naḷavars, and their priest is also a Naḷavar. At the Aṇṇamār shrine the rites of expulsion and appeasement are performed, while the rite of apotheosis, presided over by the great deity Piḷḷaiyār, occurs at the Aiyanār shrine.

All three shrines stand neglected throughout the year, except at the time of the annual vaḷarntu poṅkal ritual held in the Tamil month Āṇi (June-July). The rite opens with a pūcai, or flower offering, at the Piḷḷaiyār shrine. Once Piḷḷaiyār has been honored and has thus given his blessing, Aiyanār is offered a poṅkal by his Veḷḷāḷar priest. The priest then brings a large, curved knife out of the Aiyanār shrine and hands it over to the Naḷavar priest, who is by this time in trance. The Naḷavar priest carries the knife to the Aṇṇamār shrine, where it is waved before the stones representing the Aṇṇamār deities. Thus consecrated, the knife is carried from the temple to the courtyard. At this point both the Veḷḷāḷar and Naḷavar priests are in kalai. Paṟaiyar drummers beat out the invocations for the possessing gods. The priests stand before their respective shrines, and those who wish to address the deities are lined up in front of the little shrines. The priests, showing the physical symptoms of deep trance possession, speak to a few people in each of the rows; the most frequent topic is illness caused by sorcery. One or two persons are certai to be castigated for failing to cooperate wholeheartedly in the rituals or for failing to provide sufficient money.

Once the deities have had their say, a chicken is brought before the Naḷavar priest, who slices off its head directly in front of the Aṇṇamār and Aiyanār shrines. Next, a goat is led up to the same spot and similarly dispatched. The Veḷḷāḷars do not participate in the sacrifice, but watch attentively. For some distance away from the temple there extends a row of cocoanuts; the Naḷavar priest, still in kalai, proceeds along, chopping each in two. At each step he throws a handful of "bloodied" rice over his shoulder to coax such spirits as have been drawn away from afflicted persons by the deities, away from both the shrine and the people of the ward. The spirits are led to a junction, where more bloodied rice and cocoanuts are dropped on the ground. It is thought that the spirits pounce on them there and that later, they become confused about the way back to the people they formerly possessed. Of the offered foods, the poṅkal given to Aiyanār is deemed fit for Veḷḷāḷars' consumption, but the offerings made to the disordered beings (the spirits and Aṇṇamār) revert to the Naḷavar priest and the Paṟaiyar drummers. These Untouchables, by taking home the afflicted offerings and eating them, thus become afflicted with the same disorder which it is their ritual task to control through these rites.

IV. The Threats Posed to Order

IV.1. Introduction

The ritual confrontation with the sources of disorder produces its heroes, namely, the vaḷarntukkāraṉ, the Veḷḷāḷar patrons of the rites, who receive from them the greater measure of the benefits. Aided by the grace of the village gods and by the power of his own wife's chastity, the Veḷḷāḷar attains the fullness and richness of a life imbued with order. His crops flourish, his household prospers, the varṇāśrama dharma has been preserved, and civilization reigns in the village. Nonetheless, the victory he has attained is fragile. To maintain his power base of order, the noble Veḷḷāḷar must defend himself against the dangers posed both by the pollution of the home during the life cycle, and by the vagaries posed by fluctuations in the cosmic environment--fluctuations which, if not met by ritual defenses, could upset the fragile harmony which is order.

Pollution and the weak times of the cosmos both imperil the mystical order that Veḷḷāḷars want to establish, for they open the household to the intrusion of disordering power. When pollution occurs, it is essential not only to cleanse the household of the impurity that it suffers, but also to rid it of any disordered, afflicting powers (tōṣam) that may have intruded during the weak time. In the calendrical rites, cosmic cycles entail times of the day, of the week, of the month, and of the annual round that place the family in jeopardy; but there are also times of exceptionally good fortune. A family must protect itself during the unlucky times, and it must also take advantage of those times when ritual measures to ensure increase are certain to succeed. In the following section, a selection of the very numerous household rites Veḷḷāḷars promote is presented, illustrating their essential strategy and their role in creating the Veḷḷāḷar and the Untouchable statuses in Tamil society.

IV.2. Purity and Pollution

When a Veḷḷāḷar's family has been properly installed in a good, mystically ordered home, the stage is set for a happy and prosperous life. Nonetheless, the continued happiness and prosperity of the family depend in large part on the lord's commitment to maintaining, as far as possible, purity in the home. This is not to say that Veḷḷāḷars must maintain the great purity of the Brahman, a purity so great that one can hardly be involved in the world if it is to be maintained. It is rather that the Vellālar and his family must maintain a middling purity, one sufficient to allow them to enter temples (at least as far as the outer hall) and to carry on auspicious household ceremonies. Vellālars share this level of purity with other, touchable Sudra castes, but what distinguishes them from the others is that they use their level of purity to set in motion rites which invest them with the benefit of "increase" (palan). Kōviyars, for instance, are thought to be exactly as pure as Vellālars (considering the castes' level of corporate pollution), but Vellālars rank higher because they possess the ritual entitlement to the means of reproduction.* The touchable Sudra castes' middling level of purity is distinguished not only from the great purity of the Brahman, but also from the great impurity of those castes (Washermen, Barbers, and Paraiyars) whose task it is to deal with substances unambiguously thought impure in the Sastric tradition: menstrual blood, shavings, birthing blood, and the carcasses of deceased cattle.

But life continually poses the threat of pollution, of which Jaffna Hindus distinguish two kinds: tuṭakku (birth, death, and menstrual pollution) and tīṭṭu or tuppuravu illai (uncleanliness consequent on touching or imbibing some defiling substance). The former is the more serious of the two. Afflicting all members of the patrilineage with the exception of those who have long

*It must be stressed that no Jaffna Hindu will verbalize this point; indeed, when asked to explain why Vellālars rank higher than Kōviyars, they say, simply, that Vellālars are more pure. Yet Kōviyars cook for Vellālars, an act that demonstrates the castes' exact equivalence in purity terms. What distinguishes the two is that Vellālars are rich, having experienced the benefit of the rituals of Sudra domination; Vellālars possess the entitlement that Kōviyars lack.

resided far away, tuṭakku is described as "sorrow" or "mental agitation" (manatukku atirupti) by informants (Ryan 1980:121). It can be dispelled only by the passage of time. Pollution periods vary from caste to caste, and there is some disagreement; Veḷḷāḷars have their own list while certain upwardly mobile groups (mainly the Kaikular and certain artisan castes) claim fewer days' pollution than Veḷḷāḷars deem them to have (Table V). The purer the caste, the less vulnerable it is thought to be to pollution of this type; thus Brahmans have only eleven days' tuṭakku. The length of tuṭakku pollution is, furthermore, affected by the ritual roles of a caste, a fact evident in the ranking of Śaiva Kurukkaḷs (non-Brahman temple priests) and Paṇṭārams (Garland Makers). While insisting that all in Jaffna are Sudras save Brahmans, and consequently have a thirty-one day pollution period, Veḷḷāḷars readily admit that the Śaiva Kurukkaḷs and Paṇṭārams deserve a sixteen day period, and further admit that any vegetarian Sudra family need observe only twenty-one days' pollution. What Veḷḷāḷars deny is the claim of Kaikulars and artisans (who do not now have any temple roles in the overarching design) to a superior status in terms of pollution time. Some Veḷḷāḷars claim that Untouchables must observe a forty-one day pollution period. In any case, during the time of tuṭakku pollution the members of the afflicted household cannot enter the temple, hold auspicious household ceremonies, or enter auspicious homes.

Tuppuravu illai, the uncleanliness consequent on touching or imbibing some defiling substance, is less serious. Among the sources of uncleanliness are: "not having bathed, eating meat [esp. beef], drinking alcohol [esp. whiskey or arrack], getting a haircut, the excreta of animals, bad smells, and an untidy home" (Ibid., p. 126). While tuṭakku can be dispelled only by the passage of time, tuppuravu illai requires only a "head bath," as Jaffna Tamils put it in English, to remedy the condition. Nonetheless it is, for

TABLE V

POLLUTION TIMES OF THE CASTES OF JAFFNA

	Caste	Period of *tutakku* pollution: According to informants of the caste in question	According to Vellālar informants
Twice-Born	Brahman	11 days	11 days
Sudras	Śaiva Kurukkal	16 "	16 "
	Pantāram	16 "	16 "
	Nattuvar	16 "	31 "
	Kaikular	16 "	31 "
	Vegetarian Sudras	21 "	21 "
	Artisans	16 "	31 "
	Vellālar, Kōviyar	31 "	31 "
	Vannar (Washermen)	31 "	31 "
Untouchables	Ampattar (Barbers)	31 "	31-41 "
	Nalavar	31 "	31-41 "
	Pallar	31 "	31-41 "
	Paraiyar	31 "	31-41 "

SOURCE: Field interviews in Chavakachcheri, Sri Lanka.

its duration, as serious as tuṭakku; a person who is unclean may not enter temples, hold ceremonies, or enter clean homes. Tuppuravu illai is the term used to describe the uncleanliness of the Untouchable castes. For the Paṟaiyars, the connection between their domestic customs and their uncleanliness is straightforward; they scavenge, flay, and eat dead cattle, acts which are, for all Hindus, constitutive of impurity. The temporary impurity they experience is so heinous and so often repeated that it becomes a permanent condition for the whole caste. For Paḷḷars and Naḷavars, however, the connection between life-style and uncleanliness is less obvious; Veḷḷāḷars will say of the aṭimai Untouchables, "They fail to bathe before entering their houses," which is often untrue. To deem the aṭimai Untouchables "impure" (tuppuravu illai) is as inaccurate as deeming the Veḷḷāḷars "pure" (cuttam); just as Veḷḷāḷars lack the great purity of the Brahmans, so too do the aṭimai Untouchables lack the great impurity of the Paṟaiyar. It is rather that Veḷḷāḷars and aṭimai Untouchables are, like Sudras in the Dharmaśāstra-s, to be judged according to their domestic rituals. What distinguishes them is not that the aṭimai Untouchables are in fact more impure than Veḷḷāḷars, but rather that the latter possess an elaborate set of household rituals, those of the life cycle, that deal with both types of impurities and realign them with the powers of this world.

To be impure disqualifies one from temple and household ceremonies. That is the true stigma of impurity. The lowness consequent on impurity devolves not only from the immersion of the individual in the taints and corruption associated with corporeal life, but also from his alienation vis-à-vis the rituals which grant him the auspicious power of the landholder. Lacking that power, and what is more, being open to every kind of affliction, a polluted person threatens the ritually induced order that Veḷḷāḷars have painstakingly built up. Thus the polluted state is at once a biological and a moral matter; one is not only "unclean" but also at "fault" (kurram). The concept of fault among Jaffna Hindus would seem to truly approximate the Western notion of "sin," or a transgression against moral order. When that transgression is willful, as in the case of "stealing, telling lies, eating meat, drinking alcohol, being inhospitable, quarrelling, mistreating animals, going to temple improperly dressed, or when one is unclean or in a state of tuṭakku" (Ryan 1980:129), the result of the act is serious indeed: one's descendants are afflicted with deformities, sterility, and poverty for many generations. But this affliction is not well explained in terms of the textual Hindu concept of karma, in which very few Jaffna Hindus believe, for the affliction is not visited upon oneself in another life, but rather upon one's descendants. And it issues not from some mechanism of retribution, but rather from the openness to tōṣam that such acts entail. To be "faulted" is to invite into one's home and into one's body--and, by extension, one's descendants--all of the devastating forces which invest a person with illnesses, infertility, decrease, conflict, unhappiness, poverty, and a short, tormented life.

Since pollution is corporeal and therefore unavoidable, to be alive is therefore to be sinful; but the ritual design of Sudra domination attempts to sidestep the threat that pollution poses. The rituals of the life cycle deal with pollution which arises during the life cycles of the persons within the home. Dealing forthrightly with the eruption of impurities within the home, these rituals assume that, during the period of uncleanliness, forces of affliction will indeed enter the home and the polluted persons therein. The rites are designed to deal not only with the pollution, but also with the disorder--the evil--which the pollution has attracted, and they include procedures by which that evil can be taken away from the home. But the evil which is isolated by rituals cannot be simply discarded. In the Tamil view of things, the universe is a zero-sum game: there is a fixed quantity of evil in the world, and it cannot be destroyed; therefore when one is divested of evil, it must go somewhere:

> A man [for instance] may be cleansed of sin by worshipping god, but the sin remains in the world as potent as ever, ready to cling on to someone or something else. The plot summary of a modern Kannada novel says, 'The sin that someone did goes around someone else. Whom did the fruit of the sin done by Saṛala kill . . .?' The sin in this case is like a ghost or spirit that hovers around ready to attach itself to someone who is vulnerable.. . . [but] the sin need not be a ghost. In his novel Putra, Ramamiruthan puts in literary form the belief that a curse uttered with enough malice actually takes on form and pursues its victim. But whatever the sin may be, it is in some sense a tangible force released by the breaking of the system of order that must exist in order to insure the fertility of the earth and of the family (Hart 1979:15-16).

For Veḷḷāḷars, the repository par excellence of evil is the body of the Untouchable. As Veḷḷāḷars see it, Untouchables, by failing to bathe before they go into their houses or, in the case of the genuinely impure Untouchables by being constantly immersed in impurities, are already afflicted with evil and with the fruits of sin. They are, on that account, a logical "dumping ground" for the dangerous, afflicted substances that the rituals of the life cycle produce.

IV.3. Life-Cycle Rites: Two Examples

Rites of First Menstruation (*cāmattiya vīṭu*). A girl's first menses is said to be a very embarrassing and trying occasion for her. When she discovers that she has started to menstruate, she must go immediately to her mother and confess the news. Were she to delay, the result could be disaster for her and for her family. It is thought that, should a low caste person notice the stains before the girl announces them, a lifetime affliction will result: poverty, childlessness, widowhood at an early age, and constant adultery will be her certain fate.

Messengers are sent running to the homes of kinsmen, crying out "Periya pillai akivittal!" ("She has become a big girl!") From that moment on, the girl's life will change irrevocably: she ceases to be a child immediately, becoming instead a woman whose rights and status are strictly determined by the fact of her sexuality. She may no longer play and go about the village freely, and must be kept under strict surveillance at all times, lest she destroy the family's reputation through some lapse of chastity.

The menstruating girl must be isolated in a room, or kept in a corner of the verandah which is demarcated by a thick black charcoal line. The charcoal indicates that the space inside the line is inauspicious and polluted; anyone passing over the line (or into the isolation room) must have a "head bath" to dispel the "faults" (kurram-s) arising from contact with her.

Astrologers claim that a good chart can foretell the exact time of puberty, but the cause of the first menses is not ascribed to astrological forces. Rather, it is considered a "natural" (iyarkkai) process, one that entails the release of blood for reasons internal to the organism. Yet every natural process resulting in a release of blood must be surrounded with ritual, for blood attracts spirits and demons that can devastate a family's happiness and its power of vitality. For this reason, Jaffna Hindus say that their customs have an origin in nature: they are mandated by the faults of the organism, which make an easygoing, rule-free life impossible for anyone wishing to attain greatness. A family that failed to perform the puberty rites would be denounced as trying to "change nature" (iyarkkaikku māru), which is the most serious accusation that Jaffna folk make to one another. One who seeks to change nature places himself and his family outside the Tamil community and threatens its supernatural organization. Hence, the coercive pressure to perform household rites is quite strong; as many Tamils say, household rites have to be performed due to the authority of tradition (paramparai).

Although an outside observer may note that puberty rites impose great stress on a girl, the Jaffna viewpoint is different. No loving mother or father would think of glossing over this big moment in their daughter's life. As they view it, it is a means by which the girl can be installed in a higher status: that of a marriageable, auspicious woman who may wear a sari.

When the girl's close kin have been notified of the big event, they drop everything and go directly to the cāmattiya vīṭu ("house of attainment") to participate in the rituals known collectively by that name. They carry the supplies that will be needed for the ceremonies, which go on for several days. First, the women gather in the kitchen and prepare a meal of nourishing "raw rice" (paccai arici) to which cocoanut juice and brinjals are added. Spices and curry are omitted, however, for they are "heating", and the girl is "hot" to begin with. The fact that she is menstruating indicates that she has too much blood (the hottest of all substances) in her system. If she were to eat anything deemed "hot," it is thought that she would become very ill.

The girl has been kept in a specially prepared room while these preparations have taken place, and after a time she is led out of the room by one of the māmiyār (father's sister or mother's brother's wife), who will figure prominently in the ritual. She is veiled because the sight of her is inauspicious and constitutes a fault. In a corner of the compound, she is given a cooling "head bath" of milk and a type of sacred grass called aruku (Cynodon dactylon, var. intermedius). This shampoo is followed by a head bath with lots of cool water. After the bath, she is given a clean sari and her old garments are given to the Washerman. Though sanitary napkins are available in stores, the girl is not provided with them. The menstrual discharge soils her clothes, and so the Washerman must arrive daily to cope with the increased laundry load.

During the time of menstruation, the girl is deemed to be in a very precarious condition and to be very vulnerable to the evil eye (<u>kaṇṇūru</u>). It is thought likely that someone in the assembled crowd of kinsmen will envy the girl, and unless she is divested of the <u>tōṣam</u> resulting from the evil eye, she may be stricken with a fierce headache. To remove the <u>tōṣam</u>, three plantains are placed on a tray, each containing a wick (<u>tiri</u>) made of oil-soaked cloth. The wicks are lighted and the <u>māmiyār</u> ceremoniously wave the tray in front of the girl; this waving of lamps is called <u>ālatti</u>. They are then handed over to the Barber's wife. The soot from the lamps is the applied to the girl's forehead as <u>poṭṭu</u>, which renders her ugly to envious persons and therefore ensures that there will be no more <u>kaṇṇūru</u>. The plantains are given to the Barber's wife, who plays an important role in the rituals to follow.

The foods that have been offered to evil cannot be eaten by anyone of high caste standing, for they contain the very evil to which they have been offered. The Barber's wife removes these foods from the home and later feeds them to her family, who thus become saturated with evil. After the <u>ālatti</u>, the girl is given a nourishing draught of eggplant juice, sesame oil, and raw egg (<u>kattarikkāy cōru</u>), and eats a meal of raw red rice in the company of her close kin. She is given gifts, which are used by her parents to offset the rite's expenses. The relatives give their blessings and depart. The meals and baths go on for seven, nine, or eleven days, until the <u>māmiyār</u> deem that the menstruation is over. During this time the girl must eat only cooling and nourishing foods and must remain secluded at most times within her corner or room.

On the final day of seclusion, the big ceremony called <u>cāmattiya kaliyāṇam</u> ("attainment festivity") takes place.

It is one of the biggest events in the life cycle of a woman, and it both celebrates the attainment of reproductive power and invests her with the responsibility incumbent on one who is to bear the burden of the family's mystical welfare. No longer may she act childishly or boldly; she must show the qualities required of an adult woman.

Preparations begin early in the morning. While the women labor in the kitchen, preparing the rice meal and the trays of oil cakes, couriers deliver invitations to all of the family's bilateral kin, including those deemed tūram (distant). A temporary thatched booth is erected in the compound to accommodate the visitors, and an ornamented platform is built for the ritual. The house and compound are decorated with streamers, flags, and plaited mango leaves.

The family's kuṭimakkaḷ servants--the Barber and the Washerman--arrive, and the latter ties white cloths so that they hang under the rafters of the house, booth, and platform. The Barber's wife awaits the rites, in which she plays an essential part. Although the pollution group is patrilineal, the rites cannot occur until all of the important bilateral kin--especially the "close kin"--have arrived. Each of these persons has some specific obligation in the ritual or the preparation and serving of food. Again, the most important social group in family life is not the patrilineage, but the bilateral close-kin. In general, the males have duties in the preparation of the decorations, and the women do the cooking and perform the rituals.

When everything is ready, the girl's mother and the māmiyār escort her from her room to the bathing spot, where there is a kumpam for Piḷḷaiyār. As in every ritual, a cocoanut is broken to placate the elephant god at the inception of the rites. The girl is then seated upon a low stool, and all of her female kin (as listed above) line up to dump buckets of water upon her head. As they do so, they chant the following fixed phrase: "cakalai colvaṅkalōṭum cumaṅkaliyāka vālavenṭum!" ("May you live as one who has all wealth and as one who is well married!").

Upon completion of the cooling bath, the girl is dressed in a beatiful, expensive sari, as if she is about to be married. She is given gold jewelry to wear. Everyone has a "head bath" to dispel the kurram-s arising from contact with the still-polluted girl, and they too put on fresh or new clothes. When all have changed clothes, the puberty rite (irutu cānti, "menses-cooling") can begin.

The "attained girl" (cāmattiya pēṇ) is brought to the ornately decorated platform by her māmiyār, her mother, and other kinswomen who are well married. On the platform have been placed brass pots, brass oil lamps, paddy, and trays of food. The girl is made to stand facing these items, as if she were a goddess about to receive offerings. One of the trays of food contains a measure of paddy with a special curved iron knife (cattakam) stuck into it. This tray is intended to lure away the spirits which still hover about the impure girl, while iron, which has the property of absorbing evil, becomes imbued with the very essence of evil after the māmiyār wave it about in front of her. They pass it over the girl's shoulder to the Barber's wife, who sets it aside, to be taken with her when she leaves. Thus the fault will be removed from the household, and the Barber and his wife, who acquire a permanent stigma through repeated performance of this rite, become afflicted themselves.

Next is the final ālatti, or waving of oil lamps before the now purified girl. A brass vessel of water and a tray of plantains in which burning wicks have been placed are also waved before her. All of these materials are passed over her shoulder to the Barber's wife. Lastly, a sooty black mark is placed on her forehead to avert the evil eye, and the girl's parents then lead her back to the house. There follows a feast, a musical recital (if the family can afford to hire musicians), and sometimes a dispute. Normally all are pleased with the puberty ceremony itself, as it is a happy event for the family. But the feast provides an opportunity for nascent schisms within the family to become manifest. Should there be a serious altercation, the rite is negated and the girl must be taken to an ākama temple for a special ceremony.

People who can afford to do so unhesitatingly spend a great deal of money on puberty rites, Next to a marriage, these rituals provide a man with the best means to demonstrate his wealth and commitment to the values of the Hindu community. Of such a man it may be said, "His family is a good one; those people are of good caste. They keep their women well bound (cariyana kaṭṭupāṭatu). They are good people to get married with."

Rites of the Birthing Room. It is believed that a newly married woman who lives chastely in a good house should become pregnant within two years. The moment of conception is thought to be especially perilous for the fate and character of the child. Thus, every time that she engages in sexual intercourse, a woman must think lovingly and longingly about having a child. If she does not, it is believed that the child she conceives will have a poor personality or will suffer illnesses. If the child is not her first, a woman must be very careful to concentrate on the fetus she seeks to conceive, for the crying of her other children can distract her attention. Should she think of the other children when she conceives, the child and its brothers and sisters will be in competition all through their lives. These beliefs predispose Hindu women against birth control, for its use is viewed as a selfish disavowal of the religious duty to concentrate fully on conceiving.

The food that a pregnant woman takes should be evenly balanced between heating and cooling foods that are nourishing. Especially favored during pregnancy are milk, brinjal juice (kattirakāy cōru), black gram dhal (uḷuntuṅkaḷi), and eggs, which are deemed strengthening.

The traditional midwife in Jaffna is of the Naḷavar or Barber caste; for Veḷḷāḷars, the midwife is the spouse of the family's Barber or Naḷavar client. As in the other ritual roles that the kuṭimakkaḷ castes are asked to carry on, the midwife's role is at once secular and religious. She is asked to help not only with the birthing process but also with the propitiation of a goddess of parturition called Koṟṟiyār (or Korrippēy), a disordered spirit.

Pregnancy subjects a woman to a variety of restrictions, most of which seem to symbolize openness and easy passage. The pregnant woman is not permitted to do household work involving stopping up holes or tying. After the sixth month of the pregnancy, she may not enter the temple, as she is unclean. When labor begins, a space for the birth is prepared in an outbuilding. A vempu (margosa, Melia azadirachta) oil lamp is kept burning, for the scent is thought to be a useful prophylaxis against vicious spirits attracted to the blood to be released in the birth.

The propitiation of Koṟṟiyār involves the setting out of a full measure of rice, a serving of curry, betel leaf, and areca-nut. It is felt that the goddess Koṟṟiyār, who is a bloodthirsty spirit linked by most informants with the vicious Mū Tēvi, will busy herself with the curry offerings rather than disturb the birthing woman. A broom and a piece of iron are also placed in the room, since they are thought to absorb Mū Tēvi or other debilitating, attacking spirits.

If the labor is prolonged, the family engages a Paṟaiyar drummer to circumnambulate the temple. Paṟaiyars say that the purpose of the drumming is to control the retinue of spirits (pariyalaṅkal) that swarms around the lower deities; other informants say that the birth threatens to release pollution, which the drumming absorbs. In any case, it is believed that the drumming removes the obstacle holding up the birth. The Paṟaiyar receives nothing if he is a member of the family's kuṭimakkaḷ; he will be compensated with rice at the harvest time.

If the child is a boy, the midwife calls out loudly to the father, instructing him to "beat the roof." He should take the pestle and strike the roof tiles three times, and then throw the pestle over the roof beam. This is done, informants say, to announce the family's good fortune and pride. Cartman notes that a boy who shows cowardice will be taunted with the accusation "Your parents forgot to beat the roof when you were born" (1957:147). The birth of a daughter is not greeted with so much enthusiasm or ceremony. Indeed, the father may be indignant and curse his ill fortune at the prospect of having to pay a dowry.

The mother remains in confinement for five days more, attended by the Barber or Naḷavar midwife. She is given nourishing foods, baths made with margosa bark, rubbings with saffron paste, and an oil bath. She is never left alone. On the night of the fifth day of confinement an offering of rice and curry is made to Koṟṟiyār. This is then given to the Untouchable's wife in compensation for her services; she takes this food, along with the broom, rubbish, and the dirt that has accumulated in the confinement room, and leaves the house. She eats the food, and takes the rubbish to a road junction, where it is dumped on the ground.

The contrast between pollution and imbibed disorder in the birthing ritual recalls the similar contrast in the rites carried on at a new home. Just as the Carpenter becomes temporarily unclean from his role in propitiating the spirits, the Washerman becomes unclean from his role in taking away the soiled menstrual cloths. But neither of them imbibes the source of disorder, and consequently both are of touchable caste. In contrast, the Untouchable well-sacrificer and the Barber's wife are required to imbibe what has been offered to evil (in the sense of tōṣam, "disorder" or "disharmony," as expressly stated by informants). They thus become evil themselves and are made permanently Untouchable, bearing a stigmatized, disordered mystical condition that can never be washed away.

V. Rituals of the Calendrical Cycle

V.1. The Fluctuating Cosmic Environment

The rites of the life cycle protect the well-established home from periodic weaknesses due to the blood released at birth, puberty, and menstruation, and from the sundering of the family from the grace of the gods during times of tuṭakku affliction. Moreover, the auspicious rituals carried on after female puberty and marriage are intended to protect women from attacking, mystical agents that might afflict them with infertility, and so the household becomes a repository of chastity and of greatness. Yet the home and its occupants are still vulnerable to certain afflicting forces that can, at certain times, penetrate even the best mystical defenses.

During the course of the day, there are certain awkward times when spirit attacks are likely and defenses are weak; at these times people try to avoid places known to be infested by spirits, such as lonely groves, road junctions, crematories, shrines of certain lowly godlings, and temples of goddesses. The best time of the day stretches from dawn to noon, and there is much activity during these hours. People begin to stir at first light, when women and little children leave the house to defecate in the scrub. Men follow a little later, and by the time sunlight strikes the house, the women have prepared the food and the men are ready to go to work. Ideally, most of the day's work can be accomplished in the hours before noon, when the sun is not too hot, and when there is little danger of attack by hostile, mystical forces. At noon, people return to their homes for lunch (the heaviest meal of the day) and rest afterwards. Between dusk and midnight there is another fairly good period, although women must not venture out of the house. It is considered a good time for visiting.

Aside from the times of the day, there are other temporal cycles that impinge on the mystical order established in the homes of good caste people. Each week has its cycle of seven days, some of which possess an overall inauspicious quality, others of which are deemed lucky. In Jaffna, the days Monday, Wednesday, and Friday are thought lucky, which means that one should start a new enterprise or set out on a journey on these days. The remaining days of the week are considered inauspicious and are avoided for such purposes. However, the restrictions are quite handily circumvented. When I announced a plan to leave on a Tuesday for a trip to Colombo, I was strongly advised against it; my landlord said that it would be very dangerous. When I persisted, I was advised to start the trip on Monday, travel a few miles down the road after a grand farewell, and then return quietly. "In this way you will have started your trip on Monday. Monday is an auspicious day. You will be continuing your trip on Tuesday," I was told, "but the important thing is that you started on Monday." The days, their planetary associations, and their general character are given in Table VI.

Most feared are Tuesday, Thursday, and Saturday. It is said of Tuesday that its deity, Mars, has an open mouth (cevvāy veruvāy). The inauspicious character of Thursday is rather surprising, considering its association with Jupiter, the planet of great spirituality. Nonetheless there is a sense in which spiritual wisdom is thought to demand the cutting of bonds with this earth, and the malefic aspect of Jupiter is thought to achieve this goal in a violent way. It is said that the "bad aspect of Jupiter will cut the throat" (kaḷḷa viyāḻa kuluttai aṟuppāṉ). Saturday is, of course, the day associated with the baleful

TABLE VI

THE DAYS OF THE WEEK

English	Tamil	Deity	Character
Sunday	nāyirrukkilamai	Cūriyan (Sun)	inauspicious
Monday	tinkatkilamai	Cantiran (Moon)	auspicious
Tuesday	cevvāykkilimai	Cevvāy (Mars)	inauspicious
Wednesday	putankilamai	Putan (Mercury)	auspicious
Thursday	viyālakkilamai	Viyālan (Jupiter)	inauspicious
Friday	vellikkilamai	Velli (Venus)	very auspicious
Saturday	canikkilimai	Cani (Saturn)	very inauspicious

SOURCE: Field interviews in Chavakachcheri, Sri Lanka.

Saturn, who is deemed to be entirely malevolent towards humanity.

The character of a particular day is not judged solely by its standing in the weekly cycle, for there are monthly cycles to be considered as well. The Tamil month contains about thirty days, and corresponds to the duration of one of the twelve solar mansions (irācikal) of astrology. The year begins not in January, but rather on the first of the Tamil month Cittirai, which is the month of Aries (mētamāta cūriyan), the first of the solar mansions. The lunar cycle, on the other hand, is not symmetrical with the cycle of months. It is marked off by lunar days (titi) and the cycle of lunar days comprises a fortnight, which begins with either the full moon (pūranai) or the new moon (amāvāci). There are fourteen days named titi-s aside from the full and new moon days, and every month contains--with some overlap--two lunar fortnights.

The two fortnights possess the same cycle of lunar days, whose names refer to their ordinal standing in the cycle (e.g., *pañcami*, "the fifth"), but they are actually quite different. The first fortnight of the month, which is the waxing time of the moon, is thought auspicious and bright; it is called *vaḷar piraikkālam*, "the growth fortnight," when all new enterprises are bound to meet with success. The second fortnight is thought inauspicious and dark; it is known as *tēy piraikkālam*, the "decrease fortnight." In addition, certain of the lunar days are said to have auspicious qualities regardless of which fortnight they appear. Among these are the fourth *titi*, *caturtti*, which is especially propitious for worshipping Piḷḷaiyār; the thirteenth *titi*, *tirayōtaci*, which is sacred to Śiva; and the full moon day, *pūraṇai*, which is always auspicious and pleasing.

On the auspicious days of the lunar cycle the very orthodox may undertake a fast (*viratam*), which is thought to confer special benefits on the devoted. There is more to *viratam* than abstention from food; indeed, the point of fasting is not so much to deny oneself as to isolate the mind from its sensual involvement (*kāmam*), which before Lord Śiva is a *kuṟṟam*. Thus the fast may involve abstaining only from breakfast and lunch, while in the evening a light, vegetarian meal may be taken. The very orthodox will restrict their intake of food to cocoanut milk, cow's milk, and fruit on fasting days.

Another important determinant of a day's qualities is its *nakṣattiram*, or lunar mansion, of which there are twenty-seven The moon remains in one of its mansions for about one day, but the *nakṣattiram* cycle does not match the cycle of fortnights or that of months. Another cycle is that of the twenty-seven planetary conjunctions, or *yōkam*, which are not of the same duration as the *nakṣattiram*-s; still another cycle is that of the eleven units of time (*karaṇam*). To decide properly on the character of any particular day, one must take into account five factors: the day (*vāram*), the *titi*, the *nakṣattiram*, the *yōkam*, and the *karaṇam*. A day may be judged excellent (*amirtta*), in which case any enterprise may be undertaken with success; good (cirttam), in which a person should not be discouraged from trying to start an enterprise or taking a trip (but should not expect overwhelming results); or bad (maraṇam, "death," or kari nāḷ, "bad day"), in which case nothing at all should be undertaken. The calculations required to arrive at these judgments are prodigious, so in practice people look up the prognosis in the Pancāṅkam.

The Tamil year begins in Cittirai, with the first solar mansion, Aries. There is a New Year ceremony (varaṣup-pirappu), and it is universally agreed that Cittirai is the proper time for the inception of the year. Yet it is quite evident that, from the standpoint of ritual organization, the year really begins in the month Tai (Jan./Feb.). My justification for this assertion is that, in the Hindu view, the year of the human being is equal to a single day of the gods, and the "morning" of the year is not Cittirai but rather Tai. The parts of the year are compared to the times of the day; for instance, the unlucky times of the year, in which no new enterprises should be undertaken or marriages made, correspond to the awkward times of the day.

The month Tai is thought to represent morning, and it a very auspicious time indeed. Tai begins after the winter solstice (Dec. 21), but it is nonetheless said, wrongly, to begin on the very day that the sun begins its northward course; the months from Tai to Āni, which corresponds to noon, are with one exception--Māci--very auspicious (Table VII). The rituals carried on during the morning of the gods stress happy, auspicious rites, in which (with one exception) the ritual emphasis is on increase, life, fertility, spiritual growth, and salvation.

The summer solstice occurs on June 21, but it is not recognized in the Tamil calendar until two or three weeks later, at the inception of the month Āṭi (July/Aug.). Āṭi heralds the inauspicious afternoon of the gods, and the rituals from this period until Puraṭṭāti (Sept./Oct.) stress the danger of mystical attack. Again, there is one exception.

Throughout this period the manes and spirits are disposed to attack the home, to penetrate the best defenses, and to destroy the family's happiness; it is an unlucky time.

The autumnal equinox occurs on September 21, but it is not recognized in the Tamil calendar until two or three weeks later: the first of Aippaci (Oct./Nov.), which is the beginning of the night of the gods. Night is generally a good time, so that the months from Aippaci to Mārkali (Dec./Jan.) are fairly lucky. The rituals carried on in this period emphasize (again, with a single exception) the theme of night; two evening lamp festivals are observed.

The seasons in Jaffna correspond well with the calendar, lending a climactic underscoring to the cycle of auspicious and inauspicious months. In general, the middling or inauspicious months tend to occur during times of climactic shifts (Table VIII). Māci (Feb./March), along among the "morning" months in having a less than auspicious character, heralds the return of heat; Āṭi (July/Aug.) is a time of futile showers and vexing thunderstorms, brought on by disturbances related to the southwestern monsoons. Temperatures drop in Puraṭṭāti (Sept./Oct.), and the northeast monsoons begin in that month; they are well entrenched by Aippaci, when the temperature stabilizes at a level considered "cold" by Jaffna standards: the mean monthly temperature for December is 77°F. The rains taper off in Mārkali, and the cool temperatures persist until their steep rise once again in February. The seasons do not shape the lucky and unlucky months of the calendrical cycle, which is calculated by astrologers, but they are nonetheless entirely consistent with it. The "morning of the gods" is, for example, the harvest season in Jaffna, when there is abundance.

Hindus maintain a remarkable ambivalence about astrological influences as a determinant of fate. On the one hand, people say that one's fate is "written on the head" (talaiviti) by astrological forces at birth, and that these

TABLE VII

THE MONTHS OF THE YEAR

	English	Tamil	Time of "Day"	Quality	Solar House
Winter Solstice Dec. 21					
Morning of the gods	Jan./Feb.	Tai	Morning	Auspicious	Capricorn
	Feb./March	Māci	Morning	Middling	Aquarius
	March/April	Paṅkuni	Mid-morning	Auspicious	Pisces
	Arpil/May	Cittirai	Mid-morning	Auspicious	Aries
	May/June	Vaikāci	Forenoon	Auspicious	Taurus
	June/July	Āṉi	Noon	Auspicious	Gemini
Summer Solstice June 21					
Afternoon of the gods	July/Aug.	Āṭi	Afternoon	Unlucky	Cancer
	Aug./Sept.	Āvaṇi	Afternoon	Middling	Leo
	Sept./Oct.	Puraṭṭāti	Dusk	Unlucky	Virgo
Autumnal Equinox Sept. 21					
Night of the gods	Oct./Nov.	Aippaci	Night	Auspicious	Libra
	Nov./Dec.	Kārttikai	Night	Auspicious	Scorpio
	Dec./Jan.	Mārkaḻi	Pre-dawn	Middling	Sagittarius

SOURCE: Field interviews in Chavakachcheri, Sri Lanka.

forces will shape the overall contours of a person's life.* On the other hand, certain rituals, lifestyles, and deities are thought to protect people from the malevolent influences that periodically arise. Without denying that their fate may be inescapable, Hindus in Jaffna do all they can to avoid whatever depradation seems to be in store for them according to their horoscope or to the Pancāṅkam. A properly constructed house, for example, protects its female occupants from the influences that might render a woman sterile, and few Hindus with the means omit the astrological calculations that properly situate a house with respect to cosmic emanations.

It is believed that the astrological emanations striking a person at the time of birth are predictive of twelve basic qualities or experiences, which are the twelve houses of the horoscope. The most important astrological condition at the time of birth is the position of the moon against the twenty-seven lunar mansions, which are far more important in Hindu astrology than the twelve solar mansions (irāci). When drawing up a horoscope, the astrologer first determines the nakṣattiram of birth, and then fills in each of the twelve houses with a particular rote order of planets (Sun, Moon, Mars, Mercury, Jupiter, Venus, Saturn, and the two lunar nodes, Rāku and Kēṭu); the sequence starts with a particular planet depending on the nakṣattiram. He also fills in the twelve solar houses. Each house is then evaluated,

---

*This fate is said to be a person's karma, or retribution for acts done in a previous lifetime. Nonetheless, the concept of karma--supposedly a universal of Hindu belief--is very weakly developed in Tamil culture. Bad acts done in one's own lifetime, for example, are thought to pose far more peril to one's descendants than to one's reincarnation. Many Jaffna Tamils deny the validity of the metempsychosis tradition in Hinduism, and most of them recognize its application only in very limited (mostly astrological) contexts.

TABLE VIII

THE SEASONS IN JAFFNA

Month	Rain	Temperature	Luck
Tai (Jan./Feb.)	little	very cool	good
Māci (Feb./March)	none	warming	middling
Paṅkuṉi (March/April)	none	hot	good
Cittirai (April/May)	none	hot	good
Vaikāci (May/June)	none	hot	good
Āṉi (June/July)	none	hot	good
Āṭi (July/Aug.)	little	less hot	good
Āvaṇi (Aug./Sept.)	none	warm	middling
Puraṭṭāti (Sept./Oct.)	little	cooling	poor
Aippaci (Oct./Nov.)	monsoon	cool	good
Kārtikkai (Nov./Dec.)	monsoon	cool	good
Mārkaḻi (Dec./Jan.)	monsoon	cool	good

SOURCE: Field interviews in Chavakachcheri, Sri Lanka.

and the prognostication is made according to traditions about the interaction or conjunction (*yōkam*) of the house's ruling *nakṣattiram*, planet, and solar house. Thus each celestial body can be said to emanate one of three basic radiations, depending on its conjunction with others; these emanations may be positive, neutral, or negative.

The twelve houses are each likened to parts of the body, and the emanations of specific celestial bodies are themselves addressed specifically to bodily parts and processes. A full accounting of these influences would fill a volume; suffice to say here that, in esoteric astrological canon as well as in unsophisticated Hindu belief, the health, the character, and the career of the body are thought to be deeply subject to planetary and other celestial influences, which produce balance or imbalance. Any kind of disability resulting from astrological forces is termed *tōṣam*, or more specifically, *kiraka tōṣam*, the affliction of the planets. Of these, the most feared are *cevvay tōṣam*, the affliction of Mars, which "heats" the bile too much; *caṉi tōṣam*, the affliction of Saturn, which "cools" the phlegm with its dark, dull, frigid, and slow nature; and *nāka tōṣam*, in this case referring to the affliction of the two lunar nodes, *Rāku* and *Kēṭu*, which are "serpents" causing sterility.

In spite of the notion that the astrological conditions at birth stamp one's fate on one's head, the rituals of the annual round are precisely intended to insulate a person from the very emanations which are supposed to affect his or her fate. They are also intended to take advantage of unusually beneficent periods to fortify the household's mystical order. Some of the festivities are carried on within the house, but there is usually very little question that the household is carrying on the appropriate rite, which is taken to symbolize commitment to the Śaivite virtues that become "good-caste" people (*nalla cātiyarkaḷ*). Veḷḷāḷars claim that, during the heyday of their power and dominion, they prohibited the performance of these rites among the Untouchable castes, permitting only the respectable castes (e.g., Kōviyar, Goldsmiths, and Brahmans) to carry them on. It is still true that few Untouchable households celebrate the full complement of annual ceremonies, simply because they are often quite expensive to put on properly. A Vel̤l̤āl̤ar family that makes a grand show of its life-cycle and calendrical ceremonies will be well known as wealthy; or, to put it in terms more appropriate to Hindu thought, they will be known as a family possessing the great power of mystical order and the consequent ability to give gifts.

V.2. A Calendrical Rite (*tai poṅkal*)

The first day of the month Tai is about three weeks later than the actual winter solstice, but it is nonetheless thought to mark the start of the sun's northward course. It is a time of thanksgiving and celebration, for it marks a change in the weather, which has been dreary and cool. On the first day of Tai, young boys rise before dawn and raise a huge bonfire, which is called pōki poṅkal. On the following day, tai poṅkal, everyone in the household rises early for the poṅkal ceremony, which divines the future of the household for the year to come.

The poṅkal ceremony takes place in a kōlam (ordered space) made for Pil̤l̤aiyār. A kumpam of the god is placed in the kōlam before sunrise, and close to the kumpam are arranged in a bunch a number of cow-dung balls symbolic of Pil̤l̤aiyār, made during the previous month. A poṭṭu of holy ash, sandalwood paste, and vermilion powder is applied to each one. Lamps are lit, and incense is burned to give a sweet odor to the proceedings. A large earthenware pot has been set to boil within the kōlam, and in it is a mixture of milk and water. The fire is fed with palm fronds, and all eagerly await the outcome of the boiling, for the direction in which the solution boils over is thought to indicate the fortunes of the household during the year to come. When the milk boils firecrackers are lit in quick staccato bursts. The direction in which the milk overflows is carefully noted, but it always seems to overflow in the auspicious direction. Rice, along with brown, green, and white gram, and sweets (jaggery, cocoanut, and raisins), is placed into the pot.

When the *poṅkal* is cooked, some of it is taken out and spread on plantain leaves with a cocoanut on each, and other sweet, refreshing offerings--limes, plantains, pomegranate, and mango--are added. Opposite the fire sits a tray of flowers in water. The male head of the household picks up one of the flowers and, facing the sun, asks for the return of its warmth and brilliance. He circumnambulates the square three times, falls to the ground, and places the flower within the *kōlam*. The rest of the family follows suit. Afterwards, some of the *poṅkal* rice is thrown over the roof of the house to appease any envious spirits that might have been watching, and the family enjoys a *panti* festival. The cow-dung Piḷḷaiyārs are taken back to the shrine room, together with some of the milk-rice on a plantain leaf.

At evening, two or three members of the household gather the cow-dung Piḷḷaiyārs together with the milk-rice offering, and take them to be thrown into sacred waters. According to Hindu tradition, they should be thrown into the Ganges or some other sacred river; however, there are no rivers at all in Jaffna, and so a temple pond, or even the sea, suffices for this purpose. Several families may join in this procession.

After the *poṅkal* ceremony, the family's *kuṭimakkaḷ* servants approach the house asking for gifts, and do so with substantially more familiarity than they would on other occasions. In one instance, a Paḷḷar laborer ascended the steps to the verandah begging for gifts, which normally he would not receive for his audacity and temerity. But on *tai poṅkal*, the mystical affliction and the impurity of Untouchables are substantially abated by the altogether auspicious celestial environment, which is the result of the sun's return to its warming, brightening northward course.

The day following tai poṅkal is judged especially auspicious for securing health and fertility for cattle, which are regarded with love and affection by many Hindus. Veḷḷāḷars keep cattle for milk, for dung, for draught plowing, and for pulling carts; they are a cornerstone of agrarian productivity and a foundation of marketing ability for the average farmer. Veḷḷāḷars desire health and increase for cattle nearly as much as they desire them for themselves.

A ceremony takes place in the cow shed, which is carefully swept and smeared with cow-dung. A kōlam of rice flour is made, with men taking the primary roles in this rite. In the center of the kōlam a figure is drawn of a conch shell (caṅku), which symbolizes the Vaisnava god Krishna, the guardian of cows. By late evening, when the cattle have returned to the shed, everyone has taken a head bath, and the cows are then bathed as well. While this is done, the implements required for the milk-rice ceremony are set up in the kōlam. Facing the east are a cow-dung Piḷḷaiyār, a kumpam for Krishna, and a framed lithograph of that god. In front of each object of worship is placed a plantain leaf, on which the worshippers spread rice, betel leaf, areca-nut, and plantains. A cocoanut oil lamp and incense sticks add light and smoke to the offerings.

The rite begins with the breaking of a cocoanut for the god Piḷḷaiyār, and a new ceramic pot is placed on the hearth for the rice boiling. The pot is ornamented with mango and betel leaves, and filled with a mixture of milk and water. When it boils, firecrackers are lit, the lamp is waved before the pot, and rice is placed in the pot ceremonially, each handful being waved before the pot three times before it is thrown in. The rice consists entirely of raw red rice, to which is added green gram (payaru), jaggery, and more milk. On each of the plantain leaves some of the cooked milk-rice is placed, as an offering for the respective images; camphor is lit, and the lamp is waved before the images in adoring worship. Each of the cows receives a poṭṭu, a garland of flowers, and a serving of the consecrated milk-rice. Next the family sits down to eat the remainder of the offering.

The rice that grows in the green expanse of the paddies will not be harvested until the returning sun has made the bunches golden, but shortly after tai poṅkal, a few partially ripened bunches are harvested for a ceremony of thanksgiving. The male head of the household goes to the field on the auspicious day for the rite, which occurs on a day in Tai set out in the Pancāṅkam. He gathers a bunch of the partly ripened rice, brings it home, and places it on a large winnowing fan (culaku). This fan is kept in the shrine room of the house. He lights a lamp and camphor, ties together a few sheafs of the grain, and hangs them from a rafter. The rest is hung from a rafter of the verandah or placed in the sun to dry. After two or three days in the sun, the rice is dry enough to be hulled, and thus made into raw red rice, which will be boiled on the full moon day of the month (Tai pūcam). The ceremony, which is a poṅkal or milk-rice offering, occurs in the mid-morning. It lacks the ceremony and detail of tai poṅkal or maṭṭu poṅkal; the boiling, for instance, is done in the kitchen, and instead of making a kōlam the offerings are merely taken to the shrine room of the house. But its importance should not be underestimated. To "take the first fruits" of one's rice is to participate physically in a process that was initiated with the construction of the home and with the Veḷḷāḷar family's resolution to confront and control the powers of this world. From the benefit of palaṉ deriving from that confrontation, the family has earned not only prestige, but also the ability to ensure the fertility of the earth that it controls. Thus, to take the first fruits is tantamount to gaining closure on the remarkable ritual process by which a dignified, civilized life is created on this earth.

Chapter 6

THE NATURE OF SUDRA DOMINATION

> Who is as alive as he who,
>   though now dead,
> once gave a gift,
> and who is as dead as he who,
>   though now alive,
> once took one?
>
> --Irāmāvatāram, trans. Shulman (1980:334)

The ritual design of Sudra domination might well be summarized as an attempt to establish heaven (śrī) on earth, at least to the degree possible, by situating Veḷḷāḷar communities advantageously with respect to cosmic, divine, human, and demonic powers. At the heart of the design is the assumption that the Sudra, like the goddess Mariyammaṉ or the useful demons, can be ordered so long as he stands correctly within the vortex of powers which surround him. It is precisely the intention of the rituals to so situate him. The rites' goal, however, is not to purify the Veḷḷāḷar, as might be thought if they were equated with the purification rites enjoined in the Śāstra-s. On the contrary, their intention, by controlling and, as it were, focusing the powers of the world, is to create in the person, family, fields, and household of the Veḷḷāḷar an auspicious environment that renders him immune to day-to-day impurities and bestows upon him the enchanting benefit of increase (palaṉ).

While he is judged inferior to the Brahman, whose purity is employed to help create and sustain the ritual foundations of Veḷḷāḷar prestige, the Veḷḷāḷar with his auspicious condition nevertheless stands superior to those non-Brahmans who emulate the Brahmanical style of separation and independence from life's polluting exchanges. The Vel̤l̤āl̤ar's auspicious condition, which fosters the bounteous reproduction of all life and legitimates his claim to master the agrarian means of reproduction, is conferred upon him when he is shown before the village to possess primacy in imbibing the sanctified substance of the gods themselves and to dwell within the compass of their radiant power. Whether the rites are "transcendental" or "pragmatic," "Brahmanical" or "non-Brahmanical," "textual" or "non-textual," the aim is all along exactly the same, and reveals the comprehensive and architectonic syncretism which Tamil folk--Brahmans and Sudras working together for centuries--have made of the Gangetic and the Dravidian traditions in Indic civilization.

The Vel̤l̤āl̤ar achievement is highly esteemed among Tamil Hindus of all castes because it very successfully reconciles the unresolved conflict of Hindu society. As Heesterman defines it, this conflict issues from the "insoluble problem"--death--with which "all tradition is essentially concerned." In the Hindu tradition, "as the oldest ritual texts make clear, society is felt to be based on the alternation of life and death; and consequently, participation in society's web of relations is felt to be tantamount to continual involvement with death" (1972:101). The high standing of the Brahman stems from his having partly transcended the problem by turning his back on life, but the price he must pay is to forego a lusty involvement in life's alluring affairs. Alternatively, to be involved in life is to become involved with death; it is, therefore, to submit to the blunting of one's spirituality and the lowering of one's status. Yet the Hindu tradition, as O'Flaherty notes (1972:38), demands both strategies of a man: he is supposed to separate himself from this world and get in touch with the infinite; yet, at the same time, he is supposed to marry and to father sons so his ancestors' shades will not be neglected in the obligatory annual obsequies (*śraddha*). The Veḷḷāḷar way is not that of the Brahman; indeed, the Veḷḷāḷar is inferior to the Brahman, but by no means is his achievement less celebrated. What the Brahman achieves by separating himself from this world is easy enough, while Veḷḷāḷars accomplish what had been deemed difficult, if not impossible: they throw themselves into this world with a profound lust for the mundane, for the soil, for farming, and for the battle to win fame. And yet at the same time they achieve a transcendence--not of the individual, but rather of the social collectivity, within whose ordered precincts flourishes *śrī*, everlasting life. It is for this reason that, at least traditionally, the Veḷḷāḷar had no quarrel with his seemingly low *varṇa* rank, that of the lowly Sudra. The index of his great victory, before which all Hindus would have to stand in amazement, was that he could be so low, so mundane, and indeed so impure, and still bring before everyone the miracle of *śrī*.

Just as the Veḷḷāḷar possesses an entitlement which makes his lack of great purity irrelevant, so too does his low status counterpart, the *aṭimai* or "left-hand" Untouchable, possess a disorder (*tōṣam*) that makes his lack of great impurity irrelevant. Veḷḷāḷars rank below the Brahman exemplars of purity, but due to their power, they stand above the non-Brahmanical emulators of the Brahmanical style. Similarly, the *aṭimai* Untouchables rank above the Paṟaiyar exemplars of impurity; but owing to their disorder, they rank below the non-Untouchable castes that, like the Washerman and fishing castes, are far more involved with blood and with death. The entitlement of the Veḷḷāḷar and the disorder of the Untouchable serve, in short, to warp the Sastric ranking framework, which would impute high status and Aryan privileges only to those castes that follow the purity ideal and try to separate themselves from worldly affairs.

But it is essential to distinguish the "warping" that this Tamil ideology of rank introduces from that postulated by Dumont (1981) and Mandelbaum (1970), who have come to similar conclusions when faced with the anomalies of Sudra domination. Both authors have postulated the presence on the Indian scene of a Western form of domination, one based on the strategies of calculating, rational actors who are ready and willing to subvert their tradition if it serves their economic and political interests. Dumont has pointed out that this strategy, which is indistinguishable from the arbitrary, selfish individualism of the bourgeois capitalist, has at least some ancestry in the classical texts, viz., in the concept of artha, or "action conforming to selfish [and individual] interests." The claims of the Sudra dominant caste to high status--claims which are put forward in myriad rituals of giving and taking, of serving and being served, and of the village deities--are depicted in the literature as devices to shore up a power which, judged in traditional terms, has only the weakest foundation in ancient tradition. As Geertz has recently reminded us, this view of political ritual blends only too well with the "'great beast' views of the state that . . . locate its power in its threat to harm." For such views,

> the function of the parade and ceremony of public life is to strike terror into the minds that threat confronts.. . .it is a dark noise to impress the impressionable and to induce in them a trembling awe.. . . [Or] the conception of state ceremony is more one of mystification, in the sense of the spiritualizing of material interests and the fogging over of material conflicts. Political symbology is political ideology, and political ideology is class hypocrisy (1980:122).

Ritual, in these views, is a device or artifice used to confirm and to increase the strength of those whose primary aim is to attain mastery and domination over others. Resonating with this view is the idea that it is the coercive force of Sudra domination which maintains the status inequality of village life from generation to generation, as the caste system comes to be reproduced without revolutionary change. However appealing this assumption may appear to us, it is nearly useless for comprehending the intention of Sudra domination.

So far from using rituals to achieve wealth and political power, the Sudra dominant caste uses its wealth and mastery over subordinate castes to create rituals whose ultimate aim is to establish Hindu civilization in its Dravidian recension and to preserve--under South Indian conditions--the spirit, at least, of the social order exemplified in the varṇāśrama dharma. To be sure, the form of social order that Sudras establish departs from the Sastric ranking paradigm; but from the Veḷḷāḷar standpoint, as it is revealed to us in their myths, their temple inscriptions, and their rituals, the discrepancies of the Sastric paradigm and the Tamil caste system are very minor matters considering the great victory that has been achieved: the preservation of Hindu civilization. It is of course true that the encompassed ideology, the quintessentially Tamil ranking ideology that constitutes as meaningful the curiously anomalous ranks of Veḷḷāḷars and of the aṭimai Untouchables, contradicts in many respects the encompassing, Sastric ideology. But this contradiction, evident to an outside observer, is hardly relevant to the Brahmans, the Sudras, and the compliant kuṭimai or "right-hand" castes whose interests are well met by emphasizing the smooth synchronization of the two ranking systems. The contradiction is indeed there, and it is emphasized in the rebellious strategies of the "left-hand" castes. Nonetheless, Veḷḷāḷars by no means intend to subvert or warp any aspect of their tradition when they establish their domination. On the contrary, they firmly believe and will indeed state that in doing what Veḷḷāḷars do (including the imposition of opprobrious features of dress, etc., on Untouchables) they are acting in consonance with ancient obligations and traditional rectitude.

If Vel̤l̤āl̤ar domination is ill comprehended by defining it as arbitrary and pragmatic with respect to tradition, it is even more misunderstood by the suggestion that it represents the presence on the Hindu social scene of selfish individualism. The Vel̤l̤āl̤ar achievement is a collective, not an individual, attainment. The deities in all the village rites, for instance, focus their blessings not on individuals so much as on lineages and on kindreds; the patron represents not merely himself but also his kin group, which shares in both the benefits and the obligations stemming from the bond that has been forged with the deity. So far from representing the presence of a form of individualism on the Indian scene, Sudra domination instead reveals to us an attempt to invest _śrī_ in a self-perpetuating human community, from which individuals must ultimately be sundered by disease and death. Indeed, a Vel̤l̤āl̤ar who becomes afflicted deems himself sundered from the benefits of village ritual, and throws himself on the mercy of the autochthonous, miracle-working pilgrimage deity (Pfaffenberger 1979, 1980). When a man sickens and dies, the rituals that had once given him vitality fail him, and he becomes a danger to his kinsmen and to the order that has been established in the village. In short, Sudra domination is a community achievement, which abandons individuals without mercy when they are no longer capable of receiving the benefits of the ritual process.

The aim of Sudra domination, furthermore, is not mastery over men and land as much as it is the attaining of greatness, fame, and generosity--the qualities of the "great man" (_cāṉṟōṉ_) of ancient Tamil literature. A form of mastery certainly emerges, limited in scope and hedged about with obligations, as Vel̤l̤āl̤ars seek fame as the creators of agrarian abundance. Yet the domination that Vel̤l̤āl̤ars establish, especially under the traditional quasi-stateless conditions of Dravidian political systems, is sharply limited by the role of the ritual entitlement process in creating the statuses of Vel̤l̤āl̤ars and of the aṭimai Untouchables. Under traditional conditions, Vel̤l̤āl̤ars could create only the most limited domain, one bounded, finally, by the maximum extent of face-to-face relations in which identities, established and publicly confirmed in ritual, are known in a locality. Vel̤l̤āl̤ar power, such as it is, stands only to the extent that an individual can be invested with a publicly known status, which then absorbs him and constitutes his "caste" identity. Where a man is not known, his status and identity--beyond the rough clues of dialect and manners that cannot be disguised --do not exist, and he may therefore define them as he sees fit. On the periphery of Vel̤l̤āl̤ar domination (the dry lands, the jungles, and the cities), other non-Brahman castes pursue their various strategies of repudiating (or reproducing) Vel̤l̤āl̤ar control and establishing an autonomous niche in the overarching political framework of Dravidian society. Within the limited domain of Vel̤l̤āl̤ar authority, the traditional great men of the village functioned not so much as exploiters, but rather as redistributors, basking in the prestige which accrues to those who, despite their lowly, mundane state, nonetheless bring to this world the ambrosia of the gods.

That Vel̤l̤āl̤ars celebrate their achievement by reveling in their mundanity is at once the victory and the frailty of Sudra domination. The very foundations of Sudra authority presuppose the legitimate grounds on which it may be resisted or reproduced. Unless we are willing to recognize the limitations and frailty of Vel̤l̤āl̤ar domination, we shall be hard pressed to comprehend why it has persisted for so many centuries in the traditional South Indian social formation. We are tempted to suppose that Vel̤l̤āl̤ars have maintained caste relations in Tamil villages because they possess incontrovertible and irresistible control over them. In this we are abetted all along by the "great beast" theories of domination which have become deeply imbedded in the way Western-oriented scholars view the universe. While it is certainly true that the dominant cultivating caste uses force to uphold its claims to prestige and to the management of agrarian reproduction, I believe it is more correct to say that the Dravidian social formation was reproduced not because Veḷḷāḷar domination was so strong, but rather because it was so weak. Rooted in a system of ritual entitlement that could integrate only the smallest of realms, Veḷḷāḷar domination--notwithstanding the fact that it is founded in beliefs profoundly accepted by everyone in the system--could hardly stem the tide of legitimate mobility efforts, one outcome of which was to reproduce Veḷḷāḷar domination on the periphery of settlement.

Sudra domination, in sum, is not essentially about domination in the Western sense of coercion, ideological mystification, and mastery. Those truly concerned with mastery would surely have chosen some more comprehensive and less vulnerable formula of rule. It is rather that Sudra domination is essentially about the obligation, which only the courageous take on, to make of this wicked and afflicted life a mirror of _śrī_ and of the peace which is heaven, reproducing under South Indian conditions the essence (if not the exact form) of the civilizational order mandated by the _varṇāśrama dharma_. We should not be surprised, then, that dominant Sudra cultivators in South India possess a high rank. In the Tamil view of the universe, it is undeniable that--as it was written centuries ago in the _Caṅkam_ poetry--"this world is because these men are."

APPENDIX I: GLOSSARY OF INDIC TERMS*

ākama. Sacred writings, especially the temple-building manuals, which are of medieval, South Indian provenance.

ākama kōyil. A temple, staffed with Brahmaṉs, which is built and maintained according to the temple-building texts (ākama-s).

akaṅkāram. Egotism, selfishness, rashness; a demonic characteristic.

Ammaṉ. Village goddess (kirāma teyvam), esp. a virgin goddess who must be ritually "cooled" in the rite called kuḷirtti ("cooling, refreshing offerings") if the village is to be free from drought and from infectious diseases.

aṉṉāvi. Teacher; in Jaffna ritual, the holder of the ropes attached to the flesh of the kāvaṭi dancer.

apisēkam. Anointing rite which establishes the authority of the king (from the Sanskrit abhisēka); in temple worship, anointing rite which establishes the sanctity of the deity.

artha*. One of the four ends of life as outlined in the varṇāśrama dharma: the selfish pursuit of wealth, power, and pleasure (Sanskrit).

aruḷ. The grace of ākama deities, and in particular, their granting of an ambience in which benefits (palaṉ, "increase") may be experienced.

aruṟcakti. "Grace-force," aruḷ + cakti (power)

āśauca*. The impurity consequent upon birth and death which disqualifies agnatic kinsmen from participation in auspicious rituals (Sanskrit). *See also* tuṭakku.

atikār. An authoritative person with the legitimate right to command; a chieftain, esp. in the sense of a landholder possessing authority by virtue of ritual entitlement (from the Sanskrit adhikāra).

aṭimai. "Aboriginal" or "stranger" castes in the Jaffna caste system, defined as "slaves" in the Dutch colonial period (probably inaccurately). These castes (Koviyār, Naḷavar, Paḷḷar, and the no longer extant "Chiandos") were incorporated into the rural framework of Veḷḷālar domination by coercion, as were the "left-side" agricultural laborers of South India (the Paḷḷars were known in South India as a "left-side" caste). The term appears to be derived from the root aṭi, "bottom of a thing, foot, beginning, source," hence, aboriginality equals lowness.

āvi. Ghost, especially of a recent suicide.

bhakti*. Devotion and love for God (Sanskrit). Tamil: pakti.

cakti. Power, strength, vitality, esp. as it arises, in women, from chastity (karpu), and, in men, through a connection (totarpu) with a powerful female.

cakuṉam. An omen or portent, esp. one which in its very nature is not a sign of misfortune but is the very substance of misfortune, e.g., the appearance within the household of a wild creature.

cāṇḍāla*. The outcaste or Untouchable in the Sanskrit textual tradition, distinguished from respectable Sudras on grounds of a lack of domestic rituals and other estimable customs.

cāṉṟōn. The "great man" of the ancient Tamil literature, the one who is full of the power granted to him by the chastity of his wife and by the ordering of his sacred objects.

cantaṉam. *See* piracātam.

cantati. The patrilineal kin group in Jaffna, linked to the sapinda lineage of the classical Hindu tradition. In Jaffna as in the texts, the lineage is felt to consist of all those who share "one body" (orē otampu). But in Jaffna (as opposed to the classical tradition) the cantati is counted to include three generations both ascendant and descendant from Ego. Women change their cantati membership on marriage, joining their husband's group. Cantati members share death pollution (tuṭakku) and together enjoy the benefits should one of them serve as a temple patron (yajamāna) at an ākama shrine.

*Non-Tamil terms are marked with an asterisk.

cānti. A cooling, refreshing rite, which removes the "heat" (cutu) and depradation (kurai) of demonic influences (tōsam).

capam. A curse.

capa tōsam. The affliction resulting from a curse.

cāti. "Caste," in the sense of a specific and biologically distinct quasi-species.

cāttiri. Astrologer.

contakkārar. Kin, those bound together by possessing the "same body" (orē otampu). In Jaffna, this term refers to the bilateral kindred, which is further subdivided into kittiya contakkārar ("close kin") and tūra contakkārar ("distant kin").

cummā. Freely, ordinarily, easily, without restriction, carelessly.

cūran. Demon (literary).

cuttam. Purity, cleanliness, esp. that resulting from a bath.

cuttam illātu. Impurity, esp. that resulting from contact with impure objects and personages. See also tīttu, tuppuravu illai, tutakku.

cutu. "Heat," esp. of the body, a popular understanding of the Ayurvedic tradition of medicine, in which health is understood to be disrupted by imbalances in the natural harmony of the body's three humors (wind, phlegm, and bile).

ekkaccakkamāna neram. "Awkward times," viz., of celestial transition, in which demonic and other afflicting forces are in the ascendant.

garbhagrha*. See mūlastānam (Sanskrit).

ista teyvam. The desired god, the beloved (bhakti) god, chosen by a person to help him or her overcome "obstacles" (kastam) or affliction (tōsam).

jajmān*. The landholder and master of many persons of subordinate caste status (from the Sanskrit yajamāna) whose privileges issue from ritual entitlement (Hindi).

jajmani system*. The system of caste interrelationships first described by Wiser (1958) in a North Indian village. Emphasizing the interdependence of families of many different castes, the system focuses on a landholding family who maintains hereditary and durable relations with their servants and helpers, who are in turn compensated with a share of the food-growing family's produce.

kalai. Incarnation, esp. the appearance of a deity in the body of his or her priest (pūcāri).

kannūru. Evil eye, lit. "eye misfortune," an affliction resulting from an envious glance.

karpu. The chastity of a woman, esp. virginity before marriage and faithfulness to her husband afterwards, which produces a power (cakti) of benefit to her family.

kastam. Difficulty, obstacle, trouble, esp. one resulting from demonic or astrological depradations.

kāttu mirānti. Bumpkin, primitive, Veddah, "fool of the jungle."

kattuppātu. Social and sexual order, esp. in the sense of the civility resulting when the eighteen castes (the conventional epithet for the jajmani subordinates of the Sudra dominant caste) perform their proper roles and women are sedulously secluded.

kāvati. Shoulder-pole, a carried wooden yoke decorated with peacock feathers, tinsēl, colored paper, a lime, and often containing a small container of milk. A common feature in ritual, the kāvati is carried by those who perform vow fulfillment (nērtikkatan).

kettavarkal. "Bad people," low castes, sorcerers, Untouchables, Muslims.

ketuti. Evil, loss, reduction, esp. as a result of human envy, fear, and anger.

kiraka tōsam. Disorder consequent upon the malevolent aspect of planets (esp. Saturn) in one's astrological chart. See tōsam.

kirāmam. Village; the unit of space defined by the limits of power of the village goddess (Ammaṉ).

kirāma teyvam. Village deities, the gods of the Sudras, esp. the village goddess (Ammaṉ).

kittiya contakkārar. "Close kin," in Jaffna, a bilateral kindred including any and all persons with whom Ego feels to be closely related (often including some persons whose genealogical relations are unclear).

kōlam. A purified, ordered space, within which the apparition of the gods is possible and suitable.

koṭūramāṉa. Disordered, angry (said of a deity).

kōyil. Temple, lit., "king's house."

kōyilmaiyam. Temple axis, power space.

kula teyvam. Tutelary deity, the protector of a bilateral kindred, an agnatic lineage, or the ward of a caste in Jaffna religious life.

kuḷir. Cool, coldness, esp. in the popular understanding of the Ayurvedic medical tradition, as a disorder (tōṣam) of the phlegm; hence, "phlegmatic," in the extremity, an illness (potentially fatal) manifesting itself in indolence.

kuḷirtti. Cooling, refreshing offerings, esp. the offerings made to ensure the pacific temperament of the goddess.

kumpam. A decorated brass vessel which serves as a representation of the gods in rituals.

kuṅkamum. *See* piracātam.

kuṟai. Waste, devastation, esp. that caused by demons.

kuṟainta cāti. Low caste, lit., "caste [found] wanting."

kuṟṟam. Impurity, offense, sin, transgression.

kuṭimai. "Professional" castes (conventionally eighteen in number) in the Jaffna caste system; each is presumed to possess some inherited fitness (tanmai, "nature, essence") that qualifies it for a specific traditional occupation (both "religious" and "secular").

kuṭimakkaḷ. The Veḷḷāḷar lord's servants and retainers.

liṅkam. Stone representation of Śiva.

maṇāvalakkōlam. "Ordering the bridegroom," a ritual in which a godling is treated to a ritually induced ordering and becomes capable of bestowing benefits on his worshippers.

mantiram. Sacred incantation, which controls deities and spirits.

mantiravāti. Sorcerer.

mariyātai. Honors, esp. those given by the priest to the temple patron (yajamāna) in ākama temple ritual.

maṭai. Rice meal offering made to ancestral shades (pitir-s) at the annual, obligatory obsequies; also presented to lowly godlings and goddesses who are presumed to have once lived as men and women.

mleccha*. Barbarian, member of a group dwelling outside the compass of Hindu civilization and opposing its basic tenets (Sanskrit).

mukti. Liberation; absorption into the body of Śiva.

mūlastānam. The sanctum sanctorum of the ākama shrine; the womb-like chamber in which the seed of divinity is kept and nurtured.

muṉi. Demon.

muṟai. Rules, order, esp. the rules of ritual by which civilization and dignity are achieved.

nāka tōṣam. "Snake trouble," the affliction (tōṣam) of serpents.

nalla cātiyarkaḷ. "Good caste people" (as opposed to keṭṭavarkaḷ) who observe the restrictions (kaṭṭuppāṭu) incumbent upon the civilized.

nampikai. Faith.

nāvūru. "Tongue misfortune," the affliction resulting from envious praise or curses.

nērttikkaṭan. Vow fulfillment.

palan. Benefit of a rite; growth, increase resulting from worship, gain, result, advantage, reward.

palaṅkālattu muraikaḷ. Ancient ways, the ancient Tamil customs (murai) by which dignity and civilization may be achieved.

paṅku. Share, esp. that of a temple or a field held by a group of kinsmen.

panti. Feast of kinsmen following a ritual.

pariyalaṅkaḷ. Retinue of spirits attached to a shrine.

pariyāri. Ayurvedic physician.

pēy. Spirit.

pēy āṭṭam. The "dance" which is deemed to reveal spirit possession.

pēy piṭikkiratu. Spirit possession, a potentially deadly affliction.

piracātam. Consecrated offerings, which include (at the minimum) vīpūti (holy ash), cantanam (sandalwood paste), tīrttam (consecrated water), pū (flowers), and kuṅkamum (vermilion powder).

pitir. Ancestral shades.

poṅkal. Milk-rice.

poṭṭu. Sacred forehead mark of Śaivites, made with sandalwood paste (cantanam), holy ash (vīpūti), and vermilion powder (kuṅkamum); refers also to the black smudge often applied to childrens' foreheads to ward off the evil eye.

pūcai. Pūja, the offering of flowers.

pūcāri. Non-Brahman priest who often uses ecstatic trance states (kalai) to communicate with the deities.

Sastric*. Of or relating to the Dharmaśāstra-s, the classical legal manuals.

Śrī*. Everlasting life, youth, vibrancy; the possession of the gods (Sanskrit).

talaiviti. Fate (lit., "head-writing"), discerned in an astrological chart, and supposed to represent one's karma (retribution) for actions in a previous existence.

tāntōnri teyvam. "Self-born god," one manifested by his or her own volition without any invocational rituals.

tīrttam. Bath, esp. a pilgrimage site associated with a sacred spring or river (e.g., Keerimalai); *see also* piracātam.

toṇṭu. Services to the deities provided by various castes in temple rituals.

tōsam. Disorder, esp. the imbalance of the three bodily humors in Ayurvedic medicine; more generally, an affliction brought on by attacking forces, such as autochthonous deities, spirits, or cosmological emanations, typified by madness, sterility, ill fortune, "heat" (cūṭu), and the decrease of fertility.

toṭarpu. "Biological" connection, such as that provided by kinship, by the rite which links the temple owner to the divine substance in the temple, or by divine incarnation (kalai).

tuppuravu illai. Impurity, uncleanliness, esp. that consequent upon "not having bathed, eating meat, drinking alcohol, getting a haircut, the excreta of animals, bad smells, and an untidy home" (Ryan 1980:196); used also (euphemistically) to refer to the impurity (permanent) of Untouchables. For touchable castes, tuppuravu illai is dispelled by a bath.

tuṭakku. Pollution consequent on a cantati when a birth or death occurs within it.

upacarittal. To treat with civility; the sixteen reverences due to a king or lord.

uyir. Life, breath.

vaḷarntukkāran. Pot-giver; a ritual office at the shrines of village deities, usually shared with other members of the priest's bilateral kindred. The pot-giver is obliged to present a large pot of milk-rice at the deity's annual festival. *See also* vaḷarntupponkal.

vaḷarntupponkal. "Large pot of milk-rice," a ritual which establishes the greatness of Sudra pot-givers.

vanni. Dry jungles.

varṇa*. Caste-category; one of the four Sastric categories (Brahman, Ksatriya, Vaisya, Sudra) (Sanskrit).

varṇāśrama dharma*. Duties of the four stages of life (āśrama) and four caste-categories (varna-s) as enshrined in the classical legal texts (Dharmaśāstra-s); more broadly, the holistic design of caste interdependence that characterizes the essence of Hindu social tradition (Sanskrit).

vēḷvi. Blood sacrifice; the giving of a life (uyir) to a deity or demon.

vīpūti. *See* piracātam.

viratam. Fast.

yajamāna*. Patron of the rites in the classical ritual tradition (Sanskrit).

APPENDIX II. RITUAL ROLES OF THE CASTES OF JAFFNA

Caste	Rite	Deity Propitiated and/or Ritual Duties	Suitability of Caste for Role	Compensation
Brahman	dispelling poḻlution	assembled gods	inherited fitness, learnedness, purity	raw rice, cocoanuts, cash
"	haircutting rite	Kantacāmi, Ammaṉ	"	fruit, camphor, cash, milk rice, oil cakes (which the priest himself cooks)
"	wedding	assembled gods	"	cash, copious amounts of rice
"	thirty-first day rite	assembled gods	"	sandals, umbrella, copious amounts of rice, cocoanuts
"	annual obsequies	assembled gods	"	rice, cocoanuts, raw vegetables, curry spices, fruits, cash
"	ordering the bride-groom	Piḷḷaiyār	"	rice, cocoanuts, cash
"	temple rites	temple deities	"	salary
Śaiva Kurukkal	funerary rites	assembled gods	"	rice, cocoanuts, cash
"	temple rites at certain non-Brahman temples	temple deities	"	salary

APPENDIX II -- *continued*

Kōviyar	wedding	none; duties are to carry the groom's palanquin, to cook the feast, and to serve the guests	sudra status, attitude of reverence and desire to be of service	rice, cash, meal that the family also eats
"	milk-rice kulirtti	cook offerings for Amman	"	"
"	temple rites	cook offerings for gods, assist in temple ceremonies	"	rice, cash
"	funerary rites	none; duty is to carry the bier of the deceased	"	rice, cash, meal that the family also eats
Goldsmith	gold melting rite	none; duty is to forge the tali	inherited fitness	cash
Pantāram	ordering the bridegroom	make garland for the ordered demigod	"	cash, rice, cocoanuts
"	temple rites	make garlands for deity; assist in preparing the god's image	"	"
Nattuvar	ordering the bridegroom	none; duty is to play auspicious music	"	rice, cash
"	wedding	"	"	cash

APPENDIX II -- *continued*

Carpenter	laying the foundation	appease c̄uran with new foundation items	inherited fitness	role is included in the Carpenter's salary for constructing the home
"	occupying the new home	appease Mū Tēvi	"	"
Washerman	menses	none; duty is to remove soiled menstrual cloth	"	share of annual rice crop
"	dispelling pollution	"	"	"
"	attainment festivity	none; duty is to tie white cloths on roof rafters and remove soiled menstrual cloths	"	share of annual rice crop, share of panti feast
"	wedding	none; duty is to tie white cloths on the rafters of the wedding booth	"	cash, share of annual rice crop, portion of family's feast
"	funerary rites	none; duty is to tie white cloths on the rafters of the "head room where the corpse is kept	"	cash, rice, share of annual rice crop
"	ordering the bride-groom	none; duty is to tie white cloths for the temple festival	"	"
"	temple rites	"	"	"

APPENDIX II -- *continued*

UNTOUCHABLE RITUAL ROLES				
Barber	birthing	Korriyar, Mū Tēvi are propitiated by the Barber midwife	inherited fitness	cash, rice, curry spices offered to disorder, share of rice crop
"	hair cutting rite	affliction (tōsam) of the child is removed	"	"
"	ablution	affliction (tōsam) of the girl is removed by the Barber's wife	"	cash, rice and curry offered to disorder, share of rice crop
"	removal of evil eye	affliction (kānnūru) of the girl is removed by the Barber's wife	"	cash, afflicted offerings, share of annual rice crop
"	menses cooling	affliction (tōsam) of the girl is removed by the Barber's wife	"	"
"	wedding	none; shaves groom	"	cash, share of annual rice crop, portion of family's panti feast
"	funerary rites	controls spirit of the deceased by facilitating the spirit's exit from the body and by keeping a portion of the remains for one month	"	"

APPENDIX II -- *continued*

Naḷavar, Paḷḷar, or Barber	birthing	Korriyār, Mū Tēvi are propitiated by the Naḷavar or Paḷ-ḷar midwife	none; can be done by any low status person	rice and curry which have been offered to disor-dered deities
"	funerary rites	none; tend pyre	"	pollution; meals, arrack, cash
"	summer solstice	shades of ancestors	"	maṭai offerings
"	annual obsequies	"	"	"
"	maṭai	Kāḷi	"	"
"	milk-rice kuḷirtti	none; duty is to clean grounds, climb trees to get cocoanuts	"	cash, arrack, part of offerings
"	ordering rites for demigods	demigods; sacrifice goat and chicken to dispel peripheral spirits	"	portion of the afflicted offerings
"	ordering the bride-groom	clean grounds, pick cocoanuts	"	cash, arrack, part of offerings
"	temple rites	"	"	"
"	cutting a well	well-spirit	"	all of afflicted offerings
Paraiyar	birthing rites	retinue of spirits controlled by drumming	inherited fitness	cash, share of annual rice crop

APPENDIX II -- *continued*

Paraiyar	funerary rites	none; duty is to announce the death	inherited fitness	cash, share of annual rice crop, cloth from death room
"	milk-rice kulirtti	Amman, made manifest by drumming	"	cash, share of annual rice crop
"	ordering rites for demigods	demigods, made manifest by drumming	"	share of animal sacrificed to disordered, peripheral spirits
"	temple rites	retinue of spirits, controlled by drumming around perimeter of temple	"	cash, arrack, share of annual rice crop

SOURCE: Field interviews and observations near Chavakachcheri, Jaffna District, Sri Lanka, 1973-1975.

BIBLIOGRAPHY

Anonymous (trans.)
1827 Hindu History of Ceylon. *Asiatic Journal and Monthly Register for British India and Its Dependencies* 24:51-54, 153-55.

Appadurai, Arjun
1974 Right and Left Hand Castes in South India. *Indian Economic and Social History Review* 11:216-60.

Appadurai, Arjun, and Carol Breckenridge
1976 The South Indian Temple: Authority, Honor, and Redistributions. *Contributions to Indian Sociology* n.s., 10:187-209.

Arumainayagam, K.
1976a Caste in Jaffna. *Tribune* (Colombo), May 9, 1976, pp. 18-19.
1976b Caste in Jaffna - 2. *Tribune* (Colombo), May 29, 1976, pp. 10-11.

Babb, Lawrence A.
1975 *The Divine Hierarchy: Popular Religion in Central India.* New York: Columbia University Press.

Baldeus, Phillipus
1958-1959 A True and Exact Description of the Great Island of Ceylon. P. Brohier, trans. *Ceylon Historical Journal* 8: nos. 1-4. Originally published 1672.

Banks, Michael
1957 "The Social Organization of the Jaffna Tamils of North Ceylon, with Special Reference to Kinship, Marriage, and Inheritance." Ph.D. dissertation, Cambridge University.

1960 Caste in Jaffna. In *Aspects of Caste in South India, Ceylon, and North-West Pakistan.* E.R. Leach, ed. Pp. 61-77. Cambridge: Cambridge University Press.

Basham, A.L.
1954 *The Wonder That Was India.* New York: Grove Press.

Beck, Brenda E.F.
1969 Colour and Heat in South Indian Ritual. *Man* n.s., 4:553-72.

1970 The Right-Left Division of South Indian Society. *Journal of Asian Studies* 29:779-98.

1972 *Peasant Society in Koṅku: A Study of Right and Left Subcastes in South India.* Vancouver: University of British Columbia Press.

1974 The Kin Nucleus in Tamil Folklore. In *Kinship in Indian History.* T.R. Trautman, ed. Pp. 1-28. Ann Arbor: University of Michigan Center for South and Southeast Asia Studies.

Beck, Brenda E.F.
1976 Centers and Boundaries of Regional Caste Systems: Toward a General Model. In *Regional Analysis, II, Social Systems.* Carol Smith, ed. Pp. 255-88. New York: Academic Press.

Béteille, Andre
1969 *Caste, Class and Power: Changing Patterns of Stratification in a Tanjore Village.* Berkeley: University of California Press.

Bharati, Agehananda
1965 *The Tantric Tradition.* London: Rider.

Bremen, Jan
1974 *Patronage and Exploitation: Changing Agrarian Relations in South Gujarat, India.* Berkeley: University of California Press.

Cartman, Reverend James
1957 *Hinduism in Ceylon.* Colombo: M.D. Gunasena.

Casie Chetty, Simon
1847-1848 On the History of Jaffna, From the Earliest Period to the Dutch Conquest. *Journal of the Ceylon Branch of the Royal Asiatic Society* 3:69-79.

Chelliah, J.V.
1962 *Pattupattu: Ten Tamil Idylls.* Tinnevelly: South Indian Saiva Siddhanta Works Publishing Society.

Clothey, Fred
1969 Skanda-Sasti: A Festival in Tamil India. *History of Religions* 8:236-59.

David, Kenneth
1974 And Never the Twain Shall Meet? Mediating the Structural Approaches to Caste Ranking. In *Structural Approaches to South Indian Studies.* H.M. Buck and G. Yocum, eds. Pp. 43-80. Chambersburg, PA: Wilson College Press.

1976 Hierarchy and Equivalence in Jaffna, North Ceylon: Normative Codes as Mediators. In *The New Wind: Changing Identities in South Asia.* K. David, ed. Pp. 179-226. The Hague: Mouton.

Dumont, Louis
1957 *Une Sous-Caste de l'Inde du Sud. Organization sociale et religion des Primalai Kallar.* Paris: La Haye.

1981 *Homo Hierarchicus: The Caste System and Its Implications.* Complete Revised English Edition. Chicago: University of Chicago Press.

Elmore, Wilbur Theodore
1915 Dravidian Gods in Modern Hinduism: A Study of the Local and Village Gods of Southern India. *University Studies (University of Nebraska)* 15:1-149.

Fabricius, J.P.
1910 *A Dictionary: Tamil and English.* Tranquebar: Evangelical Lutheran Publishing House.

Farmer, B.H.
1957 Ceylon. In *India and Pakistan: A General and Regional Geography.* O.H.K. Spate, ed. Pp. 745-86. London: Methuen.

Geertz, Clifford
1980 *Negara: The Theatre State in Nineteenth Century Bali.* Princeton: Princeton University Press.

Gluckman, Max
1965 Ritual and Office in Tribal Society. In *Essays on the Ritual of Social Relations.* M. Gluckman, ed. Pp. 53-88. Manchester: Manchester University Press.

Goffman, Erving
1963 *Stigma: Notes on the Management of Spoiled Identity.* Englewood Cliffs, NJ: Prentice-Hall.

Gonda, Jan
1965 *Change and Continuity in Indian Religion.* The Hague: Mouton.

1969 *Ancient Indian Kingship from the Religious Point of View.* Leiden: E.J. Brill.

Gough, E. Kathleen
1955 The Social Structure of a Tanjore Village. In *Village India: Studies in the Little Community.* McKim Marriott, ed. Pp. 36-52. Chicago: University of Chicago Press.

1960 Caste in a Tanjore Village. In *Aspects of Caste in South India, Ceylon, and North-West Pakistan.* E.R. Leach, ed. Pp. 11-60. Cambridge: Cambridge University Press.

Gould, Harold A.
1964 The Jajmani System of North India: Its Structure, Magnitude, and Meaning. *Ethnology* 3:12-41.

Hardgrave, Robert L.
1969 *The Nadars of Tamilnad: The Political Culture of a Community in Change.* Berkeley: University of California Press.

Hart, George L., III
1973 Woman and the Sacred in Ancient Tamilnad. *Journal of Asian Studies* 32:233-50.

Hart, George L., III
1974 Some Aspects of Kinship in Ancient Tamil Literature. In *Kinship and History in South Asia.* T.R. Trautman, ed. Pp. 29-60. Ann Arbor: Center for South and Southeast Asia Studies, University of Michigan.

1975 *The Poems of Ancient Tamil: Their Milieu and Their Sanskritic Counterparts.* Berkeley: University of California Press.

1979 The Nature of Tamil Devotion. In *Aryan and Non-Aryan India.* M.M. Despands and P.E. Hook, eds. Pp. 1-30. Ann Arbor: Center for South and Southeast Asia Studies, University of Michigan.

Heesterman, J.C.
1964 Brahmin, Ritual, and Renouncer. *Wiener Zeitschrift für die Kunde Süd- und Ostasiens* 8:1-31.

1972 India and the Inner Conflict of Tradition. In *Post-Traditional Societies.* S.N. Eisenstadt, ed. Pp. 97-114. New York: W.W. Norton.

Hitchcock, John T.
1958 The Idea of the Martial Rajput. *Journal of American Folklore* 71:216-23.

Hocart, A.M.
1950 *Caste: A Comparative Study.* New York: Russell and Russell.

Hubert, Henri and Marcel Mauss
1964 *Sacrifice: Its Nature and Function.* W.D. Halls, trans. Chicago: University of Chicago Press.

Hudson, Dennis
1978 Siva, Mīnākṣi, Viṣṇu--Reflections on a Popular Myth in Madurai. In *South Indian Temples: An Analytical Reconsideration.* B. Stein, ed. Pp. 107-18. New Delhi: Vikas Publishing House.

Hutton, J.H.
1961 *Caste in India: Its Nature and Function.* Oxford: Oxford University Press.

Inden, Ronald B.
1978 Ritual, Authority, and Cyclic Time in Hindu Kingship. In *Kingship and Authority in South Asia.* J.F. Richards, ed. Pp. 28-73. Madison: South Asia Studies, University of Wisconsin-Madison.

Indrapala, K.
1969 Early Tamil Settlements in Ceylon. *Journal of the Ceylon Branch of the Royal Asiatic Society* n.s., 8:43-63.

Kanakasabhai, K.
1966 *The Tamils Eighteen Hundred Years Ago.* Tinnevelly: The South India Saiva Siddhanta Works Publishing Society.

Kane, P.V.
1974 *History of Dharmaśāstra* (Ancient and Medieval Religious and Civil Law). Vol. II, Part I. 2nd Ed. Poona: Bhandarkar Oriental Research Institute.

1975 *History of Dharmaśāstra* (Ancient and Medieval Religious and Civil Law). Vol. IV. 2nd Ed. Poona: Bhandarkar Oriental Research Institute.

Kaulācāra, Ramachandra
1966 *Śīlpa Prakāśa: Medieval Orissan Sanskrit Text on Temple Architecture.* A. Boner and S.R. Sarma, trans. Leiden: E.J. Brill.

Kearney, Robert N.
1973 *The Politics of Ceylon (Sri Lanka).* Ithaca: Cornell University Press.

Kinsley, David
1977 *The Sword and the Flute: Kāḷi and Kṛṣṇa, Dark Visions of the Terrible and the Sublime in Hindu Mythology.* Berkeley: University of California Press.

Kramrisch, Stella
1976 *The Hindu Temple.* Delhi: Motilal Banarsidas.

Kumar, Dharma
1965 *Land and Caste in South India: Agricultural Labor in the Madras Presidency During the Nineteenth Century.* Cambridge: Cambridge University Press.

Leach, Edmund
1960 Introduction. In *Aspects of Caste in South India, Ceylon, and North-West Pakistan.* E.R. Leach, ed. Pp. 1-10. Cambridge: Cambridge University Press.

1968 Ritual. *International Encyclopedia of the Social Sciences.* New York: Macmillan.

Lewis, J.P.
1884 Tamil Customs and Ceremonies Connected with Paddy Cultivation in the Jaffna District. *Journal of the Ceylon Branch of the Royal Asiatic Society* 8:304-33.

1890 Temples and Superstitions at Chavakachcheri. *Orientalist* 4:5-6.

1920 Folklore from North Ceylon. *Folklore: A Quarterly Review of Myth, Tradition, Institutions, and Custom* 36:176-85.

Lingat, Robert
1973 *The Classical Law of India.* J. Duncan M. Derrett, trans. Berkeley: University of California Press.

Ludden, David
1978 Ecological Zones and the Cultural Economy of Irrigation in Southern Tamilnadu. *Journal of South Asian Studies* n.s., 1:1-13.

Maloney, Clarence
1975 Archaeology in South India: Accomplishments and Prospects. In *Essays on South India.* B. Stein, ed. Pp. 1-40. Honolulu: University of Hawaii Press.

Mandelbaum, D.G.
1966 Transcendental and Pragmatic Aspects of Religion. *American Anthropologist* 68:1174-91.

1970 *Society in India.* Berkeley: University of California Press.

Marriott, McKim
1976 Hindu Transactions: Diversity Without Dualism. In *Transaction and Meaning: New Directions in the Anthropology of Exchange and Symbolic Behavior.* B. Kapferer, ed. Pp. 109-42. Philadelphia: Institute for the Study of Human Issues.

Mayer, Adrian
1966 *Caste and Kinship in Central India: A Village and Its Region.* Berkeley: University of California Press.

Mencher, Joan
1970 A Tamil Village: Changing Socioeconomic Structure in Madras State. In *Change and Continuity in India's Village.* K. Ishwaran, ed. Pp. 197-218. New York: Columbia University Press.

Michell, George
1977 *The Hindu Temple.* New York: Harper and Row.

Moffatt, Michael
1979 *An Untouchable Community in South India: Structure and Consensus.* Princeton: Princeton University Press.

Mootoothamby Pillai, A.
1907 Kailaya Malai. *Ceylon National Review,* January, 1907, pp. 280-85.

Navaratnam, C.S.
1964 *A Short History of Hinduism in Ceylon and Three Essays on the Tamils.* Jaffna: Sri Sanmuganatha Press.

Nilakanta Sastri, K.A.
1966 *A History of South India, From the Earliest Times to the Fall of Vijayanagar.* Delhi: Oxford University Press.

Nyrop, Richard et al.
1971 *Area Handbook for Ceylon.* Washington: U.S. Government Printing Office.

O'Flaherty, Wendy D.
1973 *Asceticism and Eroticism in the Mythology of Siva.* London: Oxford University Press.

1976 *The Problem of Evil in Hindu Mythology.* Berkeley: University of California Press.

Oppert, Gustave
1893 *On the Original Inhabitants of Bharatavarsa or India.* Madras: Lawrence Asylum Press.

Otto, Rudolph
1958 *The Idea of the Holy: An Inquiry into the Non-Rational Factor in the Idea of the Divine and Its Relation to the Rational.* London: Oxford University Press.

Pandey, Raj Bali
1969 *Hindu Saṁskāras (Socio-Religious Study of Hindu Sacraments).* 2nd ed. Delhi: Motilai Banarsidas.

Pathmanathan, S.
1978 *The Kingdom of Jaffna, Part I. (Circa A.D. 1250-1450).* Colombo: Arul Rajendran.

Pfaffenberger, Bryan
1979 The Kataragama Pilgrimage: Hindu-Buddhist Interaction and Its Significance in Sri Lanka's Polyethnic Social System. *Journal of Asian Studies* 38:253-70.

1980 Social Communication in Dravidian Ritual. *Journal of Anthropological Research* 36:196-219.

1981 The Cultural Dimension of Tamil Separatism in Sri Lanka. *Asian Survey: A Monthly Review of Contemporary Asian Affairs* 21:1145-57.

Pieris, P.E.
1914 *Ceylon: The Portuguese Era, Being a History of the Island for the Period 1505-1658.* Colombo: The Colombo Apothecaries.

Raghavan, M.D.
n.d. *Tamil Culture in Ceylon: A General Introduction.* Colombo: Kalai Nilayam.

Redfield, Robert N.
1962 The Folk Society. In *Human Nature and the Study of Society: The Papers of Robert Redfield.* M. Redfield, ed. Pp. 231-53. Chicago: University of Chicago Press.

Redfield, Robert and Milton Singer
1954 The Cultural Role of Cities. *Economic Development and Cultural Change.* 3:53-73.

Renou, Louis
1953 *Religions of Ancient India.* London: Athlone Press.

Ryan, Kathleen
1980 "Pollution in Practice: Ritual, Structure, and Change in Tamil Sri Lanka." Ph.D. dissertation, Cornell University.

Selvanayagam, S.
1966 Market Gardening in the Jaffna Region: A Study of Inuvil-Thavady Villages. *Ceylon Journal of Historical and Social Sciences* 9:172-76.

Seneviratne, H.L.
1978 *Rituals of the Kandyan State.* Cambridge: Cambridge University Press.

Shulman, David Dean
1980 *Tamil Temple Myths: Sacrifice and Divine Marriage in the South Indian Saiva Tradition.* Princeton: Princeton University Press.

Somasundaram Pillai, J.
1959 *Two Thousand Years of Tamil Literature.* Tinnevelly: South Ind: Saiva Siddhanta Works Publishing Society.

Srinivas, M.N.
1952 *Religion and Society among the Coorgs of South India.* Oxford: Oxford University Press.

1959 The Dominant Caste in Rampura. *American Anthropologist* 61:1-16

1968 *Social Change in Modern India.* Berkeley: University of California Press.

Stein, Burton
1969 Integration of the Agrarian System of South India. In *Land Control and Social Structure in Indian History.* R.E. Frykenber ed. Pp. 175-216. Madison: University of Wisconsin Press.

1977 The Segmentary State in South Indian History. In *Realm and Region in Traditional India.* R. Fox, ed. Pp. 3-51. Durham: Duke University Program in Comparative Studies on Southern Asi

1978 *South Indian Temples: An Analytical Reconsideration.* New Delhi: Vikas Publishing House.

1980 *Peasant State and Society in Medieval South India.* Oxford: Oxford University Press.

Suntheralingam, R.
1974 *Politics and Nationalist Awakening in South India, 1852-1891.* Tucson: University of Arizona Press, for the Association for Asian Studies.

Tennent, Emerson
1860 *Ceylon: An Account of the Island Physical, Historical, and Topographical, with Notices of Its Natural History, Antiquities, and Productions.* 4th Ed. London: Green, Longman, and Roberts.

Thuraisingham, S.D.
1953 Agriculture in the Northern Division. *Tropical Agriculturalist* Oct. - Dec., 1953:267-79.

Thurston, Edgar
1909 *Castes and Tribes of Southern India.* Madras: Government Press.

1912 *Omens and Superstitions of Southern India.* New York: McBride, Nast, and Company.

Wadley, Susan
1976 Power in Hindu Ideology and Practice. In *The New Wind: Changing Identities in South Asia.* K. David, ed. Pp. 133-57. The Hague: Mouton.

1980 *The Powers of Tamil Women* (ed.). Syracuse: South Asian Series, Foreign and Comparative Studies Program, Maxwell School of Citizenship and Public Affairs, Syracuse University.

Whitehead, Henry
1916 *The Village Gods of South India.* London: Oxford University Press.

Wirz, Paul
1954 *Exorcism and the Art of Healing in Ceylon.* Leiden: E.J. Brill.

1966 *Kataragama: The Holiest Place in Ceylon.* D.B. Pralle, trans. Colombo: M.D. Gunasena.

Wittfogel, Karl
1957 *Oriental Despotism: A Comparative Study of Total Power.* New Haven: Yale University Press.

Wiser, William H.
1958 *The Hindu Jajmani System: A Socio-Economic System Interrelating Members of a Hindu Village Community*. Lucknow: Lucknow Publishing House. Originally published 1936.

Adultery, 201
Aiyaṉār, 156, 183f, 192f
Alcohol, 14, 50f, 90, 187, 196
Ammaṉ, 109, 145, 148, 155f, 160ff, 163f, 165f, 173, 190
Aṇṇamār, 184f, 190, 192f
Anti-Brahman movement, 31, 32, 49
Antiprimitivism, 96f, 101, 121f. *See also* Wilderness; Jungle
Appadurai, Arjun, 23, 62
Artisans, 38, 83ff, 91, 196, 197 (Table V)
Arumainayagam, K., 90, 93
Astrology, 100, 122, 125f, 134, 214-18
Atimai-kutimai distinction, 38, 39 (Table I), 40ff, 45f, 227. *See also* Kutimakkal; Right and left castes; Untouchables •
Ayurveda, 66, 98, 99, 122

Babb, Lawrence A., 144
Baldeus, Phillipus, 36f
Banks, Michael Y., 9, 26, 35, 36, 38, 40-51, 54, 61, 89, 90, 92f, 96
Barber (Ampaṭṭar)
 impurity of Barbers, 52, 195
 kutimai category, Barber members of, 40, 90
 kutimakkal category, Barber members of, 45, 174
 occupation, 40
 pollution time, of Jaffna Barbers, 197 (Table V)
 population, of Jaffna Barbers, 47 (Table II)
 ritual role, 202-9, Appendix II
 status in Jaffna, 39 (Table I)
 status in South India, 38
Basham, A.L., 1, 6, 80
Beck, Brenda E.F., 5f, 8f, 23, 27f, 145
Benefit of ritual. *See* Ritual, Fertility
Béteille, Andre, 9, 12, 83
Bharati, Agehananda, 68
Birth, 206-9
Blacksmiths (Kollar), 38, 39 (Table I), 47 (Table II)
Blood, 97, 106, 172, 185f, 193
Brahman (Pirāmaṉ)
 above "right-side" vs. "left-side" distinction, 23
 alliance with Sudras, 21f, 25, 27f, 32, 91, 95
 anti-Brahman movement, 31, 32, 49
 artisans' claim to Brahman status, 84
 dominant caste, Brahmans as, 26f, 31
 fallen Brahmans, 54f, 88
 inauspiciousness of begging Brahman, 101
 Jaffna Brahmans
  colonization, 35
  pollution time, 197 (Table V)
  population, 26, 47 (Table II)
  purity, 35f, 198
  rank, 39 (Table I)
 landowners, 4
 lower than Paraiyars, 54f
 Mariyammaṉ, Brahman ancestry of, 163
 occupation, 7
 plowing, Brahman disdain for, 5f
 privileges, 22
 purity, 4f, 52, 164, 194f, 198, 223
 rank, 4, 7, 13, 33, 81f, 224
 relation with king, 68f
 religious duties, 7, 63
 status in South India, 9, 15f, 15n, 21ff, 31, 38
 temple rituals, 24, 61, 78, 112, 118, 147, 149, 190
 Teyvayāṉai, Brahman ancestry of, 164
Breckenridge, Carol, 62
Breman, Jan, 41

Cakti (power), 66, 151f, 166, 171. *See also* Women
Calendar
 annual round, 213ff
 awkward times, 180, 209
 days of the week, 210f
 fortnights, lunar, 211f
 lunar days, 211f
 lunar mansions, 212
 planetary conjunctions, 212
 seasons, 214

Caṅkam
 era, 21
 literature, 136-41. *See also* Tamil literature
Cāntār, 39 (Table I), 40, 47 (Table II), 90, 153, 175
Cantati. *See* Kinship
Carpenter (Taccar), 38, 39 (Table I), 47 (Table II), 130-34, 143, Appendix II
Cartman, Rev. James, 61, 152
Casie Chetty, Simon, 147
Caste, inadequacy of concept, 30f
Chastity. *See* Women
Chelliah, J.V., 95
Cold (kulir), 98f, 173
Colonial period
 Jaffna, 35ff, 38, 42, 42f, 61, 114
 South India, 33f, 89
Conflict, 95f, 98, 127, 199
Contakkārar. *See* Kinship
Coppersmith, 38
Coromandel Plain, 20, 21, 24

David, Kenneth, 54, 55, 79, 81, 84, 96
Death, 97, 101, 104, 108, 180f, 224
Demons, 95, 101, 106f, 130, 135, 149, 179-93
Dharmaśāstra, 1, 2, 8, 11, 14, 33, 49, 56, 136, 198, 225
Disorder (toṣam)
 arises in Untouchables from afflicted prestations, 58f, 121f, 121f, 135, 143f, 148, 193, 203, 205, 208f, 225. *See also* Prestations
 autochthonous powers, disorder of, 58f, 96-110, 121f, 180, 203
 consequences of disorder, 121ff, 128, 135. *See also* illness
 dangerous power arising from disorder, 58, 110, 121ff, 139
 impure persons susceptible to disorder, 121, 198ff
 origins of concept, 135-41
 ritual roles and disorder, 143f, 148, 193, 203, 205, 208f, 225, Appendix II
 unchaste women susceptible to disorder, 139f
 Untouchables, disorder of, 58, 110, 121ff, 135f, 139, 143f, 193, 203, 205, 208f, 225
Dominant caste, 4f, 8, 9, 10f, 12, 15
Dowry, 97
Dravidian civilization, 1, 2, 8, 16, 17-19, 26, 30ff
Dreams, 101
Dumont, Louis, 1, 2, 5, 6, 9, 12-15, 19, 26, 56, 83n, 226

Eighteen kuti-s, 35. *See also* Atimai-kutimai distinction; Untouchables; kutimakkal
Elmore, Wilbur, 2, 136
Emotions, ethnophysiology of
 anger, 98, 121, 128, 184
 confusion, 105, 122, 180
 cruelty, 106, 180
 disobedience, cravings for, 98, 106
 egotism, 106, 180
 envy, 105, 109f, 127
 happiness, 108, 110, 121, 134, 199
 hate, 105
 irascibility, 97, 107f
 lust, 99, 105
 malice, 105f
 sorrow, 196
Entitlement, to means of reproduction, 57, 62, 70, 81, 92, 148f, 160, 165
Evil eye (kaṇṇuru), 110, 127, 170

Fabricious, J.P., 40
Farmer, B.H., 42
Feces, 107
Fertility
 of the earth
  benefit of temple ritual, 66, 79ff, 148. *See also* Ritual
  ensured by an ordered patron's ownership of the land, 68f, 81, 148f, 222. *See also* Land tenure
  ensured by the worship of demigods, 189
  ensured by the worship of Kāli, 158
  fields devoted to temple support flourish, 65

Fertility (*continued*)
legitimacy of the yajamāna's claim to the instruments of reproduction, 70
threatened by spirits, 158
symbolized by Valli, 164f
Vedic sacrifice and fertility, 67
of the village
ensured by worship of Mariyamman̲, 145
of women
destroyed by spirit attacks, 105f, 108, 121
destroyed by the substance of wilderness beings, 98
ensured by domestic ritual, 124, 134
Firewalking, 191

Gangetic civilization, 1-3, 13, 15f, 18, 20, 21, 24, 95, 136f. *See also* North India
Geertz, Clifford, 10, 226
Ghosts, 101f, 104
Gifts. *See* Prestations
Gluckman, Max, 69
Goffman, Erving, 123
Goldsmith, 38, 39 (Table I), 47 (Table II), Appendix II
Gonda, Jan, 11, 18, 67ff, 72
Gough, Kathleen, 26, 31
Gould, Harold, 8, 67

Hanuman, 188
Hardgrave, Robert, 13f
Hart, George L., III, 21, 82, 137-41, 179, 200
Health
cattle, 221
children, 100
family, 102, 134
pregnant women, 99
Veddahs, 121f
villagers, 164, 172f
Heat (cūtu), 98f, 105, 110, 122, 173
Heesterman, J.C., 67, 224
Hitchcock, John, 11
Hocart, A.M., 38
Household
design, 124-35
intrusion of snakes, 99
rituals, 130-35, 200-9, 219-22
Hubert, Henri, 67
Hudson, Dennis, 153
Hutton, J.H., 35

Illness, 98, 105f, 109, 121f, 128, 140, 154, 164, 171ff, 189, 191, 199
Imposed features, 15, 52, 92f, 122f
Impurity
Barber, 52, 195
Carpenter, 143
defined, 7, 13
disqualifications from ritual, 7, 71, 198
"false" impurity, 10, 13ff, 15f, 52, 57
impotence of impurity as a rationale for low rank in South India, 88, 96, 143
immunity to pollution, 82, 146, 190
Ksatriyas, 11f
kurram ("faults"), 126, 128, 130, 133, 172, 199. *See also* Sin
leather, 51f, 143, 146
lifestyles exemplifying impurity, 15f
menstruation, 106, 201
Nalavar, 36, 49ff
openness to affliction, 198ff. *See also* Disorder
Pallar, 13, 36
Paraiyar, 4, 13, 51, 57, 143, 146, 195, 225
pollution times of the castes of Jaffna, 197 (Table V)
Sudras, 7
threat to order, 194
tīṭṭu, 52
toddy-tapping, 14f
tuppuravu illai, 13, 46, *defined*, 196
tutakku, 195f. *See also* Kinship
types of pollution, 195ff
Untouchables, 198
Vellālar, 15n, 82, 146, 190
Washerman, 143
Inden, Ronald, 11
Indrapala, K., 35

Jaffna Peninsula
caste system, 35-52
center of Tamil culture in Sri Lanka, 17
climate, 42, 214
cultural relation with South India, 27ff, 31
ecology and agriculture, 42ff
origins of Tamil culture in the Jaffna Peninsula, 35ff
Jajmani system, 70ff, 84f, 87, 174
Jungle, 108, 114, 121f, 125, 152f, 179. *See also* Wilderness; Antiprimitivism

Kaikkular, 39 (Table I), 47 (Table II), 87, 196, 197 (Table V)
Kāḷi, 109, 155-60, 165-72
Kallar, 12, 23, 83
Kanakasabhai, K., 95
Kane, P.V., 7, 50, 67, 79f
Kannaki, 162ff, 187
Kaṉṉimar, 152ff
Kantacāmi, 114ff, 170. *See also* Murukan
Karaiyar, 39 (Table I), 47 (Table II), 120f
Karma. *See* Metempsychosis
Kataragama, 115, 117ff, 164, 188
Kaṭṭavarāyar, 185ff, 190
Kaulācara, Ramachandra, 79
Kearney, Robert, 45
Kingsley, David, 138
Kinship
agnatic lineage or patrilineage (cantati), 61, 99, 148, 154f, 159, 168, 195f, 204
bilateral kindred (contakkārar), 132, 150, 154f, 159, 165f, 167, 169, 204
King, 11f, 20, 23, 27, 35, 67, 83, 140f, 145ff, 152f
Koṅku Nāṭu (Coimbatore District), 27, 28, 34
Kōviyar, 39 (Table I), 40, 45, 47 (Table II), 174, 195, 197 (Table V), Appendix II
Korriyār, 207f
Kramrisch, Stella, 61, 73, 79
Ksatriya, 7, 9, 11f, 33, 56, 68, 80n, 83, 86
Kumar, Dharma, 41
Kuṭimai-aṭimai distinction. *See* Aṭimai-kuṭimai distinction.
Kuṭimakkal, 40, 45, 57, 174

Laksmi (Srī, Cī Tēvi), 107f, 124
Land tenure, 22, 24, 29, 30, 44f, 69
Leach, Edmund, 17, 89
Left and right castes. *See* Right and left castes
Lewis, J.P., 151, 163, 180, 183
Liberation (mukti), 103f, 110f, 142
Lingat, Robert, 7
Ludden, David, 22ff, 31

Maloney, Clarence, 20f
Mandelbaum, David G., 2, 6, 10, 12, 30, 32, 70, 84, 148, 226
Maravar, 12, 15, 23, 83
Mariyamman̲. *See* Amman̲
Marriage, 97, 121, 189
Marriott, McKim, 18
Masons, 38
Mauss, Marcel, 67
Mayer, Adrian C., 11
Mencher, Joan, 27
Menstruation, 107, 200-6
Mental health, 98, 121f. *See also* Emotions
Metempsychosis (Hindu doctrine of reincarnation), 102f, 199, 214-18
Michell, George, 61
Misfortune, 100, 122
Moffatt, Michael, 51, 91n
Mootoothamby Pillai, A., 118
Mukkuvar, 39 (Table I), 47 (Table II)
Murukan̲, 64, 76, 114-18, 132, 164, 184, 188. *See also* Kantacāmi
Mū Tēvi, 107ff, 150ff

Naccimār, 152ff, 155
Nadars, 13
Nākatampiran̲, 97, 175
Naḷavar
Amman rites, 174f
aṭimai category, Nalavar members of, 40
kuṭimai category, Naḷavar members of, 45
concubines, 165
diet, 49f

Naḷavar (*continued*)
impurity, 36, 49ff
link with tribal folk, 123
origin myth, 153
pollution time, 197 (Table V)
population, 47 (Table II)
priest, 186, 192f
ritual roles, 192, 207ff, Appendix II
status in Jaffna, 39 (Table I)
toddy-tapping, 90
Nattuvar, 39 (Table I), 47 (Table II), 190, 197, Appendix II
Nature (iyarkkai), 99, 121f, 201f
Navaratnam, C.S., 35
Nilakanta Sastri, K.A., 137
North India, 20
caste system of, 8, 26
differences from South, 2, 8, 11, 67. *See also* South India
Nyrop, Richard, 26

O'Flaherty, Wendy, 65, 138, 224
Omens (cakunam), 100f, 126, 128, 134
Oppert, Gustave, 29, 147
Otto, Rudolph, 137f

Paḷḷar
anomalous rank in South India, 25
"fallen" Veḷḷāḷars, 55, 88f
imposed features, 92f, 123
impurity, 13, 36
Jaffna Paḷḷars
aṭimai category, Jaffna Paḷḷars members of, 40ff
concubines, 165
diet, 49f
kuṭimakkal category, Jaffna Paḷḷars members of, 45
origin myth, 55, 107f
pollution time, 197 (Table V)
population, 47 (Table II)
ritual roles, 190, Appendix II
status in Jaffna, 36, 39 (Table I)
toddy-tapping, 90
Pandey, Raj Bali, 68
Panṭāram, 78, 174, 190, 196
Pantheon, inadequacy of concept, 155
Pathmanathan, S., 35
Paraiyar
"fallen" Brahmans, 55f, 88
illiteracy, 4
impurity, 4, 13, 51, 143, 146, 195, 225
Jaffna Paraiyars
drumming, 89, 168f, 171, 177, 186, 190f, 207f
impurity, 35
kuṭimai category, Jaffna Paraiyars members of, 38, 89
kuṭimakkal category, Jaffna Paraiyars members of, 45
origin myth, 54
pollution time, 197 (Table V)
population, 47 (Table II)
rank, 39 (Table I)
Mariyamman, descent from Paraiyar, 163
medieval South India, Paraiyar status in, 22ff, 31
occupation, 4, 89
rank in South India, 4, 9
"right-side" category, Paraiyar members of, 89, 96
ritual entitlement, lack of, 24
ritual role, 89, Appendix II. *See also* Paraiyar drumming
scavengers of cattle, 4, 49, 195
shoeless, 14
status consonant with the Sastric ranking paradigm, 15, 195
successful incorporation, 89
erumpaṭai, 185
faffenberger, Bryan, 32n, 113, 142, 148, 228
ieris, P.E., 35, 145
ilgrimage, 64, 228
iḷḷaiyār, 64f, 76, 113f, 116, 131, 132, 134, 170, 184, 186, 190, 192f, 204, 219ff. *See also* Veḷḷāḷar
olitical organization, 24, 26
ollution. *See* Impurity
otters, 38, 39 (Table I), 47 (Table II)
restations
afflicted with disorder (tōsam), 135f, 143f, 148, 193, 203, 205, 208f
duty to give gifts, 69, 81
greatness of giver, 63, 69, 81, 178f, 223 (epigram)
threshing-floor distributions, 22, 43, 71
to Brahmans, 7, 21f, 62, Appendix II
to kuṭimakkal castes, 46, 57, 132, 134, 149, 203, 205, 207f, 220, Appendix II
to Untouchables, 22, 135, 143f, 148, 172, 193, 200, 203, 205, 207ff, 220, Appendix II
Purity
Brahman, purity of, 4ff, 35f, 52, 164, 194f, 198, 223
defined, 4
dignity of the pure, 164
dominion over men legitimated by purity, 7
"false" purity, 10, 12, 15, 16, 52, 57
ranking principle of pure and impure, 16
temple, purity of, 78
Veḷḷāḷar, purity of, 5f, 15n, 16, 56, 195ff, 223

Rainfall
ensured by chastity of women, 109, 145
ensured by ordering of the king, 140
ensured by ordering the village goddess, 164, 172ff
Raghavan, M.D., 2, 40, 145
Redfield, Robert, 28, 32
Reincarnation. *See* Metempsychosis
Renou, Louis, 138
Rice, ritual value of, 46, 57, 62, 65f, 79, 131, 149, 165, 174f, 185, 219ff
Right and left castes, 9, 17, 23, 38, 82-91, 135, 227
in Jaffna, distinction absent, 38n, 40, 84, 91n
in South India, 95f
Ritual
abhiṣēka, 67, 76
benefit (palan) of ritual, 58, 61, 64ff, 69, 79f, 148f, 158, 165f, 186, 189, 193f, 222
Brahmanical and non-Brahmanical, unity in Tamil culture, 30ff, 59, 148
creation of civilization, ritual means, 227
dīkṣā, 67
entitlements, 22, 24f, 29f, 57, 62, 70, 81, 148, 224, 229
"folk" ritual, 28ff
Jaffna rituals, conservatism of, 31f
language of ritual, 17, 31
legitimation of power, 226f
organization of "caste" statuses, 30f. *See also* Caste
patrons, 61-82. *See also* Yajamāna
prestations, 62ff, 135, 149, Appendix II. *See also* Prestations
rituals of Sudra domination in Jaffna. *See also* Appendix II
ākama temple rites, 61-66, 72-82. *See also* Temples
apotheosis of demons, 187-93
appeasing demons, 186-87, 192f
appeasing the chaste suicides, 152
banishing the Evil Woman, 150
birthing room rites, 206-9
cutting a well, 134f
design of the rituals of Sudra domination, 58f, 147-50, 199, 223-25
expelling demons, 185f, 192f
family entering the house, 131ff
first fruits rite, 222
first menstruation, 200-6
laying the new foundation items, 130f
ordering the bridegroom, 189-93
tai poṅkal, 219-22
treating with civility, 78, 159
unity of the rituals of Sudra domination, 59, 148, 160
vaḷarntuppoṅkal, 166-79
samskāra, 68f
Sanskritic and non-Sanskritic, 29f, 32, 148, 159
stigmatization, 58f, 92f, 122f, 144, 160
"transcendental" vs. "pragmatic" distinction, 32, 148
upanayana, 68
Vedic sacrifice, 66ff, 70

Ryan, Kathy, 199

Sacrifice, 66ff, 70, 105ff, 109, 133, 135, 138, 141, 143, 148f, 154, 159, 169, 180, 182, 186
Śaiva Kurukkal, 39 (Table I), 47 (Table II), 78, 196
Sanskrit language, 21, 24, 29, 30, 32, 61, 64, 137, 148, 158
Sarasvati, 132
Selvanayagam, S., 44
Semen, 97
Seneviratne, H.H., 145
Shamanism, 128f
Shanars, 14
Shulman, David D., 29, 108, 112, 115, 142, 163, 165, 180, 223
Ṣin, 199
Śiva, 64f, 74, 103f, 110ff, 115, 119, 132, 156f, 184
Skanda. *See* Murukan̲, Kantacāmi
Snakes, 97-100
Somasundaram Pillai, J., 149
Sorcery, 97, 110, 127, 183, 189
South India
  caste system, 2ff, 9, 27, 30f, 41, 52, 56, 83, 92
  culture history, 19-25, 95f, 136-46
  defined, 34
  non-Brahman dominant caste, 5ff
  North India, divergence from, 2, 7, 9, 11f, 23f, 71
  regional culture, 16, 17, 21, 24. *See also* Dravidian civilization, Tamil culture
  Sastric ideal, divergence from, 1f, 4
Spirits, 101f, 104ff, 127, 130, 134, 150ff, 158, 182f, 186, 193
  spirit possession, 105, 109, 122, 127, 154, 180
Śri (deity). *See* Lakṣmi
Śrī (everlasting life and abundance), 160, 223, 225, 230
Srinivas, M.N., 32, 40, 41
Stein, Burton, 2, 12, 20-25, 29, 34, 65, 81f, 84f, 89, 95f
Sterility, 96f, 98f, 105f, 109, 122, 201
Succession to ritual office, 165, 168f
Sudra
  anomalous status in South India, 7, 12f
  dominant castes
    alliance with Brahmans, 21f, 24f, 27ff, 31f, 34, 49, 91, 95
    anomalous rank in South Indian culture, 4ff, 7ff
    jajmani relations, 71
    landholding, 14
    non-Ksatriya model of domination, 11f, 83, 86
    political power, 10
  domination
    aim, 227ff
    meaning in Tamil culture, 17ff, 55-59, 95, 147ff, 160, 223ff
    reproduction of, 11, 229f
    scholarly views on, 1-17, 226
  foreigners defined as Sudras for temple entry, 62
  impurity, 7, 71
  like ordered demons, 189
  modern meaning of Sudra status in South India, 33f
  ordering of, 189, 223
  priest (pūcari), 143
  status in Dharmasāstra-s, 6f, 71, 79ff, 198
  vegetarian Sudras' pollution time, 197 (Table V)
  Veḷḷāḷars, Sudra status of, 4, 14, 33, 56, 86, 195f
  yajamāna, Sudra status of, 72, 79ff, 82
Suicide, 104, 152-55
Suntheralingam, R., 26

Tamil culture, 32, 59, 96f, 137ff, 200
Tamil chronicles of Jaffna, 35, 118f, 147f
Tamil language, 1, 2
Tamil literature, 21, 95, 111f, 136-41, 228. *See also* Caṅkam
Tamil mythology, 108, 141ff
Tamil nationalism
  in India, 32
  in Sri Lanka, 32n
Tamil social formation, 21-25
  in Jaffna, 38

Temples, 22, 24, 35, 61-66, 141ff, 148, 164f
  home, modeled on notion of temple, 124, 126
  plan of the ākama temple, 72ff
  Sudras as temple patrons, 79f
Temple Carvers (Cīrpācāri), 38, 39 (Table I), 47 (Table II)
Tennent, Emerson, 43, 125
Teyvayāṉai, 116, 164
Theophany, 112ff, 115, 118, 147
Thuraisingham, S.D., 44
Thurston, Edgar, 12, 33, 35, 55
Trance (kalai), 128, 150, 157ff, 159, 164, 167, 169, 176, 180, 189, 191ff
Tribal peoples, 121. *See also* Veddahs
  depicted in literature, 95f

Umā Tēvi, 115, 156, 163
Untouchables
  affliction of disorder, 58f, 123, 135, 143, 148, 172, 193, 200, 225
  artificially low rank of certain Untouchable castes, 13ff
  atimai Untouchables, 40ff, 46, 49, 52, 54, 57f, 87, 90, 92, 96, 123, 143, 160, 198, 225, 227, 229. *See also* Atimai-kuṭimai distinction
  danger of, 58, 110, 121ff, 139
  impurity, 198
  inauspicious, 103
  Jaffna, Untouchables of, 36, 37 (Table I)
  kutimai Untouchables, 38, 90f. *See also* Paraiyars
  laborers, 9, 44, 87
  like disordered demons, 109
  low status ameliorated by auspicious cosmic circumstances, 220
  pollution times, 197 (Table V)
  rebellion, 87-91
  relations with Veḷḷāḷars, 5
  ritual duties of, 58f, Appendix II, *passim*
  ritual prestations, recipients of, 58. *See also* Prestations
  "slaves," 44
  status in contemporary Jaffna, 45f
  status in Dharmasāstra-s, 7
  status in South India, 9
  toddy-tappers, 13ff
  traditional rights, 22, 44f
  tribal folk, link with, 96, 122f. *See also* Veddahs

Vairavar, 170, 184, 187f
Valli, 116ff, 164
Varna, 1, 5ff, 9, 11, 83
Varnāśrama dharma, 6f, 18, 83, 89, 90, 95, 179, 194, 227, 230
Veddahs (Vēṭarkaḷ), 97, 116, 121f, 136, 164
Vellālar
  agriculturalists, 4ff, 12, 21, 35 (epigram), 36, 42f, 45, 49
  alliance with Brahmans, 21f, 24, 95
  anomalous rank, 14, 16, 25
  attitude towards Untouchables, 122ff, 143, 146, 200
  auspicious, 224
  banishes Evil Woman, 150
  caste identity, 12, 80ff
  chastity of women, 160
  chieftains, 35, 38, 164f
  communities, advantageous placement of, 223
  defenders of varnāśrama dharma, 8, 82, 179, 194, 230
  diet, 49ff
  dominant caste, 38, 45, 58f, 92, 123
  emigration, 34
  Jaffna Vellālars
    immunity to pollution, 82, 146, 190
    immunity to possession, 146
    impurity, 15n
    legends, 28
    place in the social structure of Jaffna, 38-42
    pollution time, 197 (Table V)
    population, 47 (Table II)
    rank, 39 (Table I)
    relations with artisans, 84f, 91n
    relations with king, 35
    social change, 42-46
    temple ownership, 61-65
  Koṅku Veḷḷāḷars, 27
  landholdings, 14

Vellāḷar (*continued*)
lifestyle, 5
masters of kuṭimakkal castes, 9, 36, 38, 40, 52, 174
medieval South India, status in, 22f, 31, 80f
order, exemplars of, 58f, 110, 148, 194, 198
origin myth, 85f
patron of rituals, 160f, 166, 178f, 193f, 198
Piḷḷaiyār, Vellāḷar tutelary deity, 113
plowing, 5f
political authority, 82-91
prestations to Untouchables, 135, 144. *See also* Prestations
purity, 5, 15n, 16, 56, 195ff, 223
rank, 5, 9, 12, 15n, 39 (Table I), 81f, 101, 225
rebellions against Vellāḷar authority, 83-91
relations with Untouchables, 92ff, 123, 148
respectability, 40
right-side caste, 23, 82
ritual entitlement, 25, 56ff, 59, 61ff, 148f, 160, 178
ritual ordering of, 58ff, 194, 198
Sudra status, 14, 33, 56, 86, 195f
temple patrons, 22, 61ff, 174, 178f, 192f
temple rites, 22
traditional rites, 8, 22, 24
Vaisya status, 33

Village, 74, 109, 149, 178
Village goddess, 155, 172ff. *See also* Ammaṉ
Viṣṇu, 116, 119, 147
Vows, 66, 172f, 175, 191

Wadley, Susan, 8, 88
Washerman, 38, 39 (Table I), 45, 47 (Table II), 52, 143, 190, 195, 197 (Table V), 202, 204ff, 225, Appendix II
Whitehead, Rev. J., 29f, 136, 143f
Wild creatures, disorder of, 100f
Wilderness, 101, 106, 121f, 139, 143, 147, 150, 162, 179, 188
Wirz, Paul, 117, 119
Wiser, William, 26, 70
Wittfogel, Karl, 24
Women. *See also* Fertility
"bad woman," 108f, 150ff
chastity, 108, 121, 124, 139f, 146, 147, 151ff, 189, 193
childbirth, death in, 104
cumaṅkali, 124, 128
power, 145
seclusion, 124f
spirit possession, 105f
vulnerability, 110

Yajamāna, 61f, 63f, 66ff, 72ff, 80f, 88, 158
Yama, 101f

Zero-sum game, universe viewed as, 200

Note on the Author

Bryan Pfaffenberger teaches and writes at Knox College in Galesburg, Illinois, where he has held the post of Assistant Professor of Anthropology since 1977. He researched the Tamil caste system of Sri Lanka's Jaffna Peninsula during 1973 and 1974-75, the latter study being funded by a Foreign Area Fellowship of the American Council of Learned Societies and the Social Science Research Council. He wrote his dissertation on the Kataragama pilgrimage, and received his Ph.D. (from the University of California, Berkeley), in 1977. The problem of Sudra domination provided the focus for a year's library research, funded by the National Endowment for the Humanities (1979-80), on the caste system of the Tamil lands. He has published several articles on caste and ritual in Sri Lanka. He is currently working on a comparative study of caste relations in Tamil and colonial Mexican cultures, aided by a fellowship from the U.S. Department of Education Faculty Research Abroad Program. He is married and has an infant daughter.

PUBLICATIONS
of the
FOREIGN AND COMPARATIVE
STUDIES PROGRAM

African Series

Latin American Series

South Asian Series

Lists of the publications in each of the above series may be obtained from the Publications Desk of the Foreign and Comparative Studies Program, 119 College Place, Syracuse, New York 13210 USA.

Correspondence regarding manuscripts to be considered for publication should be addressed to the Editorial Committee for the relevant series, at the above address.

MAXWELL SCHOOL

Founded in 1924, the Maxwell School of Citizenship and Public Affairs has been educating young men and women for public service and for academic and research careers for over 50 years. Today the Maxwell School comprises a unique combination of disciplinary departments (Anthropology, Economics, Geography, Political Science, Public Administration, Social and Political Psychology, Sociology), degree granting programs (International Relations, Public Affairs, Social Science, Development Planning) and professional, research oriented non-degree programs (Foreign and Comparative Studies, Health Studies, Metropolitan Studies, and Mid-Career Training). Of the School's candidates for advanced degrees about half are in the traditional social science departments and the other half in inter-disciplinary programs.